Asian American Studies After Critical Mass

Asian American Studies After Critical Mass

Edited by
Kent A. Ono

Blackwell
Publishing

© 2005 by Blackwell Publishing Ltd
except for editorial material and organization © 2005 by Kent A. Ono

BLACKWELL PUBLISHING
350 Main Street, Malden, MA 02148-5020, USA
108 Cowley Road, Oxford OX4 1JF, UK
550 Swanston Street, Carlton, Victoria 3053, Australia

The right of Kent A. Ono to be identified as the Author of the Editorial Material in this Work has been asserted in accordance with the UK Copyright, Designs, and Patents Act 1988.

First published 2005 by Blackwell Publishing Ltd

Library of Congress Cataloging-in-Publication Data

Asian American studies after critical mass / edited by Kent A. Ono.
      p. cm.
   Includes bibliographical references and index.
   ISBN 1–4051–1596–3 (hardback : alk. paper) — ISBN 1–4051–1597–1 (pbk. : alk. paper)
1. Asian Americans—Study and teaching. 2. Asian Americans—Social conditions. I. Ono, Kent A., 1964–
E184.A75A8418 2004
305.895′073′071—dc22

                                                                                    2004016172

A catalogue record for this title is available from the British Library.

Set in 10/12.5pt Minion
by Kolam Information Services Pvt. Ltd, Pondicherry, India
Printed and bound in the United Kingdom
by MPG Books Ltd, Bodmin, Cornwall

The publisher's policy is to use permanent paper from mills that operate a sustainable forestry policy, and which has been manufactured from pulp processed using acid-free and elementary chlorine-free practices. Furthermore, the publisher ensures that the text paper and cover board used have met acceptable environmental accreditation standards.

For further information on
Blackwell Publishing, visit our website:
www.blackwellpublishing.com

Contents

Notes on Contributors

Peter X Feng is an Associate Professor of English and Women's Studies at the University of Delaware, where he teaches film history, Asian American studies, and cultural studies. An expert on Asian Americans and the media, he has authored *Identities in Motion: Asian American Film & Video* (2002), edited *Screening Asian Americans* (2002), and co-edited a special issue of the *Journal of Asian American Studies* on Asian American cultural production. His articles on Asian Americans in film and popular culture have appeared in *Cineaste, Jump Cut, Amerasia Journal,* and *Cinema Journal,* as well as in *Countervisions: Asian American Film Criticism* (ed. Darrell Hamamoto and Sandra Liu, 2000) and *Aliens R Us: The Other in Science Fiction* (ed. Zia Sardar and Sean Cubitt, 2002).

Candace Fujikane is Associate Professor of English at the University of Hawai'i. Her research interests encompass the literatures of Hawai'i, Asian American literatures, and Asian settler colonialism in Hawai'i. Her work has been published in *Critical Mass: A Journal of Asian American Cultural Criticism, Women in Hawai'i: Sites, Identities, and Voices* (1997), and *Whose Vision? Asian Settler Colonialism in Hawai'i* (2000), a special issue of *Amerasia Journal* that she co-edited with Jonathan Okamura (2000).

Taro Iwata is a Postdoctoral Fellow in the Asian American Studies Program at the University of Illinois, Urbana-Champaign. He completed his doctorate in history at the University of Oregon in 2003. In his dissertation, "Race and Citizenship as American Geopolitics: Japanese and Native Hawaiians in Hawai'i, 1900–1941," Iwata examined how notions of race and US citizenship, defined and modified according to American geopolitical claims to Hawai'i, shaped the political strategies of Japanese immigrants (issei), their US-citizen children (nisei), and Native Hawaiians in prewar Hawai'i. A native of Japan, he is currently working on a transnational research project which compares the political strategies and social experiences of Japanese immigrants in colonized Hawai'i, where they were racialized and discriminated against even by Native Hawaiians, with their experiences in Manchuria, China, where they were colonial masters during the same prewar period.

J. Kehaulani Kauanui is an Assistant Professor of American Studies and Anthropology at Wesleyan University in Connecticut. As a Katrin H. Lamon Resident Scholar at the School of American Research, Kauanui is writing a book on Native Hawaiian racial formations that focuses on blood quantum policy and the legal construction of indigeneity. Her work appears in the following journals: *Political and Legal Anthropology Review, The Contemporary Pacific, Social Text, Pacific Studies, American Studies, Amerasia Journal,* and *Women's Studies International Forum.* Kauanui's research interests include race, nationalism, and citizenship; gender and sexuality; US colonialism and indigeneity, Native sovereignty politics, and Pacific Islander diaspora.

Sunaina Marr Maira is Associate Professor of Asian American Studies at the University of California, Davis. Her work focuses on youth culture, popular music, and questions of gender and sexuality in diasporic and transnational communities. Maira is the author of *Desis in the House: Indian American Youth Culture in New York City* (2002). She co-edited an anthology, *Contours of the Heart: South Asians Map North America* (1997), which received an award from the Before Columbus Foundation, and is currently co-editing *Youthscapes: Popular Culture, National Ideologies, Global Markets* (forthcoming). Maira has published numerous academic articles in addition to writing fiction and has made many presentations and invited lectures. She is one of the founding organizers of Youth Solidarity Summer, a program for young activists of South Asian descent; Diasporadics, a festival of arts and activism in New York; and the South Asian Committee on Human Rights (SACH), a grassroots group that works on issues of post-9/11 civil and immigrant rights in the Boston area.

Martin F. Manalansan IV is an Assistant Professor of Asian American Studies and Anthropology at the University of Illinois, Urbana-Champaign. His present research projects include the politics around cuisine and the senses among Asian American immigrants, return migration to the Philippines, and the construction of urban modernity in Manila. He is the author of *Global Divas: Filipino Gay Men in the Diaspora* (2003), which received the Ruth Benedict Prize for the best LGBT book in Anthropology in 2003. He is the editor of *Cultural Compass: Ethnographic Explorations of Asian America* (2000), which was awarded the Cultural Studies book award from the Association for Asian American Studies. He also co-edited *Queer Globalizations: Citizenship and the Afterlife of Colonialism* (NYU, 2002).

Anita Mannur is a Freeman Postdoctoral Fellow in Asian American Studies at Wesleyan University. Her research interests are in Asian American studies, South Asian diaspora (culture and literature), food and nationalism, and race and gender studies. She is the co-editor of *Theorizing Diaspora: A Reader* (Blackwell, 2003).

Cynthia L. Nakashima is a PhD candidate in Comparative Ethnic Studies at UC Berkeley, and co-editor of *The Sum Of Our Parts: Mixed Heritage Asian Americans* (2001). She has taught courses on Asian Americans and People of Mixed Race at UC Berkeley. Cynthia lives with her husband and two daughters in the Bay Area.

Viet Thanh Nguyen is an Associate Professor of English and American Studies and Ethnicity at the University of Southern California. He is author of *Race and Resistance: Literature and Politics in Asian America* (2002), and his articles have appeared in *American Literary History, Western American Literature, Positions,* and *Hitting Critical Mass.* He is currently working on a book about the relationship between Viet Nam and the United States.

Kent A. Ono is Director of and Professor in the Asian American Studies Program and a Professor in the Institute of Communications Research at the University of Illinois, Urbana-Champaign. His research emphasis is on critical and theoretical analysis of print, film, and television media, specifically focusing on representations of race, gender, sexuality, class, and nation. He has contributed articles to numerous journals and anthologies, in addition to co-authoring *Shifting Borders: Rhetoric, Immigration, and California's Proposition 187* (Temple, 2002) and co-editing *Enterprise Zones: Critical Positions on* Star Trek (1996). He is also editor of a companion volume to *Asian American Studies After Critical Mass,* entitled *Companion to Asian American Studies* (Blackwell, 2004). He is currently completing a book on films and videos about the incarceration of Japanese Americans during World War II, *Forgetting to Remember: Representations of Japanese American Incarceration on Film and Video.*

Helen C. Toribio is a Lecturer in Asian American Studies at San Francisco State University and at the City College of San Francisco. Her research interests are in history and social movements, Filipino studies, cultural nationalism, and late nineteenth-century American culture. She is editor of *Seven Card Stud with Seven Manangs Wild* (2002), an anthology of Filipino American writings.

Acknowledgments

There is no question that this volume would not have come to fruition without the dedicated support and contribution of an entire community of people. While I hope to be able to thank the many friends who made contributions of every sort and at every turn, I could not possibly begin to thank everyone here in this short note who has contributed in important ways to the successful completion of this volume.

David Theo Goldberg initiated the idea of such a volume in his capacity as series editor of Blackwell Companions to Cultural Studies. Without the initial germ of a concept from him, this volume and its sister volume, *A Companion to Asian American Studies*, would not have come into being. At Blackwell Publishers, Jayne Fargnoli has been the consummate editor. Prompt, kind, generous, interested, attentive, and thoughtful, Jayne moved the project along, was willing to consider changes as they occurred, maintained a superb working relationship with me, and offered the kind of close communication one needs to feel supported throughout what always seems to be a lengthy process. It was Jayne who recognized the potential for a two-volume set out of the original single volume I proposed, and it was she who shepherded the concept of two volumes through the requisite approval and marketing process at Blackwell. Annie Lenth made connections with authors and provided technical information about the publication process. Ken Provencher took the original draft and oversaw the transformation of it into something publishable. Thanks also to Margaret Aherne and Nick Brock for the copyediting, and to Leanda Shrimpton for work on the cover design.

This anthology would not have been published had it not been for the tremendous efforts of two student research assistants. Gladys Nubla and Sayako Suzuki, in particular, contributed significantly to this volume. Gladys spent her year in Urbana-Champaign helping me coordinate with Blackwell, doing first-stage copyediting of the volume, and, in general, providing intellectual labor that led to the volume's completion. Sayako Suzuki helped me in the early stages of the project at UC Davis. Thanks also go to Shoshana Magnet, who helped me do last-minute work on the final version of the volume. And thanks to Rachel Dubrofsky and Joan Chan for building the index to this volume.

Many of the authors in the volume presented early versions of their chapters at a conference held at the University of Illinois, Urbana-Champaign, February 7–8, 2003, called "New Directions in Asian American Studies." Rachel Lee, Moon-Kie Jung, Susan Moynihan, and Glen Mimura all gave wonderful presentations at the symposium that helped position and frame issues raised in this volume.

My friends and colleagues at UC Davis – Wendy Ho, Karen Shimakawa, Darrell Hamamoto, Bill Ong Hing, Kevin Johnson, Thomas Joo, Caroline de la Peña, Angie Chabram-Dernersesian, Christine Acham, Sergio de la Mora, Jay Mechling, Carole Blair, Ruth Frankenberg, Laura Grindstaff, Roger Rouse, Judy Newton, Susan Kaiser, Suad Joseph, Cathy Kudlick, Beatriz Pesquera, Michael L. Smith, Ines Hernandez-Avila, Jack Forbes, Pat Turner, and Sophie Volpp all helped to create the kind of intellectual environment necessary to envision projects like this one and provided me much support for the completion of the volume along the way.

Without the constant support and mentorship provided to me by Tom Nakayama, Herman Gray, Rosa Linda Fregoso, Keith Osajima, Sara Schoonmaker, John Sloop, Elyce Helford, Peter Feng, and Leah Vande Berg, this volume would not have been possible.

My new colleagues, friends, staff, and students at UIUC have been a constant group of supporters. James Hay, Pedro Cabán, Sundiata Cha-Jua, Kal Alston, C. L. Cole, Siobhan Sommerville, Stephen Hartnett, Christian Sandvig, Cara Finnegan, and the faculty in Asian American Studies, the Institute of Communications Research, and in ethnic studies more broadly have given me much support. Particular thanks go out to Sharon Lee, the Assistant Director of Asian American Studies, for all of the hard work she and I do. Thanks also to Mary Ellerbe, Yunchul Yoo, Kapila Sankaran, Annie Wang, and Fleming Au for staff support during our conference and during 2002–3.

My mother, Lorraine, and sister, Lori, are always in my corner. Finally, I do not know what I would have done without the support, care, and nourishment provided to me by my friend, colleague, and partner, Sarah Projansky. Sarah helped give me the time and space necessary to pursue and then complete this project and was always available to me when I hit a stumbling block or became sad whenever a contributor to the project had to pull out, for whatever reason. Sarah and Yasmin, our daughter, have been a constant source of support for me. I look forward to reciprocating again when Sarah works to complete her next book project.

Asian American Studies in Its Second Phase

Kent A. Ono

This book is titled *Asian American Studies After Critical Mass*[1] because, while not perhaps yet very much beyond – or even fully into – a critical mass, in certain ways Asian American studies has (imperceptibly? subtly? not so subtly?) entered a second phase, in part as a result of a tremendous increase in the number of Asian American scholars, students, publications, and programs nationally.[2] Categorizing fields into "phases," "waves," or "generations" – e.g., first, second, and third wave feminism – can be quite problematic as a way to conceive of social, intellectual, and political movements and genealogical transformations of fields more generally. Despite my strong hesitancy to employ such artificial conceptual organizing tools – in this case by drawing too hard of a distinction between two phases and, thus, perhaps reductively implying a break between phases that then are made to appear simpler than they really are – I nevertheless do so now so that I might talk about what I see as significant shifts in scholarly perspective. Using the terminology of *phases* allows for an alternative method of conceptualization to the familiar and traditional approach of using generational markers (i.e., first, second, third, fourth generation), which are fundamentally genetic in focus, even if employed for social reasons. Focusing on phases or political generations, versus familial ones, allows me to emphasize a consideration of the field along political, institutional, and intellectual lines.

We might loosely describe Asian American studies' first phase as concerned with national identity and issues of emergence as a political/cultural/intellectual community;[3] the second phase we might describe as a period of questioning and challenging many of the long-held precepts of the first phase. In the second phase, then, scholars seek lines of power beyond the limits of a discourse of victimhood and heroism. Key, also, to the second phase are articulations of nationalisms within the larger nationalism that simultaneously recognize and produce important historically underrepresented epistemologies, social frameworks, and organizations *and* call into question the historical conceptualization of earlier forms of nationalism. And, while there still are not even Asian American studies departments or programs, let alone faculty, at some institutions of higher learning, second phase book and journal publications, job openings, and program development are at an all-time high.

Phase 1. The history of the first phase has been told many, many times before, so this narrativization claims no uniqueness. I simply describe the first phase here in order to illustrate how this anthology developed out of second phase considerations that respond to and emerge out of a first phase. Emerging in the late 1960s United States, emboldened by student protests and growing dissatisfaction with the Vietnam War as well as the Asian targets of such a war,[4] the Third World Strike at SFSU, the larger Civil Rights movement, and more generally the strictures against racial, gender, and sexual participation in the honorific ideals internationally marketed as the freedoms of US citizenship, Asian American studies surfaced as a countercultural, counterhegemonic formation with an explicit purpose of dismantling oppressive educational and institutional structures, while simultaneously creating racially specific alternatives not only within colleges and universities but also in communities. And, it did so by employing grassroots political participatory models for social change. The early discourse was explicitly emancipatory without focusing in a limited way only on Asian Americans. For instance, in her letter to *Gidra* about the development of ethnic studies, Janice Iwanaga wrote, "Ethnic Studies should involve itself in issues of today – women's liberation, U.S. aggression in Southeast Asia, Title II, the Security Pact with Japan, low wages and poor working conditions of Third World peoples, etc., etc." (p. 5).[5] But, even though many Asian Americanists had a tacit concern for Third World peoples, their principal focus was on the post-immigration family's experience of political non-recognition, non-inclusion, and outright hostility toward all things deviating from an ostensible normative embodied way of being within the nation-state. It was, in fact, lack of privilege, lack of citizenship status, and national disenfranchisement that were the central concerns of 1960s, 1970s, and arguably 1980s Asian American studies. Asian American studies employed terms such as "self-determination," and produced a critique of institutions and institutional thinking, while challenging historically produced practices of racism within society.

Phase 2. What I am calling a "second phase" is not entirely distinguishable from the first, just as postmodernism never made a complete break with modernism, and indeed some see postmodernism as a period of modernism, rather than a distinct era in its own right. After all, first and second phase scholars often occupy the same institutional spaces (e.g., departments, or more commonly programs) or homes. Some former first phase scholars might have become second phase thinkers or have incorporated a second phase outlook into their first phase perspective. Additionally, while I am suggesting we are now in the second phase, there was, arguably, a brief transition between the two phases. Some might even argue that we are currently still in the transition stage and that this volume should have been titled "On the Cusp of a Critical Mass" or "Toward a Critical Mass." And, certainly comments such as those by Karen Shimakawa and Kandice Chuh suggest there was, at least fleetingly, a transitional moment when new phase two scholars began to recognize that "A politics of claiming legitimacy and rights as Americans . . . is clearly not wholly effective in establishing social justice" (Shimakawa and Chuh, 10). Such a moment could be seen, perhaps, as a transitional moment, a moment between nationalist activism and the subsequent period of radical questioning and rethinking of the parameters of the field's earlier concerns.

The essays in this volume challenge the tenets of the Asian American studies' nationalist tradition – that is, many of the concerns of the field's first phase – but it is not sufficient to characterize this volume as singularly transnationalist in orientation. The reconceptualization of the field that these essays (and a much broader field of scholarship) offer includes, but extends beyond, transnational concerns. Far too many levels of challenging, questioning, and reconceptualizing the field of Asian American studies, the terms of the field, and the directions it will go exist for a national/transnational dichotomy to explain sufficiently the core of the scholarship now being produced and published during the second phase of the field. Indeed neither an Asian/Asian American dichotomy;[6] a nationalist/transnationalist dichotomy;[7] a globalization/class dichotomy;[8] a race/ethnicity dichotomy;[9] nor some other dichotomy (e.g., along gender or sexual lines) is sufficient in and of itself to describe the contemporary moment in which these various tensions are being felt and addressed. Indeed, the existence of these dichotomies suggests that, together, second phase scholarship constitutes a much broader array of concerns than a transnational/national construction implies.

I would argue that the transition between Phase 1 and Phase 2 was brief and that the second phase is already in full bloom. Indeed, while in the future there might be a good deal of nostalgia for the loss of an earlier period of intense nationalism within the field, the field is nevertheless already fully engaged in questions of transnationalism, the effects of the globalization of capital products and labor, the affective dimensions of experiences of minoritized subjects, neo- and postcoloniality, queer studies, multiraciality, theories of representation, comparative and critical race studies, cultural studies, critical feminist studies, and the like. Hence, at this moment perhaps we are just beyond the cusp of, though still quite near to, the moment of critical mass.

The second phase of Asian American studies is coincident with but not the same as the larger poststructural and cultural studies turns in the academy. Stimulated by a growing concern with language primarily within literary studies but that was also shared extensively throughout all of the major social sciences and humanities, as well as in some scientific, legal and medical fields, poststructuralism and cultural studies have both significantly refigured disciplinary as well as interdisciplinary academic spaces. And, while there was at least a moment in the early to mid-1990s when Asian American studies was concerned with poststructural possibilities, Asian American scholarship, especially self-reflexive theoretical work, quickly moved beyond issues of identity, subjectivity, self-reflexivity, critique of ideology, and, to some extent, deconstruction and psychoanalysis (proper).[10] Thus, like Asian American culture more generally, contemporary Asian American studies scholarship is a culturally syncretic formation and cannot be fully understood or represented as emerging out of the broader fields of cultural studies and poststructuralism. Asian American studies irrupts out of cultural contexts of which cultural studies and poststructuralism are a part, but second phase Asian American studies makes a unique cultural and intellectual contribution in relation to this broader intellectual context. Perhaps a certain kind of maturation of thought took place within the field of Asian American studies following a moment when poststructuralism and a poststructural critique, especially the critique of essentialism, began to take shape. A substantial critique of the field internally began to emerge just at this moment, partly because of the existing language, topic, and methodology of poststructuralism, even as Asian American studies was, in the end, bound to establish a different formation. Asian American studies scholarship such as the work foregrounded in this volume, arguably, has been moved by a different set of interests than the rest of cultural studies; for instance, choosing to linger at the interstices of, for example, postcolonial and queer scholarship; feminism and cyberspace; globalization and cinema; and the like. While an internal critique has generated considerations of thoroughgoing reconceptualizations of the field, continued investment in social change, attention to the materiality of the body and of social life, strategic deployment of social structural knowledges, concern with K-12 and university pedagogy, and understanding identity as a meaningful, if fraught, category, to suggest just a few, tend to distinguish second phase Asian American studies from the broader fields of poststructuralism and cultural studies.

Thus, while cultural studies scholarship *has moved quickly in a multiplicity of heterogeneous directions, sprouting in all directions in rhizomatic fashion, the field of Asian American studies, perhaps in part because it is more strongly yoked to the first phase, has moved in a slightly different direction.* The commitment to drawing attention to historical context and to power, to social relations, and to structured inequity remains a key feature within contemporary Asian American scholarship. This move within the field of Asian American studies not to follow, in lockstep fashion, poststructural and postcolonial scholarly directions, has in many ways led to the setting of new terms, with each contribution representing a point within a larger contour of what Asian American studies can be said to have become. If there were a single term to describe the interstitial space where Asian American studies is in its current formation it might be said to be at a site of "tension." Those occupying spaces within what might loosely be called the contours of the field have asked: whether to focus panethnically or panracially and hence to be Asian American studies or ethnic studies; whether to give into neoliberal restructuring and accede to globalization pressures that move us toward theorizing new transnational identities or to remain faithful to earlier immigration, acculturation, and citizenship models and maintain a commitment to a national identity; whether to reframe Asian American studies in terms of marginalized subfields within its rubric (such as queer, Southeast Asian, South Asian American, or Pacific Islander/American currents) or simply to retain the political, materialist, historical bases of the field, which may tend to privilege East Asian American studies; whether to continue along a theoretical and analytical axis – often accompanied by an exegesis of literary texts or non-literary texts put through the grind of literary critique – being brought to the field by luminary younger figures who are in their own right positioned centrally in the field or to maintain what many would consider a responsible approach to studying Asian Americans that accounts for communities, focuses on politics, and maintains a much sharper materialist edge to its social critique. These are four of the myriad tensions currently facing Asian American studies as a field and they demonstrate that "tension" is in many ways definitive of the current positioning of the field in relation to its past and future.[11]

The title of this volume, especially the "After Critical Mass" part of the title, is worth considering seriously: Precisely what lies ahead after a moment/concept of critical mass has been reached/created? Those writing in the second phase face many significant challenges and difficulties. For, while the field has been in transition, so has the larger geopolitical environment. For instance, a transnational critique of the field's nationalism may risk, at times, facilitating political currents of neo-conservatives who are working very hard to wish away what they see as an ornery, time-worn, "minority critique."[12] Additionally, just as holding fast in support of affirmative action programs can sometimes feel duplicitous among those of us challenging fixed notions of racial identity, holding onto a conception of Asian American studies – and more broadly Asian American identity – while calling for a thoroughgoing revision of the field in terms of phase two exigencies is fraught with contradictions. Moreover, there is a serious and fundamental pedagogical issue at stake: how does one make relevant to students, members of the general public, and even our own community members issues that seem necessarily theoretical in nature. Use of the term "obscurantism" itself illustrates the tension between the pull of academic, linguistic, professional, elitist, and scholarly interests and the pull of political, class, personal, community, and social ones. Relatedly, how might our concerns over cultural politics interface with material effects in public spaces and everyday lives? How will a second phase critique respond to fast-changing political exigencies, such as the relatively recent maelstrom emerging around Wen Ho Lee, the Los Alamos scientist falsely accused by the US government of revealing US nuclear scientists to China, repeated news items about Indonesia as a terrorist state, numerous South Asians and Arabs illegally detained without legal cause after 9/11, and current political media concern and fascination with North

Korea? When the temperature of relationships between nations rise, we are once again thrust into the situation of having to defend our (and others') very existence, including having to defend: the right to live where we live, our own and our family's relationship with Asia, and sometimes our right to exist on the planet. We are forced into narrow spaces from which to speak as a result of someone else's fiction about who we must be. We narrow ourselves to attempt to fit into an identity that does not fit. We are backed into the corner and, as a result, often feel forced to take action in the name of a contingent telos[13] or, as Gayatri C. Spivak called it, "strategic essentialism,"[14] even when we know the narratives being woven to set the terms of the discussion are not the ones we would have chosen had we had the representational power to have chosen them in the first place. Thus, in the process of moving into a second phase come many fraught questions about cultural politics that are and will continue to have to be addressed.

Within the academy itself, perhaps the most difficult challenge to contemporary Asian American studies is the meeting ground between Asian and Asian American studies.[15] On the one hand, area studies were, as has been documented in much detail elsewhere,[16] an effect of post-Cold War US expansionism that held as much an academic ethnographic desire for scholars as it did a national (anthropological), racialist, and neocolonial desire to fix the non-US subject as an exotic other; to map the particularities of cultural differences; and to "understand" the past and potential future enemy, thus refining hegemonic currents for politicians. On the other hand, Asian American studies, which emerged out of 1960s panracial and panethnic movements, included its own internal contradictions, including the dominance by many leaders who held rather narrow understandings of Asian American identity tied to an authentic, and often quite violent, premodern Asian masculinity.[17] Advocating for a meeting ground between Asian studies and Asian American studies may appear to be an obvious step, and in periods of economic downsizing, such a collusion may also seem pragmatic if not necessary,[18] but such a relationship is troubled. The foundations of Asian studies stem from an orientalist desire; and it is precisely a response to that desire and media projects that helped produce such a desire that led, in part, to the emergence of an Asian Americanist critique. A profound difference in academic legitimacy exists between the two fields, with Asian American studies historically being subject to a disproportionate share of tenure and promotion denials. The fact that Asian American studies in so many locations was the result of student protests leads to the self/other construction of it as a "political field," while Asian studies' self/other construction is as an academic one. There are, of course, so many other tensions to mention, but these are sufficient to suggest that the commingling of Asianist and Asian Americanist concerns will require significant attention and concerted effort within the second phase.

It is quite possible that these various tensions experienced within Asian American studies are, in fact, endemic to conceptualizing the field at this particular juncture. Perhaps such tensions are, in certain ways, definitive of what it means to be the field Asian American studies, to have to create methodologies for embracing historical political and cultural contradictions as they emerge, to choose – at points – the political without having fully set the terms of the context in which political action takes place. Perhaps we can begin to imagine, from the kind of scholarship represented in this volume, how to proceed from here.

Gathered in this volume is the work of creative intellectuals who have adopted new approaches to research. Growing out of a rich tradition of Asian American studies scholarship grounded in the study of history, literature, and sociology (among other fields)[19] is a heterogeneous group of scholars asking diversely textured questions directed at the interstices – indeed the "heart" – of contemporary social life. Each chapter addresses a "decentered" area within Asian American studies, with the purpose of foregrounding how the field could be reconceived as if this marginalized set of concerns were in fact central. How would the field look if attention to queer Asian America, Asian American youth, Asian American cinema studies, Asian American food culture, feminism, Pacific studies, Filipino American studies, mixed race, comparative Asian American/Native Hawaiian and comparative race studies, and transnationalist work were in fact the core, central elements of the field (as they are in this volume), rather than the periphery? This volume aims to highlight different frames of emergent, critical Asian American studies scholarship. Each essay is an original piece of scholarship, and while the goal of the volume was to highlight multiple areas of emergence, it was impossible, because of the purpose, scope, and size of this project, to address all areas.[20] The mode of analysis of each project is definitively interdisciplinary, yet each contributor poses critical questions that address foundational issues within historically defined disciplines. As a result, each essay has the potential to shape second phase Asian American studies. And, as a result second phase Asian American studies has the potential to shape questions of the larger academy. The ideas presented here should stimulate thought, conversation, concern, and – hopefully – even more new directions.

While it might have been preferable to have had no sections in the book, and then just to have had the essays organized arbitrarily (or alphabetically), it is worth addressing the fact that common themes of identity, disciplines and methodologies, and representations do emerge out of this collection. I have chosen to group the essays loosely according to these categories, not necessarily to suggest that some essays emphasize a certain theme more than others (because, for instance, some essays address all three themes simultaneously), but rather to suggest possible ways to think about the interconnections among the essays and to draw attention to possible conversations that might be had across the various chapters. Thus, the essays are grouped into broad sections called "representations," "disciplines and methodologies," and "identities."

Representations

The essays in the representations, section all also address disciplines, method-ologies, and identities, but they focus attention on issues of representation in ways that challenge, significantly, the particular way Asians, Asian Americans, and people generally are seen. Furthermore, they challenge Asian American studies to come to grips with a complex theory of representation that goes beyond the literary and textual to the cinematic and cultural. Furthermore, they point out the ways in which Asian American texts help to refigure what representation is and can be.

Viet Thanh Nguyen considers the role ambiguity might play in a theory of power that, at its core, assumes the goal of social equity and other political ideals within leftist politics. He attempts to understand "the political" by considering how scholars have theorized the concept and by analyzing cultural artifacts that require discussion of the political. He finds that, while commitment is an import-ant part of political efforts, ambiguity is more so when conceptualizing power. As a result, the crucial questions for him become: "If commitment is necessary for any opposition to domination and abuse, then can ambiguity be used to manage ethically the inevitable use of power? And if ambiguity can hamper resolve and introduce self-doubt, then what role can it play in political critique and mobiliza-tion?" To address his questions of what and where is the political, Nguyen considers cultural memory relating to representations of the Vietnam War. He compares three memorials: Maya Lin's Vietnam Veterans Memorial; the Vietnam War Memorial of Westminster, a jointly funded memorial by South Vietnamese and Americans; and the War Remnants Museum in Ho Chi Minh City. This comparative study addresses both the conceptual differences among the artistic projects as they relate to political action and each memorial's political incom-mensurability with the others. It also calls attention to the vastly differential socioeconomic circumstances circumscribing the production of each monument and thus the context out of which each artwork emerged. Differential contexts of production undergird these artistic works' capacity to represent formal and technical elements and point to the profound issues confronting scholars in trying to address and respond to historical events that led to the deaths of three million people. What happened to the Vietnamese under communism should then also matter to Asian Americans, if an Asian American methodology is one that not only questions abusive power but also ponders the ethical management of it.

Peter X Feng argues for an Asian American theory of representation that is able to attend to the complex ways in which Asian Americans have been positioned within mass media. He argues that the field requires a theory of representation, minimally an awareness of representational strategies. In particu-lar, he suggests that in Asian American studies scholarship, thus far, studies of cinema have mostly been dominated by a literary film analysis and, as a result, have had little to no sense of apparatus. A theory of apparatus is important because it allows us to critique documentaries, which literary critique is ill-equipped to do. Moreover, Asian American studies must contend with issues of the "ethnographic," since Asian American studies has relied heavily on ethnography and ethnographic film, as it has been important in teaching and research for discussions of political and cultural representation. Without sufficient interrogation of representation of the ethnographic, Asian American studies is unable to address in any critical and substantive way the filmic. Feng illustrates this theory by examining the work of three different filmmakers; both critical and encouraging of their work, he highlights many of the ways in which representation functions. While there are various approaches to representation, as illustrated by the three films, consideration of the various representational modes allows, at least, for a conversation about representation, which leads to deliberation about representational strategies.

Anita Mannur demonstrates how the study of food culture is important to Asian American studies and illustrates this through a literary critique of three Indian American texts. She theorizes the way in which consumption, more generally, is a racializing process; eating immigrant food, she suggests, is key to that process. Literature about food, food preparation, and the consumption of food, then, is an important site for the investigation of the discursive processes of racializing immigrants. Mannur provides analysis for three texts: Chitra Bannerjee Divakaruni's (1997) self-exoticizing novel *Mistress of Spices*, Geeta Kothari's (1999) autobiographical essay, "If You Are What You Eat, then What Am I?," and Jhumpa Lahiri's (1999) short story, "Mrs Sen's." Through her analyses of these texts, Mannur suggests that, while the issues of assimilation, identity, cultural difference, and stereotypes have been central to Asian American studies historically, studying such issues in relation to a study of food culture acknowledges the intimate ways in which these very phenomena that we typically study through a sociological, historical, or literary approach do not quite address the everydayness of food and food's interrelationship with our bodies.

Identities

While identity is key to these essays, just as it is for all essays in the volume, also critical to this group of essays are issues of sovereignty of thought and existence, scholarly methodology, material reality, and the shape of the field of Asian American studies. Identity is not the end, by any means, of the scholarly work; rather, it is one point among many leading to consideration of quite complex issues of community, solidarity, disenfranchisement, and collective action, often in particular historical (e.g., post-9/11), cultural (e.g., the specificity of Hawai'i as a colonized state within a colonized nation), and racialized (e.g., Filipina/o, queer, mixed race) contexts.

Candace Fujikane argues that Asian Americans must foreground Native nationalisms in Asian American studies by examining their roles as settlers in a colonial nation-state. She critiques the antinationalist sentiment in Asian American studies that has grown out of critiques of racist American nationalism and a masculinist and heteronormative Asian American cultural nationalism. She suggests that efforts to equate Asian American and Native Hawaiian concerns, or at times to co-opt Native Hawaiian interests as if Asian Americans were representatives of Native Hawaiian communities, have led to negative effects on Native Hawaiians. Tracing moments in history when Asian American settlers have been at odds with Native Hawaiian activism, Fujikane calls for a recognition of the rights to land and self-determination for Native Hawaiians. Although some Asian Americanists argue that we are beyond "claiming America," such antinationalist sentiment can end up opposing indigenous nationalist struggles in the United States in ways that stake a settler claim, now in the poststructuralist form of an "egalitarian non-belonging" that elides the contemporary struggles of Native peoples. Moreover, she suggests that a commitment to immigration models, to citizenship models, to discussing state minorities, and to US racism within Asian American cultural politics may be problematic if we fail to recognize Native struggles and the ways that our own intrasettler struggles obstruct their decolonization efforts. By drawing on the work of Huanani-Kay Trask and through a critique of her own work and the recent work of Kandice Chuh, she argues that, as Asian Americans, we must hold ourselves accountable for the ways our settler scholarship undermines Native struggles for self-determination.

Martin F. Manalansan IV suggests that the world has changed substantially and dramatically in terms of LGBT life in the United States. Notable ideologues have said as much and popular cultural texts (such as *Queer Eye for a Straight Guy*) bear out this claim, providing evidence of a profound transformation. Nevertheless, while change does exist, important experiences of queers of color continue to go unnoticed. The make-over of the queer community on screen and in the public eye is not, in fact, a transformation that reaches queer of color communities generally, or in the same manner. As Asian American studies scholars, we would do well to pay attention to the lives, bodies, and voices of queers of color in everyday life. Ethnographic method is one way to do this. Through analysis of the life narratives of queers of color, it becomes clear that all is not well; the make-over does not translate into real social/structural transformation. Moreover, race becomes an important aspect of research on sexuality in the model Manalansan offers. The intersection of LGBT studies and Asian American studies might profitably provide a space in which to address the material inequities and social problems that continue to exist, despite the make-over. This essay critiques the very idea of progressive transformation to suggest how it is, in fact, quite conservative and functions in the service of mainstream heteronormative (and homonormative) nationalist and capitalist ends.

Cynthia L. Nakashima addresses the significance, but historical downplay of, mixed race Asian Americans within the history of Asian American studies. She implores Asian Americanists to learn about mixed race Asian American experiences and provides a perspective informed by mixed race discourse from which to understand and make sense of Asian American studies. She draws attention to the relationship between mixed race Asian American discourse and Asian American studies pedagogy. At every step, she works against easy dichotomies. Especially in her discussion of monoracial and mixed race Asian Americans, she challenges assumptions based on biological phenotype. For her, adding and stirring is not a sufficient approach to addressing the study of mixed race within Asian American studies, since the additive model of addressing center/periphery issues is insufficient to social transformation. She demonstrates a way of looking at Asian American studies that incorporates mixed race perspectives into the very notion of Asian American studies.

Disciplines and Methodologies

The essays in the disciplines and methodologies section do address identities and representations, but they also challenge the politics of Asian American studies, the basis for subfields within it, and the methodologies used to conduct research. Thus, they call into question the way we do Asian American studies and the degree to which Asian American studies scholarship performs acts that need to be considered in political terms.

J. Kehaulani Kauanui interrogates the power relations among scholars of Asian American studies and Pacific Islander studies. She questions the grounds for an "APA" or "API" category, specifically the use of the "P" within those categories, and suggests that the desire among Asian Americanists to assume or to wish for a collaborative aim between the two groups is, both geographically and politically, misguided. Kauanui discusses the recent debate about whether to change the name of the Association of Asian American Studies to "include" Pacific Islanders as well as past organizing around Pacific Islander studies. She challenges the field to address its own racializing of and inclusionary (incorporative) politics in relation to Pacific Islanders and to assess the power relations in place when Asian Americans include Pacific Islanders, not out of genuine coalition politics, but out of a felt need among Asian Americanists for such an association. She further challenges the field of Asian American studies to self-recognize strategies and processes of incorporation of South Asians and Filipino Americans under and within the "Yellow" categories. Importantly, she questions why Asian Americanists feel the need to incorporate Pacific Islanders and Pacific Islander politics but do not feel the same need to incorporate other politically distinct groups such as African Americans or Latinas/os, for instance. Kauanui suggests the possibility for comparative research understood as research comparing two distinct groups: Asian Americans and Pacific Islanders.

Sunaina Marr Maira challenges Asian Americanists to study youth and to do so by paying attention to what youth, themselves, have to say. Youth have not been a central topic of research within Asian American studies historically and have only recently become a commonly discussed area of study within the field. Maira demonstrates the significance of studying youth in Asian American studies, but she points out many problematic ways in which youth have been conceived in Asian American studies research to date. She challenges past sociological theories that lack a complex view of race relations, studies that view youth either in a fetishistic way or see youth symptomatically as evidence of what is wrong with culture. She also challenges Asian American studies research that simplifies the cultural field of gender, race, and nation in the process of studying youth. Maira points to the need for a methodology that combines the study of symbolic culture with that of material forces in the field, more generally. She says Asian American studies needs a theory of "cultures, structures, biographies." She uses material from her own ethnographic research to develop a theory of "youthscapes" attentive to global and colonial exigencies. With her study of youth responses to 9/11, her approach builds on, improves, and otherwise produces important additive elements missing in research on youth within Asian American studies and cultural studies, more generally. Her admittedly cultural studies approach to the study of youth emphasizes ethnographic methodology as used in the earlier versions of British cultural studies versus the traditional cultural studies methodology of literary textual analysis in the United States, which leads her to a "joint production" between researcher/subject as it is applied to the post-9/11 context. Maira suggests how the particular conceptualization of youth taking on specific practices of cultural citizenship – flexible, multicultural, dissenting – that she develops in her essay affects the way we should want to conceive of youth studies within Asian American studies.

Helen C. Toribio problematizes the field of Filipino American studies, particularly Filipino American history, as they exist in relationship to Asian American studies and Asian American history. She suggests that the field of Filipino American studies continues to require serious discussions in the process of formulating an identity. She begins by questioning the concept of Asian American, goes on to discuss and question the historical specificity of the concept Filipino American, and then suggests the need for and realization of a field of Filipino American studies. Toribio reviews a significant amount of Filipino American studies scholarship, especially historical work, and points toward the places where research has been produced and where additional research is needed.

Through analysis of and examples comparing Native Hawaiian, Japanese American, and white cultural politics in Hawai'i, Taro Iwata demonstrates the significance of a comparative approach to the study of Asian American history. His essay shows how important it is to pay attention to power relations both within and outside of the Asian American community across time. Over-attention to white racism and a victim narrative in theorizing race relations within Asian American studies has tended to draw attention away from aspects of Asian American power. Asian Americans are not always the victims in power struggles; overlooking such a point can lead to a blanket desire for Asian American panethnicity, as each struggle to overcome victimhood leads to group empowerment. As a result of an assumption of white racial oppression, Asian Americanists have, for the most part, failed to address: (1) Asian American privileges resulting from white domination, (2) Asian American privileges resulting from our own domination, (3) differential power relations among Asian American ethnic groups, and (4) the effect of Asian American domination on groups outside of the Asian American community. Iwata's comparative approach enriches possibilities for Asian American studies by centering power relations interethnically and interracially, rather than maintaining a strict dichotomous model of white racism and victimized people of color.

The essays collected together in this volume suggest Asian American studies is at a point of maturation at which scholars, such as the ones represented here, are willing and able to sustain serious reconsideration and critique of the field of Asian American studies, its history, and of "Asian American" as a concept. With significant hindsight, they are able to question and explore the desire for and politics of legitimation, the strategies for equitable distributions of wealth and knowledge, the grounds for association, the need for better terms and method-ologies, the lack of attention to particular people, the need to reconceive whole paradigms, the importance of solidarity and recognition of politics beyond the academy and field, the need for renewal and reconsideration of the past, the importance of both interdisciplinary and disciplinary thought, the economic marketing of identity, and the profound need to recognize what matters beyond one's self. All of this is conducted with marvelous energy and care, which suggests the incredible potential for continued vitality of thought, perspective, and action within the second phase and beyond.

NOTES

1 I have used the term "critical mass" to pay homage to the use of the term by Asian Americanists, e.g., to the journal *Critical Mass*. By using it, I mean that there are now a significant number of people working in the field of Asian American studies, that there are many programs and some departments, that scholarship within the field is robust, that one can depend on annual conferences happening, that there are important book awards available in the field, etc. Peter X Feng helpfully pointed out to me that the term is often used in the field of physics to mean the amount of nuclear material needed to create

a chain reaction. I might also add that in organizational and business contexts, critical mass refers to the point at which an organization undergoes a fundamental shift in its identity as a unit resulting from a change in the way it operates. I thank Sarah Projansky for calling my attention to Patricia Hill Collins's discussion of critical mass as a "catalyst for some other, larger action to occur"; a small group that sets political action into motion; and the point at which "hype turns into reality"; and when people take action resulting from critique (Collins 1998: 242). Collins suggests that the concept is key to thinking about everyday struggles for freedom by African American women and that conceptualizing the term may be key to future freedom struggles (243). These many ways of thinking about critical mass are useful in thinking about Asian American studies and critical mass. On the one hand, critical mass means the point at which certain functions (scholarly, political, activist) are possible; on the other it refers to a significant change in what the field is and what general kinds of issues are considered to be germane to it. Additionally, it suggests the moment at which highly significant transformations of thought and action become, first, imaginable and then, possible. See also the discussion of critical mass in Davé et al. (2000).

2 I need to emphasize that without the Asian American movement, the larger struggle for civil (economic, racial, ethnic, gendered, sexual, and human) rights, and the struggles of individual and collective Asian Americans and Asian Americanists historically, the platform and foundation for the now stronger and more sizable numbers of Asian Americans in the academy – across the sciences, arts, humanities, and social sciences – would not have been laid.

3 For two historicizations of this period, please see Omatsu (1994) and Wei (1993).

4 For a critical reading of the relationship between Asian American studies and activism and the Vietnam War, please see Viet Nguyen's essay in this volume.

5 November, 1969.

6 Key to a discussion of Asian studies and Asian American studies is Kandice Chuh and Karen Shimakawa's edited collection *Orientations* (2001).

7 For a discussion of the national/transnational divide, please see Wong (1995) and Koshy (1996).

8 See, for instance, Lee (1999). In this essay, Lee forwards class as a key, framing concept that helps to avoid certain theoretical oversights within theories of globalization.

9 This dichotomy relates to the possibility and formation of panethnic alliances under the sign of "Asian America" versus under the sign of one's own ethnic group (e.g., "South Asian American"). For a discussion of the viability of South Asian American studies under the sign of Asian American studies, please see Davé et al. (2000). Demographic changes on college campuses have, in fact, meant that ethnic specific alliances (e.g., Taiwanese or Taiwanese American student organization and Vietnamese or Vietnamese American student organizations) vastly outnumber Asian American (panethnic) student organizations on college campuses. See Le Espiritu (1992) for a discussion of historical panethnic alliances and struggles.

10 While Cheng (2002) and Eng (2001) use psychoanalysis and while Chuh (2003) uses deconstruction as methods, all three reconceive the uses of those methodologies – and thus retool those methodologies – to be useful as approaches to Asian Americanist critique.

11 Anecdotally, on the one hand, in the past few years, I have encountered scholars who have said to me personally that they are not sure whether or not they would want to apply for Asian American studies positions, because they either have real problems with the notion of Asian American studies, have published work that challenges such scholarship, or have experienced feelings of marginalization that they see as being a result of things Asian Americanists have said or done. On the other hand, I have always been intrigued by the fact that challenging or critiquing work in a given field often leads to invitations to be on panels in that field. What both of these things suggest to me is that core to Asian American studies currently is a dimension of self-reflection and self-critique; an ever-present ambivalence about one's own institutional, political, and ethical relationship to "the field"; and a sense of isolation resulting from not being understood or not being included in appropriate ways in discourse.

12 I am thinking here of the University of California regent, Ward Connerly's, (un)inspired movement to eliminate the collection of personal racial and ethnic information in the state of California.

13 See my article with John M. Sloop in the field of communication (Ono and Sloop 1992).

14 She characterizes the Subaltern Studies group as having sought to retrieve a subaltern consciousness, an act that she says is "a *strategic* use of positivist essentialism in a scrupulously visible political interest" (Spivak 1988: 205).

15 Chuh and Shimakawa's anthology on this subject addresses in significant detail the issues that emerge in discussing the relationship between Asian and Asian American studies.

16 See, for instance, Trinh (1989) and Rony (1996).

17 Wendy Ho characterizes such violence within early Asian American cultural national-ism as "warrior" like. Early cultural nationalist discourses, she writes, projected and glorified "the power of the warrior life of Asian American men and their loyal male-identified kung-fu warrior women" (1999: 91).

18 See Chuh and Shimakawa (2001).

19 See the sister volume to this volume, entitled *A Companion to Asian American Studies*.

20 For instance, one review of this manuscript noted that while two essays in the volume (Mannur and Maira) address South Asian American experiences, neither essay specifi-cally advocates for the study of South Asian American studies as an emergent area of study but instead makes a case for food and youth studies, respectively. This is a fair critique of the volume, but my goal is not to elucidate specific area or categorical studies. Issues and conceptions of identity resonate throughout each essay in the volume. For instance, Helen Toribio's essay focuses on the specific field of Filipino American history, not on studies of Filipino Americans more broadly. For an excellent essay arguing for a focus on South Asian Americans see Davé et al. (2000). For careful analysis of the role South Asians have played within Asian American legal and historical discourses, see Koshy (1996).

REFERENCES

Cheng, A. (2002) *Melancholy of Race: Psychoanalysis, Assimilation, and Hidden Grief.* Oxford University Press, Oxford.

Chuh, K. (2003) *Imagining Otherwise: On Asian Americanist Critique*. Duke University Press, Durham, NC.

Chuh, K. and Shimakawa, K. (eds.) (2001) *Orientations: Mapping Studies in the Asian Diaspora*. Duke University Press, Durham, NC.

Collins, P. H. (1988) *Fighting Words: Black Women and the Search for Justice*. University of Minnesota Press, Minneapolis.

Davé, S. et al. (2000) De-privileging positions: Indian Americans, South Asian Americans, and the politics of Asian American Studies. *Journal of Asian American Studies*: 67–100.

Eng, D. (2001) *Racial Castration Managing Masculinity in Asian America*. Duke University Press, Durham, NC.

Ho, W. (1999) *In Her Mother's House: The Politics of Asian American Mother–Daughter Writing*. AltaMira, Walnut Creek, CA.

Koshy, S. (1996) The fiction of Asian American Literature. *Yale Journal of Criticism* 9(2) (Fall 1996): 315–46.

Lee, R. (1999) Asian American cultural production in Asian-Pacific perspective. *Boundary 2* 26(2) (Summer 1999): 231–54.

Le Espiritu, Y. (1992) *Asian American Panethnicity: Bridging Institutions and Identities*. Temple University Press, Philadelphia, PA.

Omatsu, G. (1994) The "four prisons" and the movements of liberation: Asian American activism from the 1960s to the 1990s. In: Karin Aguilar San-Juan (ed.) *The State of Asian America: Activism and Resistance in the 1990s*. South End Press, Boston.

Ono, K. and Sloop, J. M. (1992) Commitment to *Telos* – a sustained critical rhetoric. *Communication Monographs* 59(1): 48–60.

Rony, F. R. (1996) *The Third Eye: Race, Cinema, and Ethnographic Spectacle*. Duke University Press, Durham, NC.

Spivak, G. C. (1988) *In Other Worlds: Essays in Cultural Politics*. Routledge, New York and London.

Trinh, T. M.-h. *Woman, Native, Other: Writing Postcoloniality and Feminism*. Indiana University Press, Bloomington, IN.

Wei, W. (1993) *The Asian American Movement*. Temple University Press, Philadelphia, PA.

Wong, S-l. C. Denationalization reconsidered: Asian American cultural criticism at a theoretical crossroads. *Amerasia Journal* 21(1/2): 1–27.

PART 1

Representations

CHAPTER ONE

What is the Political? American Culture and the Example of Viet Nam

Viet Thanh Nguyen

Among Asian Americans, the idea of being political is highly pronounced, and yet their definition of the political is still vague. We do know that the driving concern for Asian American intellectual work since its beginning in the nineteenth century has been the question of how the political becomes manifest through the use and abuse of power. Identifying with those who have been abused by the powerful, Asian American intellectuals have sought to question, challenge, and overcome the legitimacy of that power and those who wield it.[1] As Lingyan Yang (2002) argues, Asian American intellectuals should speak truth to power. We must acknowledge, however, that Asian American intellectuals are generally predisposed to speaking the truth about *abusive* power, especially as it is manifest in the United States, rather than about power in general.

In that respect, Asian Americans are not unusual among the American left and the movements for a radical democratic culture that wrestle with the United States' role in globalization and imperial domination. For Asian American intellectuals and the American left, the workings of power and the political pose three challenges that exceed this concern with how power and the political are used and abused domestically. The first challenge concerns how those who are subordinated in one way or another use power themselves. The second challenge arises in an era of globalization, when we must address the role of power in the nations of origin from which the subordinated come or with which they feel allied. Finally, the third challenge may be the most difficult for those of us who see ourselves as political: confronting the neglected claim to the apolitical exercised by many of those who are subordinated. Confronting the political and working through what Ralph Ellison has called the "identity of passions" (quoted in Gilroy 1993: 111), composed of shared ideology and chosen beliefs, Asian American intellectuals can discover in Asian American experiences a form of practice, more important than identity, which can be useful for a radical left politics.

George Lipsitz (1990) gestures in this direction when he argues that ethnic minorities' "exclusion from political power and cultural recognition has allowed aggrieved populations to cultivate sophisticated capacities for ambiguity, juxtaposition and irony – all key qualities in the postmodern aesthetic" (135). In our postmodern moment, we cannot always easily reconcile ambiguity, juxtaposition, and irony with the demand for commitment that has been essential in American ethnic minorities' intellectual and political practice. Yet, ambiguity is the best word to describe the historical situation of Asian Americans. They are forever caught between the polarizing demands of a racial black–white binary that renders them invisible and a nationalism that offers only the possibilities of assimilation or alienation. Ambiguity and commitment then comprise the most difficult opposition that (Asian) American intellectuals must work through, and irony is the sign of that opposition.

Ambiguity's challenge to commitment is particularly acute when it comes to the intersection of aesthetics and politics. In his essay on "Commitment," Theodor Adorno (1977) argues that the committed artist is someone who must engage in a formal method of experimentation grounded in the material reality of history. Even as he privileges the autonomy of formal experimentation, Adorno also insists upon a narrow notion of political commitment. He is an example of the committed writers of whom Trinh T. Minh-ha (1989) speaks, "the ones who write both to awaken to the consciousness of their guilt and to give their readers a guilty conscience [...] such a definition naturally places the committed writer on the side of Power" (10–11). Trinh's skepticism about the committed writer, and her linking of commitment with "Power," seems to rule out the usefulness of power for those interested in writing about the subordinated. Yet, as Wendy Brown (1995) argues, this reluctance to use power and the willingness to reproach it as something negative are signs of impotence and submission to a political economy of globalizing capitalism and diffused, omnipresent state power that seems overwhelming (70–1). Therefore, for writers and the subordinated, two distinct if oftentimes overlapping populations, the use of power is both necessary and inevitable if they expect political action and change, either through political movements or through aesthetic practice.[2]

As a result, the crucial questions for committed artists and intellectuals are twofold. First, if commitment is necessary for any opposition to domination and abuse, then can ambiguity be used to manage ethically the inevitable use of power? And second, if ambiguity can hamper resolve and introduce self-doubt, then what role can it play in political critique and mobilization? Adorno properly draws a distinction between aesthetics and politics, and the answers to these questions differ somewhat depending on whether we are focusing on aesthetics or politics. The American war in Viet Nam and its aftermath presents us with an opportunity to consider how these questions play out in both realms, for the war is an example of what Mary Louise Pratt (1992) has called a "contact zone." In contact zones, different cultures meet in tragic but also productive ways, and in the case of the war, what we find is also a moment where aesthetics can be used to question politics, and vice versa.[3]

John Carlos Rowe (2000) has argued that American studies needs to transform itself into a study of contact zones, rather than a study of groups and separate cultures. Multiculturalism and nationalism use this logic of culture as discrete, and, in the case of the United States, both multiculturalism and nationalism can be provincial.[4] American studies, for example, does not usually study other peoples, places, or events outside of the United States, even when the United States has had great interaction with and impact upon these peoples, places, or events, and vice versa. Furthermore, when scholars consider these other places they are usually viewed through US intellectual paradigms which are considered "exportable and meaningful everywhere" (Desmond and Dominguez 1996: 476). Therefore, we look for similarities to our own location, rather than considering how a foreign perspective on our own location may be fundamentally different and may produce different results.[5]

This type of provincialism becomes glaringly, distressingly evident in the work that deals with the American war in Viet Nam. While both the United States and Viet Nam were guilty of nationalist solipsism during and after the war, the United States fostered a wealth of representations and presented them worldwide in a way the Vietnamese could not. This imbalance on the field of representation is a direct result of the inequities of globalization, in which the war played a key part as a moment of interruption. When it comes to the war and accounting for its place in the history of globalization, American studies and cultural production need to focus as much upon the impact of the war on Viet Nam as on the United States. In doing so, we will learn more about the United States than we might anticipate. As for Asian Americans, the war matters because the Vietnamese revolution helped to inspire the Asian American movement. If an Asian American methodology is one that not only questions abusive power but also ponders the ethical management of power, then what happened to the Vietnamese under communism should matter to Asian Americans as well as to those interested in the pursuit of a radical democratic culture.

If Asian Americans have tended to forget some aspects of the war and remember others, they are not unusual. From 1975 on, the American nation as a whole has struggled to reconcile the state's attempts at rehabilitating the war with popular memory of the war. According to Robert McMahon (2002), the state, during events such as presidential speeches, seeks to remember the war as another example of selfless American exceptionalism through the "discourses of heroic sacrifice, reconciliation, and healing" (171). Popular culture's depiction of the war, however, shows that there are still "widespread feelings of anguish, revulsion, and opprobrium toward the whole Vietnam experience," evident in Hollywood films and mainstream literature (175).

Maya Lin's Vietnam Veterans Memorial Wall, in both its construction and the way it is experienced by its viewers, is central to this struggle for memory and for considering the intersection of aesthetics and politics. In her book *Boundaries*, Lin (2000) acknowledges that she was "naïve" about her racial identity during the controversies around her selection and design, and she narrates the climax to a standard Asian American story: "*to some, I am not really an American*" (5:06, italics in original). Now conscious of being an Asian American, she writes that it is the "feeling of being other that has profoundly shaped my way of looking at the world – as if from a distance – a third-person observer" (5:06). While Lin may be the opposite of Adorno in her sense of political detachment, she argues for an aesthetic commitment based upon a negotiation between binaries and oppositions. Numerous Asian diasporic women intellectuals share Lin's method: writers like Theresa Cha, Le Ly Hayslip, and Maxine Hong Kingston, and critics like Ien Ang and Trinh T. Minh-ha.[6]

These writers and critics are diasporic intellectuals in the sense that Ang (2001) describes them, people whose impulse, like that of Lipsitz's minority subject, "is to point to ambiguities, complexities and contradictions, to complicate matters rather than provide formulae for solutions" (2). As a result, she "is declared suspect because her emphasis on undecidability and ambivalence leads arguably to a valuation of hybridity, which does not lend itself to the development of revolutionary strategies" (2). While Ang counters this suspicion by claiming that hybridity is not a luxury but a necessity, a space of "friction and tension" (200), she never makes it clear how hybridity can also be a space of political commitment and how the work of the diasporic intellectual can also be a practice of power. The tension that Ang identifies but never resolves between hybridity and commitment is the tension marked by this question: what is the political, and when does it happen?

Minority discourse and of course Marxism are also obsessed with this question. They sometimes resolve it by claiming in the manner of Fredric Jameson (1986) and Deleuze and Guattari (1986) that every cultural product emanating from the third world or the minority is, by definition, political. While this is true in one sense, it is as unsatisfactory as any other universal claim, both in its simultaneous exhaustiveness and its exclusion and denigration of that which is not political. Lin, who claimed that her design was apolitical, suffers the tired but enduring dilemma of all minority artists of sufficient repute: the general public always expects her, despite any claims to the contrary, to represent the entirety of a culture, a group, an event, or a political problem.

A specialized, critical audience needs to be more creative in the face of such a burden, instead of resorting to standard reflexes such as pointing to how aesthetics cannot escape politics, or how artists cannot escape their specificity into a dream of universality. These reflexes make sense in the United States, where dominant power constantly refuses to admit to the political presence in culture. Dominant power instead seeks simultaneously to commodify culture and to deny its links to the working lives of consumers and inhabitants; from the perspective of dominant power, an apolitical population is desirable. As a result, a leftist or progressive impulse to claim the political basis of culture and to decry the apolitical is understandable but is also a reaction against the mainstream. A sign of this reaction in left politics is the incapacity of the left to imagine what the apolitical might mean in a positive sense.

One political critique that we can level at Lin's memorial concerns how it inadvertently encourages American nationalism. James Young's (1993) argument about the role of monuments becomes important here; he argues that monuments "[allow us to divest] ourselves of the obligation to remember. In shouldering the memory work, monuments may relieve viewers of their memory burden" (5). What, then, is remembered and forgotten in Lin's memorial?[7] For Americans, the wall's dark mirror, engraved with 58,000 American names, compels identification with other Americans and one's self. In the discourse around the memorial, Americans remember the American veteran as the nation's other, the most visible and abject sign of a war many Americans regarded as a civil war in the American soul. Defined by what Lin calls "the power of a name" (4:09) the wall cannot memorialize, or remember, the most important other to the nation in the context of the war, namely the Vietnamese (Sturken 1977: 62–3). As designer of the memorial, Lin also divests herself of the need to remember being part of a racial minority. The absence of the body in the memorial is a key statement by Lin in this regard, as she denies the visibility that can also mark Asian difference from the American norm. Lin demonstrates what an assimilated Asian American might look like: apolitical, invisible and yet central to the American imagination (or, possibly, central because invisible and apolitical).

We can always read the apolitical aesthetic of Lin's wall politically, and yet such a reading is limited in the end because it does not acknowledge the mutually necessary relationship of the political to the apolitical. I see the desire for the apolitical on the part of the artist or the audience as a *potentially* but not inevitably utopian gesture against the futility or contradictions of what sometimes passes for political action. In the contemporary United States, for example, oppositional politics are often articulated through the politicized identities of race, gender, or sexuality. According to Brown, these identities for the left have become "wounded attachments" to past damage and an expression of reliance upon the power of the state to redress this damage, rather than moments around which to organize political movements that would fundamentally alter American society and eradicate the state (52–76). Being apolitical, in this context, might mean disaffection from the identities offered, recognizing that in one sense they are a tie to a constraining past and an omnipresent state rather than a route to an alternative future. Being apolitical can signal a desire for some other mode of practice and identification than that offered by a left stricken with a poverty of imagination.

We need to be sensitive to the varieties of identification because, as Anne Cheng (2000) demonstrates, identification is the ethical staging ground for political action and political identities (195). The question of ethics arises around how one handles the contradictory and confusing process of identification, on the one hand, and the necessary closure demanded by political identities, on the other. In this vein, David Eng (2001) argues, "our psychic identifications [. . .] never quite align with our political or politicized identities"; as a result, "it is crucial that we do not conflate our conflicted identifications with our desired identities" (26). The moment of "friction and tension" Ien Ang speaks of is the moment when identity/identification and the political/apolitical rub against each other. For Ang, this friction and tension occurs in the space and practice of hybridity, which I consider to be a space of ethical practice.

It is in this ethical space that artists produce exciting aesthetic work and where politicized intellectuals can think creatively. Most aesthetic works incorporate elements of both the political and the apolitical to one degree or another. Those works that can hold the political and the apolitical most carefully and vividly in suspension are the ones that will also hold our attention over the long run. Those works that veer too far in either direction tend to be boring or enraging (and oftentimes both). Our own position as viewers and our own sense of "taste" and "value" will, of course, determine what we consider to be political and apolitical. The critical success of Lin's wall has much to do with the way her tastes and values are in resonance with theirs, versus the other, realist statues of servicemen and nurses by Frederick Hart and Glenna Goodacre that are a part of the Vietnam Veterans Memorial. Even if I do not find their statues compelling, they are for some viewers, partially because their political celebration of the recognizable common soldier and nurse at the heart of the capital is balanced by the apolitical absence of any explicit critique of the history and politics of the war.

Lin chooses to examine the war not through the form of whole, recognizable bodies but through the idea of how bodies and minds were wounded and how it is that they can be healed. Furthermore, Lin's wall in the very abstraction of its form is an expression of the ethical tensions between identity/identification and the political/apolitical. In Lin's case, the friction and tension is between the gravity of the war and a desire to break away from it. Lin's memorial is, in her words, a "neutral ground in history" (2:05) for "contemplation" (2:03). To the extent that the wall achieves this effect for some and not for others, it is because it simultaneously represents three things: a wound, a suturing, and a scar. The war was and is a wound to which many are attached, and the wall is itself a wound in the earth. We could further read the wall's summoning of the wound as an attempt at suturing the utopian and the dystopian, on the one hand, and the past and the future, on the other hand. In 1982, the time of the memorial's commission, its utopian gesture was toward confronting the incomprehensibility of the future and death. Its dystopian gesture was toward the incomprehensibility of a massive, murderous American war machine, its weaponry manufactured by an American military-industrial complex and its spirit born from American culture itself. Finally, we could also read the wall as even more than a suture, which is only a wound that has been closed; we could read it instead as a scar, a wound that has been healed. For some, the wall can be the neutral space that Lin intends because for them the war has already become a historical, rather than a living, memory.

For many others, the war is not yet a scar. Twenty-one years after the dedication of the wall we can look at the Vietnam War Memorial of Westminster, California to see how some Asian Americans are continuing the struggle to insert themselves into the national narrative through a memory of a wound. Unlike Lin's memorial, this one is an example of an aesthetic work that submits very much, although not completely, to contemporary political demands. Located on "All American Way," the memorial is the first of its kind that commemorates both American veterans and South Vietnamese veterans. Built through a combined public and private effort, it features ten-foot tall bronze sculptures of an American soldier and of a South Vietnamese soldier. Their postures, gazes, and accoutrements visually echo Frederick Hart's realist sculpture of the three multicultural servicemen that faces Lin's wall and deliberately rebukes both its abstraction and its "gash." Behind the soldiers are two flagpoles: one flying the South Vietnamese flag, the other flying the American flag with the POW/MIA flag beneath (see figure 1.1).

The spectacular opening day ceremony for the memorial on April 27, 2003, drew 9,000 people. The ceremony featured a flyover by a National Guard Huey helicopter, an icon of the war in Viet Nam; speeches by Vietnamese and American generals and admirals, a veteran American nurse, Vietnamese American television celebrities, and politicians and judges; a variety of Vietnamese and American honor guards; the singing of both national anthems and a number of original musical creations; and a large assembly of Vietnamese veterans and others dressed in a diversity of South Vietnamese uniforms representing the army, navy, air force, and even military police. The theme of the speeches was one of remembering heroism, featuring especially the recuperation of the South Vietnamese veteran and the nation he represented. Many of the speakers felt both were neglected and forgotten in American national memory.

If the Vietnamese are excluded from the Vietnam Veterans Memorial, the Vietnam War Memorial of Westminster is a demand for inclusion but is also exclusive itself. The Vietnam War Memorial is an outcome of a protracted fundraising effort and political struggle in which the South Vietnamese's effort for recognition on the part of the larger American public is intertwined with their effort to commemorate South Vietnamese soldiers and to demonize the Vietnamese communist regime. The fundraising and design of the memorial itself was marked by controversy in ways that recall the controversy over the selection of Lin's design for the Vietnam Veterans Memorial. Some critics

Figure 1.1   The Vietnam War Memorial of Westminster, California

of the Westminster design felt that it was not realistic enough in depicting the actual nature of fighting. The artist, Tuan Nguyen, rejected this critique, arguing that he wanted to depict friendship, not war.[8] Regardless, the point of the memorial is that the South Vietnamese are a part of the American nation, albeit a troublesome part both for the state and for many Asian American and left-wing intellectuals.

The memorial commemorates an Asian American population by integrating them with traditional American narratives of war, heroism, sacrifice, nationalism, and anticommunism. The memorial, by participating in and validating these discourses through the figure of the anticommunist male soldier, renders invisible the rest of the Vietnamese American community and is certainly antithetical to many Asian American intellectuals' professed beliefs. At the same time, even as the United States wants to remember its veterans but forget the war, the memorial, with its South Vietnamese and POW/MIA flags, demands that the war itself not be forgotten. Ironically, the whole and undamaged bodies of the memorial's sculpted soldiers can only bring to mind the damaged bodies of the dead who are not represented, but who nevertheless haunt the memorial and give it meaning. This haunting impedes economic globalization and the promotion of trade relationships between Viet Nam and the United States, as the Vietnamese embassy recognized in a letter of protest to the Westminster City Council regarding the memorial.

Not surprisingly, the Vietnamese memory of the war is similarly troubled and troubling. The War Remnants Museum in Saigon, renamed Ho Chi Minh City after the war, is a perfect example of the conflict over memory in Viet Nam. The museum is the largest tourist attraction in that city, even though the Vietnamese government does not endorse it. Since its founding in 1975, the museum's name has successively changed from the Museum of Chinese and American War Crimes to the Museum of American and Puppet War Crimes, then to the Museum of War Crimes, and finally to the War Remnants Museum. The different names reflect the changing political and economic priorities of the Vietnamese government as it has sought rapprochement with China and the United States, especially after the 1986 implementation of *doi moi*, its economic renovation program that implemented free market reforms. *Doi moi* also entailed a liberalization of government attitudes toward artistic free speech, so that in the late 1980s Viet Nam witnessed a boom in literary and cinematic expression that grappled directly with the war's oftentimes disappointing legacy. The War Remnants Museum exemplifies this contradiction that *doi moi* poses for the Vietnamese state, for even as the state seeks free market possibilities, it must balance that quest with the preservation of its ideological inheritance from communism and revolutionary struggle.

The museum is a nondescript, square arrangement of small buildings occupying half a city block in downtown Ho Chi Minh City. As John Martone (2002) puts it, the museum "presents the 'victor's' point of view, but that victor certainly reaped very little by way of spoils" (478). This condition is evident in the museum's structure and presentations. The buildings housing the exhibits encompass a courtyard filled with captured American cannons, bombs, tanks, and airplanes. Inside one building, over the hum of electric fans that fail to dispel the humidity and heat, I encountered blurrily enlarged photographs of atrocities; next door, there was a glass jar containing a deformed human fetus, victim of

Agent Orange; in a darkened cell, I saw painted reproductions of torture scenes; in another cell is a recreation, down to the inhabitant, of a tiger cage where the French, and later the South Vietnamese, shackled political prisoners for years; and in one room I stopped along with a troop of Vietnamese high school students before an enlarged version of Ronald Haeberle's famous photograph capturing the last moments of a group of villagers before American troops massacred them at My Lai.

While Maya Lin insists that death is a private matter, this museum asserts that it is quite public. It is an assertion that fits with the North Vietnamese state's encouragement during the war of the need for selfless sacrifice and martyrdom on the part of its people.[9] The state repeats the memory of that sacrifice in the contemporary moment but also wishes to overcome it when convenient. Seeking further investment, especially in its tourist industry, the state encourages the idea that the Vietnamese are a people who have moved beyond their war-torn past.[10] In this context, the museum's uncomfortable exhibits, which make little effort at reconciliation, have a critical and contradictory purpose in terms of reminding the Western tourist, and the Vietnamese, of history.

In so doing, until recently the War Remnants Museum failed to memorialize the nation's other, like the Vietnam Veterans Memorial. As a result, some tourists have criticized how the museum ignores the deaths and experiences of Americans and South Vietnamese, as well as the atrocities committed by North Vietnamese and Viet Cong troops.[11] The challenge for the Vietnamese state would seem to be how to commemorate more than just the objective fact of the war, which it can do, for example, with the many exhibits of captured American weapons found all over Viet Nam. The state also needs to acknowledge the existence of death and suffering, but without alienating its own people or foreign tourists and investors.

The most recent wing of the War Remnants Museum seems to be an attempt to address this challenge. It is an exhibit, organized by the Western photographers Horst Faas and Tim Page, of photographs taken by photographers who were eventually killed or reported missing in the line of duty, also published in their book *Requiem* (1997). The exhibit and book try to acknowledge and memorialize the other, beginning with the very nature of the photographs' mounting as a partnership between a Vietnamese museum and Western photographers. The exhibit and book also include an international body of photographers, ranging from Americans and other Westerners to Japanese, South Vietnamese, North Vietnamese, and Cambodians.

As Maya Lin speaks of her own position as the outsider and the negotiator between self and other, so do these photographs speak from a similar third-person standpoint of being a witness, at least as Faas and Page introduce them. The exhibit and book ask viewers to identify not just with the object of the image, but with the subject of the perspective as well. The photographer or the artist becomes another victim of the war. As in Maya Lin's memorial, where the abstraction of the design is inevitably noticeable, the artist is the absent presence that filters our gaze at the pictures, imbuing the photographs with a layer of ambiguity and irony.

The biographies of the 135 dead or missing photographers, as well as the juxtaposition of the photographs in the exhibit and book, emphasize this absent presence. As Faas and Page point out, Western photographers and North Vietnamese photographers worked under drastically different material conditions. Western and Japanese photographers could count on unlimited supplies of film and ready access to darkrooms and film labs. In contrast, the North Vietnamese photographers had scant supplies, and were forced to develop their film in makeshift labs in the jungle, or to send their film up the Ho Chi Minh Trail for development. Their film was often destroyed or lost on the trail, or was lost when the photographers themselves died. This explains why, although North Vietnamese photographers account for 72 of the 135 photographers, their photographs make up only a small fraction of the total in the exhibit and book. The absence of these photographs weighs heavily on the book if one is looking for North Vietnamese representations (South Vietnamese ones are scant as well). The biographies of the photographers, one of the most poignant sections of the book, render this absence even more visible. While substantial sections are devoted to the lives and work of Western photographers, the biographies of South Vietnamese, North Vietnamese, and especially the twenty Cambodian photographers are extremely brief. One Cambodian photographer named Leng is not unusual in having no birth or death date and a biography that states baldly: "A freelancer with AP, Leng left no trace."

We do not have to read the exhibit or the museum itself for the voices of the dead or the missing other, searching for some essential meaning to their existence and suffering. It is more productive to read the silences, absences, and "imperfections" of the museum and its exhibits as signs of the nature of the war and its consequences. The material difference of the war for Americans versus the Vietnamese from both sides, and Cambodians and Laotians, is realized in an inverse equation. On one side of the equation are the numbers of dead and missing, and on the other side, the ability to represent and commemorate. Approximately three million Vietnamese died and 300,000 North Vietnamese remain missing versus 58,000 American dead and 2,000 missing. Military and industrial power is the variable that solves the equation, as the United States was able to exercise much greater damage on the infrastructure and people of Southeast Asia than was done to it, despite Jimmy Carter's proclamation that both sides were engaged in mutual destruction. That same power accounts for the greater production, reproduction, and export of American narratives concerning the war and its aftermath.

The *Requiem* exhibit and book – as is the Vietnam Veterans Memorial – are embodiments of this power even as they make the effort to provide some type of commemoration to the war. The material difference between the War Remnants Museum and the Vietnam Veterans Memorial is obvious. Most of the museum's exhibits would not pass muster in many small, municipal American museums; the photographs, for example, are often grainy and poorly mounted, with the exception of the *Requiem* exhibit's photographs. Paradoxically for me, however, the fascination with the museum comes precisely from these qualities that Westerners might see as amateurish and raw. If aesthetic power does derive from the friction and tension between the political and the apolitical, then the museum succeeds aesthetically through its embodiment of that struggle.

The political dimension of the museum lies in its celebration of the triumph of the war, the successful revolution for independence and reunification. Some foreign tourists construe this celebration as "propaganda," and the aesthetics of such "propaganda" clash with the recognizably Western photographic and journalistic aesthetics of *Requiem*. This clash is important, however, for while *Requiem* the book is compelling, *Requiem* the exhibit is even more compelling because of its situation in relationship to an alternative, revolutionary photographic and commemorative history relatively unknown in the United States. Likewise, that history benefits from *Requiem*'s demand for ambiguity about the meaning of the war. We can read this demand as a gesture toward the apolitical, given the politicized climate around the museum's commemoration of death and atrocity.

Shadowed by this memory of three million dead this essay has two political demands. The first is that we remember the American war in Viet Nam as being a typical, rather than an aberrant, manifestation of American policy. The second demand is to think about what the political itself means when the consequences of the ideological struggle in Viet Nam were both catastrophic on a human scale and utterly, depressingly normal on a historical scale. Faced with the paramount political problem of French and American exploitation, resulting in warfare, suffering, and death, the only response the committed may have to the second demand may be the turn to revolution and the idea of the "people," as was the case in Viet Nam. Remembering Viet Nam for the (Asian) American left has also usually been an act of revolutionary identification with the Vietnamese "people," specifically the South Vietnamese of the National Liberation Front (otherwise known as the Viet Cong) and the North Vietnamese.

"The people," however, can be a troubling concept, because "the people" are one thing *and* many, not one thing *or* many. Embedded in the concept of the people is thus the paradox of ambiguity and commitment. That paradox is the answer to the question of "what is the political?" Without ambiguity and the notion of the many, we become idealists in the name of commitment, demanding a unitary notion of the people (and hence of ourselves, if we assume the mantle of the people's representatives). Without commitment and the notion of the one, we become paralyzed by our respect for the diversity of the people, and are incapable of taking concrete political action and creating a collective political movement. Keeping this paradox of the political and the people in mind, we can recast the seemingly dated revolutionary idea of "writing for the people, by the people, and from the people," as Trinh T. Minh-ha suggests (1989: 22).

Irony is one sign of this people's writing and of commitment and ambiguity's paradox. Irony works in two registers. In one register, political ideologues and parties often use the people's name for policies that inflict crimes upon these same people. If abusive power works ironically in this register of manipulation, then the struggle against abusive power works ironically in the other register of recognition. When Lipsitz (1990) argues that ethnic minorities are "masters of irony in an ironic world" (135), he means that they can sometimes recognize the ironic ways in which they are manipulated, not only by their explicit enemies, but also sometimes by those who purport to represent them.

While irony as the sign of commitment and ambiguity's paradox is particularly important for those working in the realm of culture and aesthetics, it is hardly irrelevant for those working in the realm of "real" politics, as is evident in both postwar Viet Nam and the postwar United States. The situation in Viet Nam, where the revolution has "succeeded," is hardly an ideal comparison for the United States, but as the (Asian) American left struggles with the ethical use of power, and to understand its own use of and desire for power, it needs to observe other places where power and the state have been seized by the left. In the case of Viet Nam, this seizure of power has resulted in the communist state saturating everyday life, i.e., rendering everything as a political concern. In contrast, the postwar United States has witnessed the marginalization of the left in the territory of electoral politics and grassroots politics. As a result, the left has turned to the realm of culture for political struggle (and, according to Brown, conceded to the legitimacy of the state itself through using the discourse of equal and civil rights that the state legislates).

In both Viet Nam and the United States, what we will discover is the irony of how the political, manifest through the dominant state or the oppositional left, respectively, subverts itself by seeking to find evidence of itself everywhere. In so doing, the political ironically undermines the ambiguity of the people in the name of commitment. Certainly, the political can be found in the realm of culture, and in this context Lipsitz's claim, following upon Gramsci, that "culture can be a rehearsal for politics" is correct (16), but not only for the left. The right also recognizes the same claim. Yet, even as we can claim that culture is *sometimes* political, it isn't *always*. Nor should it be. For the academic left, as E. San Juan, Jr. (2002) argues, the idea that culture is always political is the dangerous claim that cultural studies sometimes seems to be making when it transforms everything, particularly everyday life and trivial forms of popular culture, into a site of *textual* political analysis and struggle (222–36). The sleight-of-hand overlooked in this turn to textual politics is the substitution of cultural play and negotiation for the mobilization of culture as part of a political movement.

While making these political claims on culture is nevertheless crucial, the universalization of culture-as-politics both in the academy and outside of it goes one step further. This universalization ironically dilutes the meaning of the political and enables the exploitation of the apolitical by capitalism and conservatism, which obviously prefer a docile population. In contrast to the right, the left, as Brown suggests, sees political action and awareness as constituting the practice of freedom itself (21–6). Being apolitical is then a state of unfreedom, a negative existence of defeatism, paralysis, and apathy. As a result, for the left, in a world where everything must be political if freedom is to be achieved, the apolitical becomes the perversity that the political cannot allow.

The left's tendency to read the apolitical negatively is important, but is it exhaustive? In looking at a situation like the war in Viet Nam, driven by the furies and passions of those who believed in their political visions, can we blame the apolitical in Viet Nam for being apolitical? If Hue-Tam Ho Tai (2001) is right, and contemporary Viet Nam after a bloody revolution that consumed three million lives looks very much as South Viet Nam did before the revolution, dominated by a corrupt state more interested in the exploitative pursuit of profit than in freedom, justice, or equality, then whose vision of the future during the time of the war was correct?[12] The apolitical might have had it right, after all, in deciding that the political entailed only death.

Perhaps what we might find in the political's dismissal of the apolitical is not just the righteous belief in the struggle for freedom. The refusal of politics on the part of an apolitical population also speaks directly to the very basis of the political's right to existence. By an apolitical population I do not mean those who are opposed to my political position, for they too are political. Their existence and antagonism confirms my existence as a political being. By the apolitical, in contrast, I refer instead to those who either do not recognize the necessity for politics or commitment on their part, or who do not recognize the legitimacy of the political options available to them. As a result, the apolitical defines a space of either recalcitrance against the political or resistance against the very concept or possibility of resistance itself. Ironically, if not surprisingly, while we who are political can, with the greatest respect, exterminate or punish those who oppose us, we hold the apolitical in the prison of our contempt, for not being like us, and in the ward of our fear, for not recognizing us.

Those of us who are political are then faced with a twofold ethical challenge. On the one hand, we must recognize those who do not agree with us, and on the other hand, we must also recognize those who do not recognize us. In short, we must recognize the autonomy of the apolitical even as we carry on the work of the political, whether that happens to be through political mobilization, textual interpretation, or aesthetic practice. The function of the apolitical is to cast a necessary doubt upon the political's sense of commitment, for the future to which the political are committed is inevitably shrouded in darkness.

Wartime Viet Nam was a place and communist Viet Nam is a society in which this ethical challenge was not met and has not been met. The results both during and after the war have been death and injustice on a massive scale, as those who were political on both sides prosecuted the war against their enemies and the apolitical that happened to be in the way. Realizing the failure of the American endeavor in Viet Nam or the current limits of a communist state from the perspective of a capitalist society is easy, of course. The other, harder question for us would be considering to what extent the ethical challenge of the political is met in the United States today.

Let's end with two examples to illustrate this challenge, with the first being a short story titled "Cun" from Nguyen Huy Thiep (1992), arguably the most important writer to emerge in Viet Nam during the period of *doi moi*. "Cun" is about an unnamed writer whose good friend is a literary critic, K. The writer tells us that K. "demands high standards in what he calls the character of a person. Hard work, sacrifice, dedication, sincerity, and, of course, good grammar are the qualities he requires"; "he understands our literary debates well (which I must confess I don't)" (102). The relationship between the bemused writer and the earnest critic seems analogous to the larger relationship between writers and critics in communist Viet Nam. Here the state closely regulates literature, which remains an important and central cultural expression. In short, when it comes to literature, politics is not merely textual, but has meaning for writers and audiences in terms of approval, publication, censorship and punishment, mediated by critics. This particular critic, K., tells the writer that K.'s father, the "Cun" of the story's title, only wanted to be a human being throughout his short life, but failed. Intrigued by this cryptic fragment, the writer weaves a grotesque story, set during the Japanese-induced famine of 1944 that killed about one million people in the north.

This story-within-a-story concerns a child beggar named Cun, discovered in a drainpipe. He has a beautiful face and a strangely deformed body, with a "hydrocephalic head and soft, seemingly boneless limbs." Cun drags himself along on the ground, but his beautiful face makes him a compelling beggar. Despite his body's inhuman ugliness, Cun is the only person with human characteristics on his street. Through the luck of a windfall inheritance, Cun becomes wealthy, and a beautiful but destitute neighbor persuades the naïve Cun to give her his wealth in exchange for one sexual encounter. This is the only happy moment of Cun's life. Cun lives just long enough to see her give birth to his child before an illness kills Cun. In the timeline of the story told by the writer, the child is the literary critic K. Upon reading the story, the appalled critic claims that the writer has fabricated the story, not knowing the reality; to prove the reality, the critic shows a photo of his father, "a big fat man wearing a black silk shirt with a starched collar. He also wore a neatly trimmed moustache and was smiling at me" (113).

One way to read "Cun" is as a metafictional parable about both the failure of literary criticism and the failure of the revolutionary state. Through depicting the critic as a descendant of a half-human father and a whorish mother, the story-within-a-story not so subtly mocks the critic; the story as a whole further derides the critic by showing how quickly his critical subtleties break down, turning into a naïve photo-realism. Or, even worse, we can read his reaction not so much as a break down but, rather, the fullest expression of his hypocritical aesthetic of propriety. Lost in the critic's reaction is any evaluation of the child beggar Cun, who might be a symbolic embodiment of the poor and their plight in Viet Nam, from the 1944 of the story's setting until the present. The state, in the figure of the critic, is not responsive to these conditions or their non-realist representation in as much as it is concerned with protecting its own lineage, authority, and representation. Invested in a political criticism of strict standards that has not theorized its relation to the rude world of the apolitical, the critic is stunned when confronted with the writer's intrusion into the private space of his family.

The irony in the story is found in the contrast between the critic and the writer. The critic is committed to an aesthetic but has no sense of ambiguity. The writer is equally committed to an aesthetic but, because of his sense of ambiguity about the results of the revolution, better suited to actually depicting "the people." Even the writer's sense of interpretation is finer than the critic's. The writer builds a story upon a fragment that the critic can only counter with a photograph, as if the photograph depicts the truth. Of course, the story is biased and one-sided, given that it's a writer writing about writers and critics, but where else is the writer best equipped to exact his revenge upon critics except in fiction? More importantly, what is a critic to do when confronted with allegations of hypocrisy, blindness, and the misuse of criticism's institutional – not just textual – power? Culture is the battleground where writers and critics meet, sometimes as enemies and sometimes as allies, and the political and apolitical constitute necessary weapons of choice; to adapt Kandice Chuh's argument (2003: 28), they are "collaborative antagonisms" that mutually enable each other.

During the course of this essay I have presented a series of these collaborative antagonisms: political/apolitical, realist/abstract, identity/identification, and commitment/ambiguity. In doing so, I certainly do not intend to imply that the elements of these antagonisms somehow exist separately from each other, as if they could be broken apart and aligned neatly with each other into two columns in which texts or events could be placed for easy categorization, so that, for example, only realist art could be political, or as if revolutions against oppression were unambiguous acts of commitment. Rather, these antagonisms exist within texts and events, animating them as they also animate the actors in these events and the critics and artists who create and interpret these texts. In order to make sense of what we see, we also use these antagonisms as if they were the collection of lenses found in an optometrist's refractor. In the act of interpretation or observation, we are both patient and optometrist. Seeing through two eyes separately and yet simultaneously, we experiment with an ever-changing pair of lenses until what we observe is in focus.

I end, then, with a photograph that struck me deeply when it finally came into focus for me. The concluding image of *Requiem*, the book, captures a shattered artillery site, and is the only known surviving work by the North Vietnamese photographer The Dinh (see figure 1.2). In this photograph, there is both "abstraction" and "reality." The reality is that a howitzer intrudes on the left, pointing toward a jumble of crates and equipment. The barrel of the howitzer is parallel to the body of a dead soldier, his face hidden or destroyed, one of his legs bent at the knee while the other is partially buried in the dirt. The fabric of his pants is somehow, for some reason, darker than the fabric of the rest of his uniform. Hovering over the landscape is The Dinh's shadow as he takes the photograph. The abstraction is that the soldier's corpse, the most aching sign of the real, is difficult upon first viewing to discern as a corpse amidst the wreckage, while The Dinh's shadow is as much a ghostly presence and the absence of a body as it is a real shadow. The photograph is eerily appropriate as a visual metaphor for the presence of the Asian photographers in the *Requiem* exhibit and book. They are, for the most part, shadows without stories. This shadowy existence is confirmed if we look at the back of the sole, torn print of the photograph, on which there is this pencil-written obituary: "The Dinh was killed."[13]

If the photograph is both abstract and real, it is also both political and apolitical. The Dinh was working in the service of his army, producing photographs for an expressly political purpose. Yet, the politics of this photograph is

Figure 1.2 The only surviving photograph of The Dinh (courtesy of the Requiem Collection)

hard to determine. Both the photographer and his photograph exist for us as fragments of war, their presence cryptic, haunting, and ambiguous. What we see in the photograph is our own shadow looming over the landscape, in the same way that what we experience at Maya Lin's wall is our own reflection. There is ambiguity in these subjective responses, the possibility that the photograph and the wall may not be clear-cut statements about war and death, and that they may survive the politics of their time and become "merely" aesthetic or cultural. This may unsettle us, but it shouldn't. After all, there is a sign of commitment captured in this seemingly ambiguous photograph: it is the photographer himself with his finger on the shutter.

NOTES

1 This essay has benefited from the comments of Kent Ono and the participants at the "New Directions in Asian American Studies" conference he organized at the University of Illinois, Urbana-Champaign. I also thank Rachel Lee at UCLA and Ruth Mayer at the University of Hannover for generously providing further opportunities to refine the essay before audiences. This essay would also not have been possible without Cam Vu's valuable and dedicated research assistance. Finally, Horst Faas was kind enough to provide me with the reprint permission for, as well as the digital image of, the photograph by The Dinh. As for the definition of an Asian American intellectual I am using, see the introduction to my book *Race and Resistance* (2002), where I discuss it extensively.

2 Pierre Bourdieu argues that writers, and other cultural workers, often feel an alignment with subordinated populations. This is because writers are the dominated fraction of the dominant economic class, and hence can identify with the dominated in general.

3 Marilyn B. Young has also called the war a "zone of contested meaning" (*The Vietnam Wars, 1945–1990*, p. 314), quoted in McMahon (2002: 159).

4 In addition to Rowe, other scholars who have made similar arguments about the ethnocentric limits of American studies include Friedensohn (1979), Kerber (1989), Lee (1995), and Desmond and Dominguez (1996).

5 Asian American studies, too, suffers from some of this same provincialism, marked by its tendency of relying on American perspectives, American sources, and the English language, even when it tries to become transnational. Some notable exceptions include Lai et al. (1991), Wong (1992), and Hsu (2002).

6 The oppositions and binaries they negotiate range across geography, nationality, ideology, and gender. Kingston (1989), Hayslip (1989), and Trinh (1989) have also claimed the American war in Viet Nam as central to their experience of themselves as subjects and artists.

7 There is a considerable body of scholarship on the history of Lin's memorial and its effect upon various audiences. Sturken's (1997) work makes an excellent introduction.

8 I used the following sources for information on the Vietnam War Memorial's history: Carter (2000), Gittelsohn (2003), Templeton (2003), and an article with no named author in *The Asian Voice* (2003).

9 See Malarney (2001) for this argument concerning the state's representation of death and mourning.

10 See Kennedy and Williams (2001) for more on the role of tourism in contemporary Viet Nam.

11 This discussion of tourist reactions to the War Remnants Museum stems from my informal survey of websites designed by individual tourists that document their trips to Viet Nam generally and visits to the museum specifically. The two major reactions found in these websites are, not surprisingly, guilt about American actions or anger at the museum's characterizations of these actions. See Scott Laderman's "Navigating Contested Terrain" for his own more detailed accounting of these reactions to the museum, based on tourist interviews and the museum's visitor logs.

12 Tai does not explore in detail why contemporary Viet Nam looks like pre-1975 South Viet Nam. From a capitalist point of view, as Laderman argues in "Celebrating *Doi Moi*," it may seem that this ironic result is simply a confirmation of capitalist possibility, interrupted by a period of communist misrule. From a more critical point of view, however, culpability is much more complex, if one considers the effects of the twenty-year American embargo on Viet Nam, which was essentially war by other means.

13 The description of the photograph's physical condition comes from an email by Horst Faas, June 2, 2003.

REFERENCES

Adorno, T. (1977) Commitment. *Aesthetics and Politics.* Verso, London, pp. 177–95.

Ang, I. (2001) *On Not Speaking Chinese: Living Between Asia and the West.* Routledge, New York.

The Asian Voice (January 1–15, 2003) Vietnam War Memorial gets major boost. http://www.theasianvoice.com/200211_03/html/vietnam.html (April 28, 2003).

Bourdieu, P. (1993) *The Field of Cultural Production.* Columbia University Press, New York.

Brown, W. (1995) *States of Injury: Power and Freedom in Late Modernity.* Princeton University Press, Princeton.

Carter, C. J. (June 15–21, 2000) War waged over memorial statue. *Asianweek.* http://www.asianweek.com/2000_06_15/bay2_vietnamstatue.html (April 28, 2003).

Cheng, A. (2000) *The Melancholy of Race.* Oxford University Press, New York.

Chuh, K. (2003) *Imagine Otherwise: On Asian Americanist critique.* Duke University Press, Durham.

Deleuze, G. and Guattari, F. (1986) *Kafka: Toward a Minor Literature.* University of Minnesota Press, Minneapolis.

Desmond, J. C. and Dominguez, V. R. (1996) Resituating American Studies in a critical internationalism. *American Quarterly* **48**(3): 475–90.

Eng, D. L. (2001) *Racial Castration: Managing Masculinity in Asian America.* Duke University Press, Durham.

Faas, H. and Page, T. (eds.) (1997) *Requiem: By the Photographers Who Died in Vietnam and Indochina.* Random House, New York.

Friedensohn, D. (1979) The mid-life crisis of American Studies. *American Quarterly* **31**(3): 372–6.

Gilroy, P. (1993) *The Black Atlantic: Modernity and Double Consciousness.* Harvard University Press, Cambridge.

Gittelsohn, J. (April 28, 2003) For some, memorial is vindication. *Orange County Register.* http://www.ocregister.com (April 28, 2003).

Hayslip, L. L. with Wurts, J. (1989) *When Heaven and Earth Changed Places.* Doubleday, New York.

Hsu, M. Y. (2002) *Dreaming of Gold, Dreaming of Home: Transnationalism and Migration Between the United States and South China 1882–1943.* Stanford University Press, Stanford.

Jameson, F. (1986) Third-world literature in the era of multinational capitalism. *Social Text* **15**: 65–88.

Kerber, L. J. (1989) Diversity and the transformation of American Studies. *American Quarterly* **41**(3): 415–31.

Kennedy, L. B. and Williams, M. R. (2001) The past without the pain: the manufacture of nostalgia in Vietnam's tourist industry. In: Tai, H.-T. H. (ed.) *The Country of Memory: Remaking the Past in Late Socialist Vietnam.* University of California Press, Berkeley, pp. 135–63.

Kingston, M. H. (1989) *The Woman Warrior.* Vintage International, New York.

Laderman, S. (n.d.). Celebrating *Doi Moi*: Neoliberalism and Travel Guidebooks for Vietnam. Unpublished manuscript.

Laderman, S. (n.d.). Navigating contested terrain: memory and meaning at the War Remnants Museum. Unpublished manuscript.

Lai, H. M., Lim, G. and Yung, J. (eds.) (1991) *Island: Poetry and History of Chinese Immigrants on Angel Island, 1910–1940.* University of Washington Press, Seattle and London.

Lee, B. (1995) Critical internationalism. *Public Culture* **7**(3): 559–92.

Lin, M. (2000) *Boundaries.* Simon and Schuster, New York.

Lipsitz, G. (1990) *Time Passages: Collective Memory and American Popular Culture.* Minnesota University Press, Minneapolis.

Malarney, S. K. (2001) The fatherland remembers your sacrifice. In: Tai, H.-T. H. (ed.) *The Country of Memory: Remaking the Past in Late Socialist Vietnam.* University of California Press, Berkeley, pp. 46–76.

Martone, J. (2002) Historic truths/looking at earth. *Public Culture* **14**(3): 477–92.

McMahon, R. J. (2002) Contested memory: the Vietnam War and American society, 1975–2001. *Diplomatic History* **26**(2): 159–84.

Nguyen H. T. (1992) Cun. *The General Retires and Other Stories.* Oxford University Press, Singapore, pp. 102–14.

Nguyen, V. T. (2002) *Race and Resistance: Literature and Politics in Asian America.* Oxford University Press, New York.

Pratt, M. L. (1992) *Imperial Eyes: Travel Writing and Transculturation.* Routledge, New York.

Rowe, J. C. (2000) *Post-Nationalist American Studies.* University of California Press, Berkeley.

San Juan, E., Jr. (2002) *Racism and Cultural Studies: Critiques of Multiculturalist Ideology and the Politics of Difference.* Duke University Press, Durham.

Sturken, M. (1997) *Tangled Memories: The Vietnam War, the AIDS Epidemic, and the Politics of Remembering.* University of California Press, Berkeley.

Tai, H.-T. H. (2001). Faces of remembering and forgetting. In: Tai, H.-T. H. (ed.) *The Country of Memory: Remaking the Past in Late Socialist Vietnam.* University of California Press, Berkeley, pp. 167–95.

Templeton, A. (April 28, 2003) Let it be a place of healing. *Orange County Register.* www.ocregister.com (April 28, 2003).

Trinh, T. M.-h. (1989) *Woman, Native, Other.* Indiana University Press, Bloomington and Indianapolis.

Wong, S.-l. C. (1992) Ethnicizing gender: an exploration of sexuality as sign in Chinese immigrant literature. In: Lim, S.G.-l. and Ling, A. (eds.) *Reading the Literatures of Asian America.* Temple University Press, Philadelphia, pp. 111–29.

Yang, L. (2002). Theorizing Asian America: on Asian American and postcolonial Asian diasporic women intellectuals. *Journal of Asian American Studies* (June), 139–78.

Young, J. (1993). *The Texture of Memory.* Yale University Press, New Haven.

CHAPTER TWO

Ethnography, the Cinematic Apparatus, and Asian American Film Studies[1]

Peter X Feng

At a time when foreign-born Asian immigrants living in the US outnumber US-born Asian Americans, bringing with them linguistic and cultural backgrounds that may make their communication with dominant US culture problematic, visual culture generally and film specifically have the potential to eclipse English-language literature as modes of expression (on the one hand) and socialization (on the other). It is in this context that Asian American studies increasingly incorporates cultural studies approaches (in addition to well-established literary studies methods), but the field risks promoting superficial textual analyses uninformed by medium-specific traditions. For example, literary scholars who turn to cinema have overwhelmingly privileged feature-length fiction at the expense of other important cinematic modes (a failing that might also be observed of film studies generally, although many scholars specialize in the documentary, the experimental film, the short subject, and non-commercial modes such as the home movie).

Given Asian American studies' central aims – to document and explore Asian American experiences and to counter dominant discourses about Asian-ness – the field has a complicated and richly problematic relationship to ethnography. Asian American cinema studies in particular must consider cinema's roots in ethnography – a driving force behind the technological development of cinema and a discipline combining scientific discourse with a political project (virtually) inseparable from imperialism (during the turn of the century period when cinema developed).[2] In addition, Asian American cinema studies has insufficiently examined the legacy of 1970s film theory (especially semiotic and feminist approaches falling under the umbrella of "apparatus theory") focusing on questions of representation, enunciation, spectatorship – in short, the ideological underpinnings of the cinematic apparatus generally (as opposed to the ideological operations of specific texts).

These issues come to a head when we consider how Asian American Studies as a field deploys texts. Even as current scholarship (cultural studies) emphasizes the ways in which Asian bodies have been rhetorically constructed (e.g., Lisa Lowe, David Palumbo-Liu, Anthony W. Lee), in the classroom we often sidestep questions of rhetorical construction when examining texts. The fact that this is happening at the same time that the field of literary studies seems to be increasingly turning to the novel and away from poetry is intriguing and suggestive. There was a time when literature and poetry were synonymous terms – reading literature required appreciation of poetic allusion and thus a poetic tradition – but interest in the discursive construction of novels (from Bakhtin onwards) has resulted in a number of "cultural studies" projects that have shown how (e.g.) legal discourse, medical discourse, correspondence manuals, etc., have shaped the novel – and thereby elevated the position of the novel in literary studies. The novel's representational project enables its introduction into the interdisciplinary Asian American studies classroom, while poetry is generally barred or at least is rarely invited. The *Blu's Hanging* controversy – not to belabor the point – is indicative of a certain incompatibility of these various uses of the novel – and its burden of "representation" (in multiple senses).[3] This is not to argue that literary studies has a sophisticated grasp of representation and other fields approach literature in a naïve way (although that is certainly how initial debates about *Blu's Hanging* within the AAAS were framed).[4] Rather, I am suggesting that the introduction of literary texts into the interdisciplinary classroom is fraught with danger and will be until Asian American studies develops a theory of representation.

One writer whose work reflects a sophisticated awareness of theories of representation as developed by film studies in the 1970s was Theresa Hak Kyung Cha. Cha's *Dictee* is a rare example of a text that avoids constructing a centered speaking subject (and therefore a securely-placed reading subject).[5] The text foregrounds its own constructed nature, calling attention away from what it represents and to its patterns of representation. Cha's text evokes the visceral impact of colonization and exile through a meditation on the nature of language. The title refers to a pedagogical technique used to instruct students in French grammar, wherein students are required to transcribe a dictated text (successful completion of the task requires a student to notate agreements in number and gender that are not aurally distinguishable). Language instruction is thus compared to the practice of catechism (the repetition of dogma until it becomes internalized) and related forms of interpellation. *Dictee* puts these meditations on language in the service of a "narrative" that spans the twentieth century, linking (to take but one example) Korean uprisings against Japanese colonialism in 1919 (*sam-il*) to protests against the US-installed Synghman Rhee in 1960 (*sa-il-ku*). These historical connections are made possible through a structure of identifications and disidentifications, wherein the narrator's voice quotes official discourse one moment (a 1905 letter from Rhee in Honolulu to President Roosevelt that sought to forestall the

Taft–Katsura Pact between the United States and Japan) and private discourse the next (the Calliope section is based on the personal journals of Hyung Soon Huo, Cha's mother). *Dictee* thus refuses to construct a stable position from which to address the reader, producing a corresponding disorientation in the reader. While this disorientation may be frustrating, the result (for this reader anyway) is a heightened sensitivity to narrative conventions that seek to interpellate the reader and thereby shape our consciousness.[6]

Cha's interest in the ways that written and cinematic texts position their readers (spectator-auditors) no doubt arose from her studies, especially her postgraduate work in film theory. Cha studied with Thierry Kuntzel and Christian Metz at Centre d'Etudes Américaine du Cinéma à Paris, and would include their essays in *Apparatus/Cinematic Apparatus: Selected Writings*, published in 1980. Apparatus theory emerged out of French semiotics of the late 1960s, articulating a Marxist critique of cinema as an institution strongly indebted to Althusser's concept of interpellation (the notion that our response to modes of address [hailing] indicates our investment in established forms of communication and power). At the level of textual analysis, critics such as Metz, Jean-Louis Baudry, Kaja Silverman, et al., focused on fundamental cinematic conventions of editing and camera placement and dissected the ideological implications of these conventions. Obviously much of this analysis was grounded in a Marxist critique of film as a commodity and conduit for bourgeois ideology, but apparatus theory also extended its analysis beyond commodity capitalism to examine the foundations of cinema's narrative structures in the Western tradition of the Enlightenment (later, we'll take up an aspect of this argument that is especially relevant when considering the ways that cinema obscures its own representational schemas: the ideological implications of perspective photography).[7]

I propose that Asian Americanists take up a reconsideration of apparatus theory in light of emerging scholarship in critical anthropology, work that has problematized ethnographic technique and foregrounded the role of the anthropologist in constructing (indeed, narrating) knowledge of culture(s).[8] The history of cinema's technological development is intertwined with the instruments invented by anthropologists and naturalists such as Etienne-Jules Marey to record images of human and animal movement for study. At the end of the nineteenth century, anthropology provided the scientific justification for acts of imperialism. During roughly the same period, interest in cinema as a commercial medium was fueled by the US public's interest in the Spanish–American and Philippine–American Wars: US screens were filled with "actualities" (documentary footage of distant lands) and re-enactments (short films with titles such as "The Battle of Manila Bay" and "Filipinos Retreat from Trenches"). In short, imperialism, ethnography, and cinema are mutually implicated at a fundamental level; bringing to bear the insights of apparatus theory (which focuses primarily on cinema as an established industry, but which can also provide insights into the ideological implications of the development of cinematic conventions) will result in a methodological apparatus that is sensitive to cinema's unique structures of interpellation and thus provide us with the beginnings of a theory of representation. Such a theory will enable us to imagine ways that cinema can be brought to bear against the imperialistic overtones of the ethnographic project that shapes cinematic discourse, a "disidentification" with cinema that I take to be at the heart of Asian American cinema studies.[9]

This is a project that I tentatively initiated in chapter 1 of *Identities in Motion* (2002b), a discussion itself heavily influenced by Rony (1996), and it is one that requires more space than I have been allotted here. In lieu of offering a fuller theoretical synthesis of apparatus theory and Asian American film studies, I will instead attempt to demonstrate what such an interpretive method looks like in practice, leaving the formal elaboration and synthesis of these approaches to a later date. I feel that Asian American Studies as a whole must come to grips with its own ambivalent relationship with ethnography, especially in the classroom, where a number of narrative forms are typically deployed to introduce ethnographic content without a full consideration of each medium in its specificity. I am not concerned primarily with narrative film, as both teachers and students are (more or less) well-equipped to approach feature film as a rhetorical system using methodologies derived from literary studies; it is documentary film (which we might think of as non-fiction but not as non-narrative) that concerns me most in this context.

With that in mind, I will undertake a discussion of three varied movies, all documentaries in the larger sense, which engage with questions of ethnography.[10] These three movies engage questions of knowledge and cinematic form in different ways, and each raises different questions about ethnography by positing very different relationships between maker and object of study. In addition, each of these movies represents a "new direction" for Asian American studies since none of them deals primarily with Asian American experience (narrowly defined). Trinh T. Minh-ha's first two films, *Reassemblage* (1982) and *Naked Spaces–Living is Round* (1985), depict the cultures of Senegal, Mauritania, Mali, Burkina Faso, and Togo. Ali Kazimi's *Shooting Indians: A Journey with Jeffrey Thomas* (1997) is a portrait of Canadian Iroquois artist Thomas by a Toronto-based, Delhi-born documentary filmmaker. Finally, Kimi Takesue (a multiracial filmmaker who grew up on the mainland and Hawai'i) produced *Heaven's Crossroad*, an experimental piece utilizing video footage that she shot while visiting Vietnam in 1995.[11]

None of my examples is engaged in auto-ethnography, but all involve Asian/North American makers representing other groups, in which the relations range from superficial (Takesue as tourist), to scholarly (Trinh as ethnomusicologist and resident of Senegal), and the "imagined community" of the Indian and the Iroquois "Indian."

Africa

Trinh Thi Minh-ha was born in Hanoi in 1952, grew up in Saigon, and left Vietnam in 1970 at the age of 17.[12] She trained as a composer and ethnomusicologist at the University of Illinois, where she earned both an MFA and a PhD. From 1977 to 1980 she taught music at the *Institut National des Arts* in Dakar; she returned to Senegal in 1981 to shoot her first 16mm film, *Reassemblage* (1982), a film not "about" but "near by" Senegal. She completed the manuscript for *Woman, Native, Other* in 1983; over the course of the next six years it was rejected by 33 presses, before Indiana University Press eventually published it in 1989, virtually concurrent with the first screenings of *Surname Viet Given Name Nam*. *Woman, Native, Other* includes pointed critiques of conventional ethnographic practice, critiques which Trinh had put into practice with *Reassemblage* and continued with *Naked Spaces–Living is Round* (1985).

Reassemblage is a 40-minute film that represents the Joola, Sereer, Manding, Peul, and Bassari people (among others) of Senegal. In a 1985 interview, Trinh described the strategies in play as "jump cuts, unfinished pans, fragmented compositions, multiple framings [. . . that] prevent the viewers from appropriating the content of the images by their brevity and dispersion" (1992: 213–14).[13] The film's soundtrack mixes field recordings with a meditative and fragmented voice-over by Trinh (e.g., "The omnipresent eye. Scratching my hair or washing my face become a very special act / Watching her through the lens. I look at her becoming me becoming mine / Entering into the only reality of signs where I myself am a sign" [FF 1992: 101]). Trinh notes that her first film foregrounds its "disjunctive aspect" in a fairly didactic (her word is "evident") way. By contrast, *Naked Spaces* "does not *appear* disjunctive even though it may be said to be profoundly and extensively so" (214). In contrast to *Reassemblage*'s strategy of brevity, *Naked Spaces* employs a strategy of "duration and empty (de-centered) circular motion" (214), that is less evident (and, I will contend, less successful) than the earlier film.

Naked Spaces depicts the Joola, Sereer (misspelled "Serer" on screen), Mandingo, Jaxanke, Bassari, Soninke, Oulata, Moba, Tamberma, Kabye, Konkomba, Dogon, Birifor, Bisa, Fon, and Peul peoples of Senegal, Mauritania, Togo, Mali, Burkina Faso, and Benin. Voice-over is divided among three women: Barbara Christian's voice, "the only one that can sound assertive, quotes the villagers' sayings and statements, as well as African writer's works," including those quotes by Western scholars like Chernoff. Linda Peckham's voice "informs according to Western logic and mainly cites Western thinkers" such as Barthes, Cixous, and Heidegger. Trinh's voice "speaks in the first person and relates personal feelings and observations" (FF 1992: 3). Unlike Trinh's *Woman, Native, Other*, which also quotes diverse writers, offering ambiguous attributions like "a learned man says," *Naked Spaces* risks slipping into a simplistic dualism in which African words (given voice by an African American scholar) are elevated and western words (given voice by a white, [English] accented voice) are interrogated.

But by far the most controversial aspect of the soundtrack is Trinh's decision to juxtapose field recordings and images from different regions of Africa. In a 1989 interview, Trinh notes: "in both *Naked Spaces* and *Reassemblage*, music from one group is first heard with that very group and then varingly [sic] repeated afterwards in other groups. The viewer is diversely made aware of such 'violation' of borders" (FF 1992, 124). This use of music is not overtly signaled by the film (in subtitles for example): only an attentive viewer-auditor will note that music from one section of the film is being repeated later. Trinh's aim is avowedly not pan-Africanist: she is not claiming a continuity across regions and ethnicities; nor does she intend to promote an "undifferentiated otherness" (1992: 124). Rather, Trinh's stated intent is indeed to challenge established conventions of anthropological filmmaking directly, as she makes clear in this extended passage (taken from an interview with Scott MacDonald):

> to rectify the Master's colonialist mistakes, they [cultural experts and anthropologists] have come up with disciplinarian guidelines and rules. One of them, for example, is that you always show the source of the music heard, hence more generally speaking, the music of one group should not be erroneously used in the context of another group. However, such rationalization also connotes a preoccupation with authenticity; one that supposes culture can be objectified and reified through "data" and "evidences." Here the use of sync sound becomes binding, and its validation as the most truthful way of documenting is taken for granted.
>
> [. . .] when circumstantial and history-bound methods and techniques become validated as the norms for *all* films no matter who the (ahistorical) subject is, then they prove to be very dangerous: once more an established frame of thinking, a prevailing system of representation is naturalized and seen as the only truthful and "correct" way. Surely enough, these "rules" are particularly binding when it is a question of Third World people: films made on white American culture, for example, can use classical music from any European source and this hardly bothers the viewer. (FF 1992: 124–5)

(This last example is somewhat disingenuous. Trinh's comments describe a common use of extra-diegetic music [i.e., background music], but the soundtrack of *Naked Spaces* bears the auditory signature of field recording.) Trinh is certainly correct in pointing out that the cinematic convention promotes a misleading correspondence of image and soundtrack: for example, just because Joola music accompanies images of Joola architecture does not mean that the music has not been wrested out of its context (perhaps accompanying or indeed constituting a specific ritual); even more fundamentally, continuing music across a cut can function to disguise the cut in a way that Mary Ann Doane (1985) (among others) has identified as serving the ideological function of constructing a coherent subject position for the film spectator. However, since Trinh's strategies do not differ substantially (materially) from "the Master's colonialist mistakes," its deconstructive project is not fully realized.[14]

Elsewhere I have argued that Trinh's *Surname Viet Given Name Nam* is largely successful in foregrounding its challenges to documentary convention, and Trinh has articulated an effective critique of African representation in the context of her 1996 book, co-authored with Bourdier.[15] Their title, *Drawn from African Dwellings*, puns on one of the representational strategies (drawing) employed in the book and thereby emphasizes the distance of the book from the source from which it is "drawn." The book alternates chapters that focus on aspects of cultural practice (e.g., "A Drop of Milk") with chapters of illustrations – captioned but otherwise omitting text (e.g., "Picturing Soninke Dwellings" and "Picturing Bassari Dwellings"). Three of these chapters conclude with brief essays headed "Reflections" that discuss some of the representational strategies utilized in the book. The last such essay, titled "The Bird's-Eye View" (in scare quotes[16]), discusses axonometry.

Axonometric drawing, as opposed to "perspective" or "vanishing point" drawing, preserves spatial relationships, not "as they appear to one's eye, but as they are knowingly reconstructed by the eye of one's mind" (Bourdier and Trinh 1996: 227). Bourdier typically combines axonometry with an oblique, overhead view employing cutaways or semi-transparent walls, allowing a synthesis of the ground plan and the front view (not strictly speaking an "elevation," but conveying much of the same information). Bourdier and Trinh gesture toward a critique of Euro-centrism by noting that axonometric representation can be traced back to pictorial traditions in ancient China while perspective has its roots in the Renaissance (and is indeed sometimes called Quattrocento perspective). Apparatus theorists have argued that perspective representation (mechanically produced by the camera lens) serves to locate the spectator in a particular location in space and therefore organizes pro-filmic space to be observed from a specific (and ideologically determined) vantage point.[17] By contrast, Chinese scroll painting traditions do not imply a vantage point and therefore allow the spectator to identify not with the act of viewing but selectively, with the space itself. However, Bourdier and Trinh do not offer axonometry as an un-ideologically inflected system of representation. While noting that such drawings "entice a certain 'rediscovery' in the reading journey [...it] suggests thereby an understanding of how the spaces interact, while inviting the reader to imagine the experience of walking through several spaces with its offered and hidden views" (229). Bourdier and Trinh note that this invitation to "walk through" suggests a colonizing impulse consistent with the use of the technique toward military or scientific aims, but they note that axonometry maintains a "fundamental perceptive ambiguity" (228). Bourdier and Trinh conclude by noting, "In the end, it may be adequate to say that one of the paradoxes of the axonometric drawing lies in the fact that it offers a different way of viewing for every onlooker, and yet the view offered is one that nobody can ever really have" (230).

By discussing the reasons and limitations of their choice of representational strategy and by refusing to elevate axonometry as a non-western alternative to perspective, Bourdier and Trinh offer a critique of ethnographic conventions while also noting their own implication in those conventions and alternatives. But while Trinh's 1985 film attempts to expose the ideological underpinnings of ethnographic conventions, it fails to offer a reflexive analysis of the convention that it offers in its place.[18] Rather than inviting the spectator-auditor to deconstruct her cinematic project, as I argue that Trinh does in *Surname Viet Given Name Nam* (1989),[19] *Naked Spaces* provides insufficient cues and not only fails to distinguish among the peoples and regions it represents but actively conflates them.

North America

By contrast, Ali Kazimi's *Shooting Indians* is more directly critical of ethnographic and imperial discourses at the level of content, as well as indirectly critical at the level of form.[20] Since Kazimi's film is in a sense a portrait of the Iroquois artist Jeff Thomas, the film is arguably a vehicle for Thomas's own critiques of ethnographic representation. For example, one of Thomas's projects involves visiting monuments and statues devoted to so-called Indians, which he typically photographs with his teenage son in the frame, sometimes mimicking the noble poses of the "vanishing" race. Thomas describes himself as an "urban First Nations person" marginalized by romantic representations of the North American Plains Indians (http://www3.sympatico.ca/onondaga11/intro.html): he poses his son because "My son Bear, whose appearance has changed over the years, attacks the stasis that has engulfed and protected the Indian stereotype" (website, dreamescape1 page). If you visit Thomas's website, lacking contextual cues such as size or print quality, photos like "Dream/Escape: Bear Thomas – General Store" (1994) could easily be taken for snapshots from a family album. Kazimi's film provides a context somewhere in between the website and a gallery showing. By documenting the process, Kazimi's film reflexively emphasizes the construction of Thomas's photographs.

This self-reflexivity is captured in the multiple meanings of the movie's title, which alludes to Hollywood narratives organized by waging war on indigenous Americans, but which also refers to the act of photography and therefore could refer to the work of Edward Curtis, Jeff Thomas, or indeed Ali Kazimi himself. In addition, "shooting" can be taken as a participle as well as a gerund, in which case the title refers to Indians who shoot, that is, Indians who wield cameras – this time referring to Thomas and Kazimi, but not to Curtis. The multiple meanings of the title gesture not only to a layering of actions one upon the other (a mise-en-abîme of Indians with cameras photographing Indians with cameras photographing Indians with weapons) but also to the shifting politics of inclusion: as Curtis is included in some formulations and excluded in others, so (it is implied) is Kazimi linked to Thomas in some formulations and distinguished from him in others. The identification of South Asian and aboriginal American is thus continually problematized. The movie's opening narration begins by telling us:

> My journey begins where Columbus's journey was supposed to end: in India.
>
> Delhi, 1965. We have visitors from England and they have presents for us. [Two plastic figures are displayed.] These are cowboys; they are good. These are red Indians; they are bad.
>
> Toronto, 1983. It's my first year studying film as a foreign student in Canada. Here I'm called an East Indian. Here I see real red Indians in the turn-of-the-century photographs of Edward Curtis. The images seduce me: they remind me of the westerns that I saw in India. Many Canadians tell me that these kind of Indians don't exist anymore.
>
> It's 1984, one more year to go before I finish my studies and return to India. I'm hunting for the subject of a thesis film. I come across a portfolio [of Jeff Thomas's photographic portraits]. These Indians do exist, but they have no India to return to. I decide to make my film about the man who took these pictures [. . .]

This narration deftly establishes a number of Thomas's and Kazimi's themes. Thomas's critique of ethnographic photography and its attendant discourses of extinction (of the photographed) and survival of the (fittest) photographer are alluded to in the statement that "real red Indians" no longer exist. Kazimi subtly indicts his own motivations by noting that Thomas is the topic that he has been "hunting." Finally, the four paragraphs are a veritable "theme and variations" on the possibilities of an identity between South Asians and North Americans: Columbus conflated the two, the English distinguish good Americans from the bad, Canadians distinguish East Indians and red Indians, and Kazimi compares his impending return home to the experience of Thomas's photographic subjects, who have no home, no India. Through these variations, Kazimi makes clear that it is no great leap to connect aboriginal Americans and Desis, while also cautioning us against linking the two in a facile manner.

Kazimi's timeline is not restricted to this prolog, but becomes crucial midway through the film when Kazimi reveals that the project ground to a halt due to turmoil in Thomas's personal life. It is after a chance encounter eight years later "in October 1993" that Kazimi and Thomas agree to "resume [their] journey" in "September 1995." Kazimi and Thomas's reunion is shot on Hi-8 video (in the movie's only non-film sequence). Much of the ensuing sequence (shot at a Dakota powwow held in Bismarck, North Dakota) was shot in black-and-white 16mm footage, tinted blue in the final print (one effect being a more seamless transition between color and monochrome footage). Kazimi elected to shoot these scenes, and the "talking head" interview (shot in the fall of 1996) interspersed throughout the film, in black-and-white. His motivation was in part financial (black-and-white footage is cheaper, and Kazimi was shooting extensive footage for these sequences), in part thematic (to draw a comparison with Thomas's black-and-white medium), and in part aesthetic (he "wanted to play around with filmic language notions of B&W being perceived as 'archival material'"[21]). The blue tint cancels out these originary intentions, leaving the viewer to draw connections between the interview sequences and the Bismarck sequence. If the interviews are largely about Thomas connecting his personal experience to his artistic method, the Bismarck sequence draws a connection (in Thomas's voice-over) between Thomas's artistic practice and the personal satisfaction it provides him.

The last section of *Shooting Indians* involves a journey to Vancouver Island to talk with surviving participants of Edward S. Curtis's 1914 film, *In the Land of the Headhunters*. Like the infamous *Nanook of the North*, Curtis's film purported to be a documentary record of aboriginal life, and like *Nanook* the film also featured carefully staged scenes from which all signs of cultural contact with whites had been removed.[22] If the movie up to this point has been concerned with Kazimi's distance from Thomas (and the identificatory desire to bridge that gulf), the movie now extends that ambivalence and ambiguity to Curtis. Rather than condemning Curtis's work, several people affirm or appropriate Curtis's images. We are told that Maggie Frank, one of the Kwakiutl actors featured in Curtis's film, considers the film to be pseudo-home movie. (This may not be an appropriation at all, since the film she views is the 1973 restoration of the film made "in consultation with fifty surviving cast members" and featuring "a soundtrack of Kwakiutl dialogue, chanting, and singing – none of it subtitled" [(Russell 1999: 99].) For his part, Thomas expresses his belief that many of Curtis's portraits preserve the humanity and dignity of the sitters. Thomas describes

> [...] these incredibly strong portraits full of texture and humanity, strength, power [...] The other photographs, it was pretty obvious that they were constructions. The men that Curtis had photographed, they had that sense about themselves, they brought it to the camera [...] And he's held up, like I say, the poster boy, like this is the wrong thing, you know, this is what's been done to us and it represents everything evil about the white man. And I just didn't feel that way. But it's set up a dialogue for me. I think when you vilify something you have a tendency to discount it, and for me, I was uncomfortable with his work, uncomfortable enough to find out why rather than just to react to it and dismiss it [...]

In Thomas's analysis, Curtis's photographs do not need to be appropriated (as Maggie Frank does with *In the Land of the Headhunters*) for the humanity of his subjects to shine through. Neither does Thomas ascribe resistance to the photographed; rather, Thomas allows that Curtis did not necessarily frame his subjects. If the dignity of the portraits is not entirely attributable to Curtis, neither does that dignity emerge in resistance, out of the friction of the sitter "in spite of" the photographer.

Vietnam

With *Naked Spaces* and *Shooting Indians* as markers, I now want to turn to Kimi Takesue's *Heaven's Crossroad*. Takesue's first two films combined experimental and narrative techniques in carefully planned compositions. *Heaven's Crossroad* differed in that she shot the footage on DigiBeta while traveling through Southeast Asia, initially as a "diaristic tool," and only later decided to assemble the footage into "a piece about regaining sight, about being able to appreciate the world around me" (Lilien 2002). The piece is avowedly about seeing, opening with an epigram by James Elkins (1996) ("Seeing is metamorphosis, not mechanism . . . [it] alters the thing that is seen and transforms the seer") and ending with a close-up of a blind musician;[23] in between there is absolutely no voice-over, and while some segments feature underscored music, the film relies primarily on sync sound. There is no narration or even dialog – only two people speak to the camera – with the exception of a karaoke singer and the blind musician.

Unlike *Naked Spaces* and *Shooting Indians*, *Heaven's Crossroad* is not avowedly positioned in opposition to existing cinematic conventions (ethnography and Hollywood westerns). Certainly the "diaristic" impetus for the project suggests a certain framework, but to the extent that the footage is touristic (and I think the mise-en-scène suggests that the footage is not very touristic at all), in this case I think the uses to which the footage are put clearly overwhelm any remaining touristic impulse – which is to say, editing trumps photography. The epigram suggests only the loosest critique of ethnography – however, the framing of many of the images suggests an opposition in its own right. While there are a few "bird's eye" vantage points, the vast majority of the shots in the piece are notable for the ways that they refuse to document spatial relationships. The camera is often located at waist level with a slight upward tilt (low angle), excluding the horizon and other markers – particularly in the striking opening sequence, where the clarity of the digital video image, the absence of shadow, the omission of spatial markers, and the structure of the editing (jump cuts) all serve to suggest chroma-key and post-production editing.

Takesue has suggested that *Heaven's Crossroad* is about regaining sight. I would put it slightly differently – this video is an attempt to see without interpreting, to show without telling. The video tries to document without offering explanations, and as such it risks many of the same issues that render *Naked Spaces* problematic. But I think the piece's strategies of framing and editing are key. When Trinh abandoned *Reassemblage*'s fragmentary framing and editing in *Naked Spaces*, she was left with footage that does indeed document – that overlaps with ethnographic convention. *Heaven's Crossroad*, by contrast, evinces carefully composed images that deliberately disorient. It could be argued that the piece's deliberate refusal to offer conventional framing – its awareness of conventional seeing – implicitly confirms the logic of those conventions and thereby undercuts its project of finding new modes of seeing. But while it may not fully succeed in seeing anew, Takesue's video does unambiguously distance itself from ethnographic convention.

Conclusion

The three pieces discussed in this chapter each attempt to distance themselves from conventional ethnographic practice, struggling in different ways to evade or foreground their own implication in conventional cinematic language. Attention to dynamics of power and representation are inevitable when minority filmmakers turn their attention to other marginalized groups (as Trinh has pointed out when noting that her right to make films about Africa is continually challenged while that of white filmmakers is not). Asian American literary studies has been highly sensitive to questions of representation when life writing is involved: for example, much scholarship has focused on the various discursive strategies that Maxine Hong Kingston employs in *The Woman Warrior* that undercut the notion that the work is autobiographical. The assumption that Asian American artists make autobiographical work assumes that: (a) minority artists are only of interest insofar as they are concerned with subcultural and cross-cultural issues; (b) dominant artists are equipped to represent others while minority artists can only represent themselves; and (c) minority artists are defined in terms of the thematic content of their work rather than by their formal innovations. To the extent that Asian American studies is engaged in a project of auto-ethnography, the field is at times guilty of these assumptions, e.g., defining artists as "real" vs. "fake," or marginalizing the experiences of some Asian groups if they do not fit the established patterns of migration from East Asia. These assumptions serve to call attention away from the iterations of specific media, so that Asian American studies can be faulted for not fully integrating the insights of its constituent disciplines.

Film studies has long been concerned with enumerating the formal factors that distinguish it from other forms of media; this project can be connected to the field's investment in differentiating its object of study from the fields of literature, theater, etc. But while attention to form may originate in strategies of legitimation, the study of form has brought the field to a rich consideration of cinema's unique structures of interpellation. So while Asian American studies may be drawn toward film for its engagement with questions of identity, the nation, and power at the level of content, apparatus theory reminds us that such questions are profoundly shaped by cinema's formal structures and the ideological underpinnings of the cinematic apparatus (of cinema as an institution). At a moment when the linguistic and cultural diversity of Asian immigrants in the United States requires Asian American studies to interrogate established narratives of migration and acculturation, we must pay particular attention to formal aspects of communication: we cannot understand what is said without considering how it is being articulated. Cinematic discourse is so pervasive that it is easy to treat cinema and television as transparent media: it is, of course, that very fiction of transparency that signals our own imbrication in cinema's interpellative structures.

NOTES

1 I am indebted to Bernard L. Herman for discussing with me architectural representation in particular and cross-cultural representation in general. Thanks also to A. Timothy Spaulding for comments on a nascent draft of this material.
2 In this article, as in chapter 1 of *Identities in Motion*, I am following the lead of Fatimah Tobing Rony (1996).
3 I discussed some of these paradoxes in representation in an unpublished conference presentation (1999). My thinking about the conflicting senses of what it means "to represent" are greatly indebted to Spivak (1994).
4 In 1998, the Association for Asian American Studies awarded Lois-Ann Yamanaka's *Blu's Hanging* its annual prize for fiction; the award was immediately rescinded by vote of the membership. A number of scholars, critics, and artists have discussed the disciplinary and geographic differences that the controversy exposed; many of these perspectives have been usefully summarized and contextualized by Candace Fujikane (2002). In a nutshell, one faction against rescinding the award argued that the character of Ivah was an "unreliable narrator," explaining away the racist depictions of Filipinos in this fashion, and thereby casting those who would rescind the award as unsophisticated readers unfamiliar with literary studies. Many literary scholars, far from taking a stand for or against the award, were caught unprepared by the terms of debate (I'm grateful to Kandice Chuh for this observation).
5 Trinh T. Minh-ha employs excerpts from *Dictee* as epigrams for a special issue of *Discourse*, "She, The Inappropriate/d Other" (1986–87).
6 The essays collected by Kim and Alarcón (1994), particularly Elaine H. Kim's "Poised on the In-Between," discuss the ways in which the text may produce a visceral reaction among diasporic Koreans seeking an unproblematic link to the Korean nation. For a discussion of one diasporic Korean artist's response to *Dictee* (Yunah Hong's video, *memory/all echo*), see Jennifer Guarino-Trier's essay in Feng (2002c).
7 Rosen's (1996) *Narrative, Apparatus, Ideology* provides an excellent introduction to the key writings, and Rosen's introductory essays are particularly helpful in contextualizing the articles that he has selected.
8 I do not pretend to be able to introduce the field of critical anthropology to the reader, but I can cite one work that has influenced my own understanding of the ethnographic project, Ruth Behar's (1996) beautifully written essays collected in *The Vulnerable Observer*.

Since I am about to discuss Trinh T. Minh-ha's films, I should also note that I first encountered chapter 2 of Trinh's *Woman, Native, Other* at a formative stage of my intellectual development; however, I have since been persuaded that Trinh's scathing critique of traditional anthropology is out of step with developments in critical anthropology. See Alexander Moore (1990) for a pointed, if somewhat defensive critique of Trinh's chapter.

In addition to responding to Moore, Sarah Williams (1991) offers a fascinating reading of the page of images *between* chapters 1 and 2 of *Woman, Native, Other.*

9 I borrow the term "disidentification" from Muñoz (1999) to describe the ambivalent critique of cinematic convention evinced by Asian American filmmakers wary of cinema's power to define identity. I discuss this ambivalent relationship at length in the introduction to *Identities in Motion* (2002b).

10 Weinberger's (1994) skeptical assessment of ethnographic cinema includes a list of 14 principles that should guide ethnographic filmmakers. Weinberger's article is the lead essay for an anthology that reprints a number of the articles cited here, including Marcus (1990) and Henrietta Moore (1990), and also includes a conversation between Nancy N. Chen and Trinh T. Minh-ha.

Hockings (1975) collects a number of important articulations about ethnographic film, including contributions from Emile de Brigard, Richard Leacock, David Mac-Dougall, and Jean Rouch. Catherine Russell (1999) elegantly discusses contemporary trends in ethnography and experimental film.

11 Correspondence with author (February 6, 2003).

12 Biographical information on Trinh is drawn from a number of sources, primarily from interviews given by Trinh and collected in *Framer Framed* (1992) and *Cinema Interval* (1999). See also my discussion of Trinh focusing on *Surname Viet Given Name Nam* in *Identities in Motion* (2002b).

13 Ukadike (1994) dismisses arguments that Trinh's style is deliberately disjunctive, calling her films "amateurish" and "structurally and aesthetically sloppy." Ukadike also calls *Reassemblage* pornographic (56).

14 Desmond (1991) argues that the film's soundtrack allows us to "run the danger of generalizing our perceptions into a vague dehistoricized sense of primitive 'African-ness'" (155).

15 Trinh's collaborator on most of her film projects and some of her books is Jean-Paul Bourdier, an architect and a professor of architecture. (Bourdier taught at the School of Architecture and Urbanism in Dakar from 1977 to 1980.) Bourdier and Trinh co-authored *African Spaces: Designs for Living in Upper Volta* (1985) and *Drawn from African Dwellings* (1996).

16 The scare quotes signify that axonometry is not technically any eye's view at all since it is not "determined by the laws of vision" (Bourdier and Trinh 1996: 28).

17 I relate Jean-Louis Baudry's analysis of identification with the camera in my essay on *The Matrix*, a contemporary film that reveals much about the US film industry's investment in the Pacific Rim (2002a).

18 I am grateful to Bernard L. Herman for the insight that *Naked Spaces* offers an incomplete deconstruction, substituting one convention for another. See also Rapaport (1995) for a discussion of *Woman, Native, Other* as deconstructionist and as "deconstruction's other."

19 *Surname* is not nearby Vietnam but about Vietnam – but in a sense it is about "about," in that it interrogates the interview and multiplies the problematics of translation.

20 The reader is referred to Francis (2002) for an extended discussion of Kazimi's film in the context of the critique of "salvage ethnography."

21 This quote and all information about the movie's production are drawn from correspondence with the author (June 4, 2003).

22 For discussion of *Nanook of the North*, see Fatimah Tobing Rony's *The Third Eye* as well as the documentary *Nanook Revisited*.

23 To be precise, the close-up is the penultimate shot, which dissolves briefly into an image of clouds.

REFERENCES

Behar, R. (1996) *The Vulnerable Observer: Anthropology That Breaks Your Heart*. Beacon Press, Boston.

Bourdier, J.-P. and Trinh, T. M.-h. (1985) *African Spaces: Designs for Living in Upper Volta*. Holmes & Meier-Africana Publishing Co., New York.

Bourdier, J.-P. and Trinh, T. M.-h. (1996) *Drawn from African Dwellings*. Indiana University Press, Bloomington.

Cha, T. H. K. (ed.) (1980) *Apparatus/Cinematographic Apparatus: Selected Writings*. Tanam Press, New York.

Cha, T. H. K. (1995) *Dictee*. Third Woman Press, Berkeley.

Desmond, J. (1991) Ethnography, orientalism and the avant-garde film. *Visual Anthropology* 4(2): 147–60.

Doane, M. A. (1985) Ideology and the practice of sound editing and mixing. In: Weis, E. and Belton, J. (eds.) *Film Sound: Theory and Practice*. Columbia University Press, New York, pp. 54–62. Reprinted from: deLauretis, T. and Heath, S. (eds.) (1980) *The Cinematic Apparatus*. St. Martin's Press, New York.

Elkins, J. (1996) *The Object Stares Back: On the Nature of Seeing*. Simon & Schuster, New York.

Feng, P. X (1999) Represent! The paradox of artistic activism for Asian American studies. Paper presented to the Association for Asian American Studies conference, Philadelphia, PA, April 1, 1999.

Feng, P. X (2002a) False Consciousness and Double Consciousness: Race, Virtual Reality, and the Assimilation of Hong Kong Action Cinema in *The Matrix*. In: Cubitt, S. and Sardar, Z. (eds.) *Aliens R Us: The Other in Science Fiction Cinema*. Pluto Press, London, pp. 149–63.

Feng, P. X (2002b) *Identities in Motion: Asian American Film and Video*. Duke University Press, Durham.

Feng, P. X (ed.) (2002c) *Screening Asian Americans*. Rutgers University Press, New Brunswick.

Francis, M. (2002) Reading the autoethnographic perspectives of Indians "shooting Indians." *Topia: A Canadian Journal of Cultural Studies* 7: 5–26.

Fujikane, C. (2002) Sweeping racism under the rug of "censorship": the controversy over Lois-Ann Yamanaka's *Blu's Hanging*. *Amerasia Journal* 26(2): 158–94.

Hockings, P. (ed.) (1975) *Principles of Visual Anthropology.* Mouton Publishers, The Hague.

Kim, E. H. (1994) Poised on the in-between: a Korean American's reflections on Theresa Hak Kyung Cha's *Dictee.* In: Kim, E. H. and Alarcón, N. (eds.) *Writing Self, Writing Nation: Essays on Theresa Hak Kyung Cha's* Dictee. Third Woman Press, Berkeley.

Kim, E. H. and Alarcón, N. (eds.) (1994) *Writing Self, Writing Nation: Essays on Theresa Hak Kyung Cha's* Dictee. Third Woman Press, Berkeley.

Lilien, J. (2002) *Heaven's Crossroads* [sic] gives original perspective on Vietnam. *The Massachusetts Daily Collegian* 29 March, 1.

Marcus, G. E. (1990) The modernist sensibility in recent ethnographic writing and the cinematic metaphor of montage. *Society for Visual Anthropology Review* 6(1): 2–12, 21, 44.

Moore, A. (1990) Performance battles: progress and mis-steps of a woman warrior. *Society for Visual Anthropology Review* 6(2): 73–9.

Moore, H. L. (1990) Anthropology and others. *Society for Visual Anthropology Review* 6(2): 66–72.

Muñoz, J. E. (1999) *Disidentifications: Queers of Color and the Performance of Politics.* University of Minnesota Press, Minneapolis.

Rapaport, H. (1995) Deconstruction's other: Trinh T. Minh-ha and Jacques Derrida. *Diacritics* 25(2): 98–113.

Rony, F. T. (1996) *The Third Eye: Race, Cinema, and Ethnographic Spectacle.* Duke University Press, Durham.

Rosen, P. (ed.) (1996) *Narrative, Apparatus, Ideology: A Film Theory Reader.* Columbia University Press, New York.

Russell, C. (1999) *Experimental Ethnography: The Work of Film in the Age of Video.* Duke University Press, Durham.

Spivak, G. C. (1994) Can the subaltern speak? In: Williams, P. and Chrisman, L. (eds.) *Colonial Discourse and PostColonial Theory.* Columbia University Press, New York, pp. 66–111.

Trinh, T. M.-h. (1982) *Reassemblage.* 40 min. Color.

Trinh, T. M.-h. (1985) *Naked Spaces–Living is Round. Motion Picture* (Spring/Summer).

Trinh, T. M.-h. (1986–87) Introduction. *Discourse* 8 (Fall/Winter): 3–9.

Trinh, T. M.-h. (1989) *Woman, Native, Other: Writing Postcoloniality and Feminism.* Indiana University Press, Bloomington.

Trinh, T. M.-h. (1992) *Framer Framed.* Routledge, New York.

Trinh, T. M.-h. (1999) *Cinema Interval.* Routledge, New York.

Ukadike, N. F. (1994) *Black African Cinema.* University of California Press, Berkeley.

Weinberger, E. (1994) The camera people. In Taylor, L. (ed.) *Visualizing Theory: Selected Essays from V.A.R., 1990–1994.* Routledge, New York, pp. 3–26.

Williams, S. (1991) Suspending anthropology's inscription: observing Trinh Minh-ha observed. *Visual Anthropology Review* 7(1): 7–14.

CHAPTER THREE

Culinary Fictions: Immigrant Foodways and Race in Indian American Literature

Anita Mannur

> Asian Americans may be haunted by the phrase "strange people but they sure can cook," finding themselves valued only in the areas of life where they are allowed to tend to the needs of the dominant group.
>
> Sau-ling Cynthia Wong (1993), "Big Eaters, Treat Lovers, 'Food Prostitutes,' 'Food Pornographers' and Doughnut Makers," 58

In the popular imagination, Asians are inextricably linked to their foodways. Filipinos, Vietnamese, and Koreans are routinely depicted as indiscriminate consumers of disease-ridden animals, offal, and other unmentionables. Chinese men are unflatteringly portrayed as the bucktoothed delivery boy, waiter, and cook, and Indians are depicted as individuals who are drawn to unpalatably fiery tastes.[1] With the notable exception of Sau-ling Wong's (1993) landmark essay, "Big Eaters, Treat Lovers, 'Food Prostitutes,' 'Food Pornographers' and Doughnut Makers," there have been few systematic attempts to map the study of culinary narratives onto studies of race and gender in Asian American literary studies. Such an omission seems particularly egregious given the ubiquity of derogatory images associated with Asian American foodways. Whether it is the Chinese waiters, cooks, or bus boys, Vietnamese shrimp boat operators, Hmong meatpackers, Filipino and Japanese labor in the plantation economy in Hawai'i in the 1930s, or Chinese labor in Alaskan salmon canneries, Asian American laborers have played a pivotal role in agribusiness, food service, and the food and beverage industry.[2] Moreover, it is through their labor that Asian Americans have become, and continue to be, racialized (M. Manalansan IV, unpublished manuscript, 2003). But the absence of any serious engagement with immigrant foodways in Asian American literary studies is an epiphenomenon of several disciplinary anxieties, elisions, and omissions. While social and labor historians and anthropologists have documented the pivotal role that Asian immigrant labor played in the development of American agribusiness, food studies scholars have been slow to understand the racial presence of Asian American labor in the fields, canneries, and shrimp boats.[3] Literary scholarship on food has been equally "color-blind" – critical methodologies inspired by formalism and structuralism have placed little importance on reading the sociopolitical implications of foodways in literature; they focus, instead, on reading the symbolic and affective value of meals and foodstuffs. With the institutionalization of postcolonial theory, however, it has become *de rigueur* to consider how the depiction of ritualized everyday activities might be a window of understanding into the lives of colonized, subjugated, or otherwise marginalized subjects.

As a field of study that has emerged in tandem with the ethnic studies movement, identity politics, and histories of invisibility and exclusion, Asian American literary studies has gravitated toward understanding the everyday as an important site of racial formation for Asian American subjects. Critics, then, cannot naïvely disregard lessons and methodologies imported from postcolonial theory, and must examine how the literary narrative about the everyday is political. Asian American literary critics are acutely aware of the paradoxical bind that envelopes Asian American authors who must, on one hand, negotiate strategies to counter depictions that have cast Asian Americans as heathens and aberrant (Kim 1982; Wong 1993; Nguyen 2002) and, on the other hand, resist the realist-representational-ethnographic impulse that draws audiences who are interested in learning about Asian American experiences from the perspective of the native informant. Literary critics have also noted that in a period of late capitalist orientalism, Asian American literature is fast undergoing a process of commodification. Ketu Katrak (1997) suggests that Indian Americans, as minority writers, must contend with a literary marketplace "eager to consume marginal cultural products [...] when the game of inclusion and exclusion is played without the players always knowing the rules" (195). Viet Nguyen (2002) further suggests that late capitalism has transformed racial identity into a commodity, with Asian America serving as a "niche market for that commodity" (145). But even a cursory glance through many recent collections and monographs yields similar results – food is never considered to be a serious topic of study. I suggest that the works I examine below do not merely reinstate Indian Americans as consuming subjects with exotically interesting foodways; rather, by reading three different modes of consumption, those moments deemed intensely social and cultural, I maintain that consumption is a racializing process that warrants closer analysis. In addition, I examine how culinary moments become productive spaces from which to critique the orientalist notion that Indian Americans are merely "ethnic" subjects with interesting foodways that symbolize their connection with a "homeland" elsewhere.[4]

To this end, I question the strain of research on immigrant foodways that follows on the heels of Herbert Gans's (1979) influential work, which postulates a symbolic relationship between identity and ethnicity. "Ethnicity," Gans contends, "takes on an expressive rather than instrumental function in people's lives" (435). Foodways, in Gans's estimation, are "ready source[s] for ethnic symbols" (436); by consuming particular foods, immigrants can feel connected with a tradition "without having to be incorporated into everyday behavior" (436). I argue, obversely, that the relationship between food and identity is never merely ethnic in a symbolic sense. Rather, the desire to consume particular foods serves to racialize immigrants in particular and powerful ways. Furthermore, I take Sau-ling Wong's point that eating and food cogently illustrate patterns of subjectification and objectification in Asian American literature. And, following literary critic Patricia Chu (2000), I argue that culinary narratives fall within the range of "acceptable" interventions – safely ethnic and non-political because they figuratively serve marginalia up on a platter.[5] The presence of so-called ethnic food in Asian American literary narratives is complexly situated within a dynamic racializing process, which in turn reconfigures prevailing notions about Asian American female subjectivity. This article serves as a foray into arguing for the importance of resituating the study of foodways and culinary practices in Asian American literary studies. I am not suggesting that culinary moments are doorways into understanding sociological truths about everyday Indian American life, nor is my aim blithely to disregard disciplinary and methodological specificities; it is, instead, to signal how Asian American literary criticism might tap into the largely unexplored terrain of food writing in order to produce relevant analyses concerning representations about everyday encounters with food, race, and gender, thereby shifting the epistemological and methodological orientation of the existing body of Asian American literary criticism. To do this, I schematically read three Indian American texts, Chitra Bannerjee's *Mistress of Spices*, Jhumpa Lahiri's short story "Mrs Sen's," and an autobiographical essay, "If You Are What You Eat Then What Am I?" by Geeta Kothari, with a view to establishing how three related modes of everyday behavior – cooking, shopping, and consuming – are sharply gendered and racialized.

Consuming Subjects

Indian grocery stores can seem intimidating with all those strange spices, unfamiliar vegetables, sacks of grains and smells of sandalwood, spices and incense.
Linda Bladholm (2000), *The Indian Grocery Store Demystified*, 12

Chitra Bannerjee Divakaruni's *Mistress of Spices* emerges against the backdrop of a fascination and revulsion with the "authentically" ethnic. Hitting the bookshelves in 1997, the novel is frequently omitted in studies and discussions about Indian American literature. *Mistress of Spices* rests uneasily within studies of Asian American literature because its overtly self-exoticizing terms routed through the culinary imaginary approximate Frank Chin's (1981) concept of "food pornography," a form of cultural self-commodification through which Asian Americans earn a living by capitalizing on the so-called exoticism embedded in one's foodways.[6] As Wong (1993) notes, food pornographers superficially appear to promote, rather than devalue, one's ethnic heritage, but, "what they in fact do is to wrench cultural practices out of their context and display them for gain to the curious gaze of outsiders" (56). Telling the tale of Tilo, an Indian American curandera, who owns an Indian grocery store named Spice Bazaar located in Oakland, California, the novel constructs a narrative (in which chapters are named after spices such as turmeric, cumin, and asafoetida) that are built around highly routine activities like visits to local Indian grocery stores to procure spices and other foodstuffs that evoke the "homeland."

While the novel has understandably come under considerable fire from literary critics, both in the United States and also on the subcontinent, because it crassly packages ethnicity within a palpably exotic ethnic framework, it has been voraciously consumed by the North American mainstream reading public – perhaps *because* as a multicultural commodity it transforms the dusty immigrant enclave of the spice store into a mythically alluring terrain where so-called exotic spices can magically resolve interpersonal problems. When the book was first released, for instance, it was sold along with a packet of spices, presumably to capitalize on the ethnic-exotic appeal of the thematic focus. In the novel, the storeowner, Tilo, is an aging Indian immigrant described as an "architect of the immigrant dream" (28). The novel explains that Tilo's role is to help only her own kind – the South Asian community. All others "must go elsewhere for their need" (68). As these individuals meander in and out of her store to feed their nostalgia for the immigrant homeland, Tilo learns about their psychic and racial traumas as Indians in the United States and dispenses spices to her customers to help them negotiate their problems. But as the novel's epigraph announces, each spice, "should be taken only under the supervision of a qualified Mistress." Like other popular food novels that borrow from the magical realist tradition, notably Laura Esquivel's *Like Water for Chocolate* and Joanne Harris's *Chocolat*, food here is imbued with magical potential. It has the ability to engender love and to help characters overcome personal obstacles. But unlike these novels, the problems that Divakaruni's characters face are a direct consequence of their position as racial and ethnic minorities within the United States. Divakaruni's characters are not the model minority doctors, lawyers, and recently arrived university students who yearn for the "homeland." Instead, the characters are Haroun, a cab driver who is a victim of a racially motivated attack; Lalitha Ahuja, a battered wife; Jagjit, an alienated teenage gang member; and Ramu, an elderly Gujarati immigrant who is caught in the ebb and flow between tradition and modernity.

Consistent with a philosophy of what Vijay Prashad (2000) calls "New Age orientalism," the novel is premised on the notion that Indian Americans are besieged with problems because they are unwilling to allow "spiritual" energy to enter into, and change, their lives. Characters must chart their own journey toward a better life, and they are ably assisted by a curandera who dispenses spices that aid the individual to find the strength from within, as if ingesting turmeric or fennel in the correct doses can curb racism and sexism. In many ways, Tilo, the mistress of spices, bears a striking resemblance to the highly visible Indian American demi-god of self-help, or what Prashad calls a "New Age Sly Guru," Deepak Chopra (47).

Divakaruni's solutions to race- and class-based discrimination are not far removed from Chopra's solutions. Individuals may not participate in a form of consumption based on monetary exchange, but they must take charge of their life, and not blame others, if they are to see improvements in their everyday racial lives. But it is significant that consumption does not provide the answer to Lalitha, a woman who suffers the physical, sexual, and psychic abuse of her husband. Initially, Tilo tries to help Lalitha resolve her problems by slipping a handful of turmeric wrapped in an old newspaper into her grocery bag. When the consumption of turmeric fails to bring an end to Lalitha's abuse at the hands of her violent husband, Tilo turns to another spice. Fennel, she tells Ahuja's wife, is a "wondrous spice. Take a pinch of it raw and whole after every meal to freshen the breath and aid digestion to give you mental strength for what must be done" (104). But for Lalitha, Tilo's words are cheap, offering her little by way of a concrete strategy to extricate herself from a cycle of abuse. Faced with Lalitha's increased skepticism, Tilo searches for another solution:

> I reach for the small bag of fennel to press into her palm, but it is not there. But here is the packet on top of this stack of *India Currents* magazine, where surely I did not place it. Spices, is this a game or is it something you are telling me? There is no time to ponder. I pick up the packet and a copy of the magazine. Give her both. (105)

Shortly afterward, Tilo shortly receives a letter from Lalitha, writing to her from an undisclosed location that is later revealed to be a battered women's shelter. In her letter, Lalitha writes,

> you know that magazine you gave me? In the back were notices. One said, if you are a battered woman, call this number for help [...] the woman on the line was very kind. She was Indian like me, she understood a lot without my telling. She said I was right to call, they would help me if I was sure of what I wanted to do [...] Two women picked me up at the bus stop. They tell me if I want to file a police case they'll help me. But they warn me things won't be easy. (269–70)

As critical race scholars and analysts of domestic abuse in immigrant communities have argued, there is a racialized dimension to domestic violence but the novel fails to fully attend to the complexity of this phenomenon (Bhattacharjee 1992). Lalitha's trauma is solved not by ingesting a magical potion of spices, and by wishing for the best, but by taking a concrete step to extricate herself from an abusive situation. Lalitha ultimately takes that step, but there is a structure, however tentative, that enables her to make this "choice."[7] The problems that the other characters face, in sharp contrast, are far more easily resolved; for Jagjit and Haroun, the consumption of spices and careful love and attention can help to lessen the trauma of their experiences with racism if only they are willing to let go of the pain and suffering they have experienced. And while Jagjit rejects the notion that consuming spices will help him negotiate the everyday racialized violence he encounters because he wears a turban and doesn't speak English fluently, the text too easily slides away from offering a pointed critique of the particularities of youth experiences with racism and suggests that the problems faced by characters such as Jagjit stem from their inability to imagine a way out of their problems and into safer and better realities. A story like Lalitha's exemplifies the novel's desire to fashion a narrative attuned to the racialized encounters particular to Indian American immigrant women and the attendant failures they experience in trying to fashion lives in the United States. But in using a culinary frame that is pornographic in Chin's sense, the novel as a whole dilutes the stench of the unsavory stories with the affective overflow of the aromas and passions of Indian spices. Herein lies one of the biggest paradoxes of the novel. The novel compellingly addresses hate crimes, the difficulty faced by immigrants who toil for hours in 7–11s and gas stations, domestic violence, and the difficulties that cab drivers face, but lest these issues seem too messy for the demands of an ethnic-themed novel, the narrative turns to a version of magical realism inspired by Deepak Chopra's pop Ayurvedic philosophy and romance, commodifying a fictional conceit about Indian mysticism. Ultimately, the text enacts a version of what we might think of as palatable multiculturalism: those narratives that are messy and complicated, those narratives that signal the ways in which Indian American characters are bound up with matters of race, class and gender, give way to something less indigestible and more palatable. But that which is different cannot always be made palatable, or appealing. In the next section, I turn to another example of consumption – one that attends to how the desire to consume everyday foods is inextricably linked with one's ethnic background and also serves to racialize the Indian American subject.

Consuming Americanness

Migration engenders complex changes in the deep structures of people's everyday lives where in certain respects they celebrate the transformations and in other aspects they desperately seek rootedness. "Home" for migrants is a complex place – they hope to rebuild their homes anew, bring some of the old home with them and also fantasize about leaving their traditional homes. Migrant food practices reflect this ambivalence.

Krishnendu Ray (1998), "Meals, Migration and Modernity," 105

If *Mistress of Spices* presents Indian food as mythical, alluring and exotic, Geeta Kothari's (1999) autobiographical essay, "If You are What You Eat, then What am I?" and Jhumpa Lahiri's (1999) short story, "Mrs Sen's," are intently focused on the depiction of the non-exotic aspects of Indian culinary practices in the United States. Kothari's essay first appeared in the pages of the *Kenyon Review* and was later included in the collection, *Best American Essays of 2000*; it remains one of the few works in the series to be written by an Asian American. Speaking of the deep divisions that mark Indian Americans as "other" within the North American racial landscape, Kothari's essay offers a poignant glimpse into what it means to try to become "American" by consuming foods that are overtly coded as "American."

At first glance, her essay's title seems to echo formulaically the tired cliché, which has inspired many scholarly works on food and consumption. Framing the cliché, "you are what you eat," as a question rather than as a smug statement of fact, Kothari's title unearths a deeper ambivalence about food, race, and ontology. Her title interjects doubt, complicating a neat alignment between eating particular foods and claiming a particular identity rooted in, and routed through, race and ethnicity. The essay opens with an epigraph from Michael Ignatieff's *Blood and Belonging* (1995), "To belong is to understand the tacit codes of the people you live with," drawing attention to how immigrants must work to unravel the unwritten codes and rules of US society. Kothari's coming-of-age story is structured as a series of vignettes, in which she continually turns to food to find ways of being included and, by implication, of appearing less "foreign" to her "American" friends. In a discussion over tuna fish sandwiches, Kothari reveals:

> I want to eat what the kids at school eat: bologna, hot dogs, salami – foods my parents find repugnant because they contain pork and meat by-products, crushed bone and hair glued together by chemicals and fat. Although my mother has never been able to tolerate the smell of fish, my mother buys the tuna, hoping to satisfy my longing for American food.
>
> Indians, of course, do not eat such things.
>
> The tuna smells fishy which surprises me because I can't remember anyone's tuna sandwich actually smelling like fish. And the tuna in those sandwiches doesn't look like this, pink and shiny, like an internal organ. In fact, this looks similar to the bad foods my mother doesn't want me to eat. She is silent, holding her face away from the can while peering into it like a half-blind bird. [. . .]
>
> "What's wrong with it?" I ask.
>
> She has no idea. My mother does not know that the tuna everyone else's mothers made for them was tuna *salad*. [. . .]
>
> There is so much my parents don't know. They are not like other parents, and they disappoint me and my sister. They are supposed to help us negotiate the world outside, teach us the clues to proper behavior: what to eat, and how to eat it. [. . .]
>
> We throw the tuna away. This time my mother is disappointed. I go to school with tuna eaters. I see their sandwiches yet cannot explain the discrepancy between

them and the stinking oily fish in my mother's hand. We do not understand so many things, my mother and I. (5–6)

I deliberately quote the first vignette almost in its entirety in order to trace the contours of Kothari's troubling encounters with tuna fish. The tale of making tuna salad out of oily canned tuna fish is one of failed assimilation. Geeta, the child, wishes to eat tuna fish sandwiches because she thinks that by eating American food, she will fuse seamlessly with her friends, and move beyond her racial identity, an external mark of her difference – if she eats like them, then she becomes more like them. Her attempts to assimilate are predicated on internalizing a hegemonic view of middle America's notion about the form of a tuna salad sandwich. But, ironically, her failure to follow the implicit recipes further accentuates her difference instead of facilitating her inclusion into the world of the second grade within the lunchroom cafeteria.[8] Neither she nor her mother understands that a pink oily fish must be mixed with mayonnaise before it acquires the creamy white texture characteristic of the tuna fish sandwiches which her white friends routinely consume for lunch. Kothari's anxiety about tuna fish sandwiches poignantly captures the tensions that arise from eating foods that might be deemed unusual. Here, Kothari's essay focuses on the everyday as the site that racializes Indian Americans. It is not in some elaborate eating ritual that Kothari comes to understand her difference; it is through the mundane act of making a tuna salad sandwich in her mother's kitchen that she confronts the implicit culinary hegemony of white middle-class America, and understands how consumption alone cannot dismantle her racialized experiences.

In sharp contrast to *Mistress of Spices*, which was a popular success and critical failure, is the *Interpreter of Maladies*, Jhumpa Lahiri's Pulitzer Prize-winning collection of short stories. In part, the *Interpreter of Maladies* has appealed to a large segment of mainstream reading publics and won literary accolades because it skillfully evokes the ordinariness of the immigrant existence. But these poignant, at times heart-wrenching, tales of alienation that provide subtly pointed critiques about the racialized underpinnings of Indian American immigrant experiences are also implicitly gendered. In one of the collection's most celebrated stories, "The Third and Final Continent," the narrator is the prototypical immigrant who comes to America in search of the "American Dream." As he waxes about how far he has come from his modest beginnings as a young librarian to live a life beyond his imagination, the narrator of "The Third and Final Continent" is able to imagine "arrival" in specifically gendered terms. It is the narrator, not his wife, who imagines "arrival." Yet a story like "Mrs Sen's" that sits unobtrusively in the middle of the collection does not easily settle questions about arrival, inclusion or exclusion. By and large, literary critics have overlooked the story precisely because it seems to present a mundane problem that does not "travel" easily. In the remainder of this section, I examine how the story thematizes an alternative narrative of migration for the immigrant woman who works within the home and must implicitly uphold the burden of maintaining traditions from the "homeland."

In "Mrs Sen's," Lahiri evocatively narrates an encounter between a pre-pubescent boy, Eliot, and Mrs Sen, the immigrant wife of an Indian professor at a small liberal arts college. Over a series of afternoons, Eliot passes time with Mrs Sen, his babysitter, in the latter's home. Routed through Eliot's perception, the story narrates how the two characters develop a subtle, yet powerfully affective bond that appears to cross lines of age, race, gender, and class. Initially, Eliot passes his time within the confines of the Sen apartment that overflows with the sights and smells of Mrs Sen's home in Calcutta, India, and Mrs Sen gradually allows him to see her in that world. She is a lonely immigrant who yearns for a connection with her home and family; she spends her days imagining what she might best prepare for the evening meal, typically comprising Bengali dishes. At the same time, she recognizes that her makeshift universe of the Indian kitchen can be safely observed by Eliot, a child, but that it must be carefully hidden from the sight of his mother. Eliot marvels at Mrs Sen's culinary prowess, but before Eliot's mother comes to fetch him, all signs of Mrs Sen's "otherness," notably the smell of difference and foreignness, must be carefully covered up. Floors are scrubbed, vegetable peels are removed, and the odor of foods is masked. She does her utmost to lessen the appearance of strangeness by systematically removing anything that might reinforce her status as an "other."

When Mrs Sen ventures into the outside world, it is primarily to purchase food for the week's meals. On one occasion when she succumbs to the pressures of cultural nostalgia, she takes Eliot with her to buy fish, a staple of her culinary repertoire. As she puts it, "in Calcutta people ate fish first thing in the morning, last thing before bed, as a snack after school if they were lucky. They ate the tail, the eggs, even the head" (124). Because she cannot drive, she and Eliot take the bus. During the journey, Mrs Sen is gently reproached for carrying fish, with its pungent odor:

> The driver turned his head and glanced back at Mrs Sen. "What's in the bag?"
> Mrs Sen looked up, startled.
> "Speak English?" The bus began to move again, causing the driver to look at Mrs Sen and Eliot in his enormous rearview mirror.
> "Yes I can speak."
> "Then what's in the bag?"
> "A fish," Mrs Sen replied.
> "The smell seems to be bothering the other passengers. Kid, maybe you should open her window or something." (132–3)

When the bus driver startles Mrs Sen with his offhanded question he assumes that her request to clarify his question means that she cannot speak English. When confronted with Mrs Sen's startled look, he does not repeat his question, but questions whether she can speak English, implicitly suggesting that her failure to respond immediately to his question is a sign that she does not understand his words. Instead of addressing Mrs Sen, he speaks to Eliot, at once erasing Mrs Sen's presence and reminding her of her status as a racialized outsider. Even though she understands the bus driver's words, she does not understand that she is expected to suppress the fishy odor of otherness, so latently offensive to the other passengers on the bus. The next time Mrs Sen decides to buy some fish, she opts not to take the bus – presumably out of a desire not to be cast once again as the racialized outsider who does not understand the tacit rules of society; instead, she braves her fear, and drives to the store with Eliot in tow. The outcome, though not grave, brings a screeching halt to her affiliation with Eliot. Mrs Sen loses control of the car, hitting a telephone pole. The tentative meeting of these different worlds is instantly demolished; Eliot is taken out of Mrs Sen's care, and Mrs Sen returns to a world where she negotiates the pangs of loneliness and alienation that she feels as a woman located far away from her family with no real community to speak of besides her husband in the United States.

Like Kothari, Lahiri evocatively stages the everyday as a scene of dramatic racial encounters. It is in the mundane acts of preparing the evening meal and purchasing fish that Mrs Sen reflects on her position as a racialized immigrant. There is little in this story that can be easily digested without thinking about messy racialized bodies. Mrs Sen's Bengali foodways are not rendered exotic and colorful; indeed, she has to go to pains to hide all visible signs of difference lest she is deemed an unfit caregiver. When Lahiri does speak of culinary nostalgia, it is to tell a story of a woman who has banal, everyday concerns. There is nothing "exotic" in this tale about a woman who seeks to feed her nostalgia for India by purchasing a smelly fish. Further, "Mrs Sen's" does not "travel" easily; it speaks to, and of, Mrs Sen's particular experiences as an Indian immigrant woman, but even more to her position as a Bengali American. As sociologist Krishnendu Ray (1998) notes, "dinner is often one of the few spheres left in an American world where a Bengali can reproduce her Bengalihood actually and materially" (118). Ray argues that the drive toward commodification and the demands of Bengali patriarchy code meals as either "American" or "Bengali," "traditional" dinners or "American" breakfast. Mrs Sen's almost obsessive need to prepare a fully Bengali dinner must be read in light of her position as an immigrant woman wedded into a system of Bengali heterosexual patriarchy. Eliot, for instance, takes note of the care with which she prepares each meal, "eventually a collection of broths simmered over periwinkle flames on the stove. It was never a special occasion, nor was she ever expecting company. It was merely dinner for herself and Mr. Sen" (117). "Mrs Sen's" is not a universalist feel-good story that emphasizes the underlying humanity of the character. Instead, it subtly calls attention to how Mrs Sen's dislocation is further complicated by the implicit pressure to assimilate. Mrs Sen goes to pains to observe the tacit codes of mainstream society but fails because she calls attention to herself and all of the ways in which she and her foodways do not belong.

But following Lahiri's meteoric rise to fame, evidenced by her securing the Pulitzer Prize, her writing has become consumed and commodified in its own way, perhaps because it seems to present a palatable version of multiculturalism, one that reaffirms the view that Indian Americans enter the wider terrain of American culture easily, even though stories like "Mrs Sen's" clearly indicate the opposite. It is perhaps less than surprising that Lahiri's immediate post-Pulitzer writing venture was a short piece titled "Indian Cookout" that appeared within the pages of *Food and Wine,* a leading magazine in the food and beverage industry.[9] Lahiri writes about her own family, describing her parents as "pirates" running the equivalent of an ancient spice trade, transporting spices from India back to her home in Rhode Island in a vintage portmanteau converted into a portable pantry. Here, Indian American foodways are legible within mainstream orientalist terms. The foods alluded to are exotic spices and unusually colored powders. Gone are the smelly fish of her earlier parable about immigrants and food; the immigrant experience in this story is about commemorating nostalgic encounters with their foodways. The story thus engenders a form of "ersatz nostalgia" that allows readers without particular lived experiences or a connection to particular collective historical memories to feel a particular sense of loss for the ways of life that have been forgotten as Indians become more at home on alien soil.[10] Where the stories in *Interpreter of Maladies* unearth the racializing tendencies of food, failure of consumption, and the ways in which immigrants like Mrs Sen fall outside of our imaginations, "Indian Cookout" reaffirms that Indian American immigrants travel easily, and where they continually affirm nostalgia for the "homeland" through their consumptive practices. Here, Lahiri dishes up a narrative for a public that is hungry for visions of culinary alterity that can be considered tasty, colorful, and "exotic." Moreover, Indian Americans can be seen as the consummate minority at ease and at home in the United States – all that they seek to consume is comfortably within reach in suburbia. All that is smelly, distasteful, foreign, violent, or abnormal is carefully kept out of this story to produce a version of Indian American modernity that is line with a vision of palatable multiculturalism that avoids intimating that Indian Americans are also racialized by the foods that they choose to consume.

Digestion and Palatable Futures

If there is one sure thing about food, it is that it is never just food – it is endlessly interpretable – materialised emotion.

Terry Eagleton (1998), "Edible Ecriture," 204

While much more can, and should, be said about each of these stories, it is also clear that they are not exclusively about food; to borrow Terry Eagleton's words, the scenarios are "endlessly interpretable" (204). Here I have offered one out of several possible interpretations, a reading that attempts to locate how ethnically affirming culinary rituals, manifest at an everyday level, can morph into racializing traumas. In her analysis of alimentary motifs in Asian American literature, Sau-ling Wong isolates the image of stone bread in Joy Kogawa's 1981 novel about the Japanese Canadian internment, *Obasan*. Here, the image of processing and digesting the dense bread allegorizes the intellectual journey the reader must undertake in order to "get through the narrative complexities" (Wong 1993: 21) and grapple with the moments that attest to the violent racism, injustices, and traumas intrinsic to the internment experience. In fact, all of the works I have discussed in this article offer up morsels for hungry readers. My own ambivalence about Chitra Divakaruni's novel is twofold. On the one hand, the text blatantly peddles ethnicity; on the other hand, the stories (such as Lalitha's) are not so easily digested. Divakaruni evocatively narrates Lalitha's suffering without casting her as a hapless victim. The simple act of shopping in the type of ethnic grocery store that catches the erudite foodie's fancy is literally turned on its head. Ultimately, spices are not able to heal subjects, but it is the overpowering aroma of spices wafting through her novel, masking the stench of the disquieting stories, that is cause for concern. Meanwhile, Kothari's short story does not even pretend to speak of an easy racialized identity; at each twist and turn of her intellectual journey she must ask herself what it means to be an Indian American and what role food will play in affirming her sense of who she is, ethnically and racially. And even if Mrs Sen does not view herself in racialized terms, the rituals in which she engages to affirm her ethnicity as a dislocated Bengali American in turn racialize her when she must enter into the outside world.

For Asian American literary studies to continue to grow as a field, it will need to think about its relationship to other spheres, both discursive and material. In this brief essay, I have focused on a specific ethnic grouping, Indian American, within the rubric of Asian American literature. While my observations are intended to be tentative and particular to Indian American literary culture, the overall framework that I have offered here can be applied to other Asian American contexts. While the type of concerns with assimilation, cultural differences, and existential differences central to these texts have been, and continue to be, important foci within Asian American literary criticism, current models of inquiry do not adequately situate the everydayness of food. Indeed, food, and in particular its ability to racialize Asian American bodies in an everyday setting, remains largely ignored within the field. Far too often, literary studies discard the everyday in its attempt to not be ethnographic. But as I have argued here, Asian American literary studies cannot *not* engage seriously with food and consumption because culinary practices are also sites of Asian American racial formation;

instead, culinary fictions, read through and against the construction of immigrant subjectivities and positioning, are fertile sites upon which to complicate the notion that immigrant realities for Asian Americans are only about effecting gustatory pleasure.

NOTES

I am grateful to Dale Hudson, Gladys Nubla, Kent Ono, and Cathy Schlund-Vials for sharing their thoughts about this essay, and to Martin Manalansan for allowing me to read from his work in progress.

1 As cultural critic Robert G. Lee (1999) notes, yellow face minstrel songs, such as Billy Rice's "Chinese Ball," had a particular and peculiar fascination with Chinese foodways. The Asian body is racialized through real and imagined foodways and consumptive practices; what makes Asians, particularly the Chinese, appear to be so viscerally offensive is that they are indiscriminate consumers of foods deemed offensive.

2 In 1982, the Vietnamese Fisherman's Association in Galveston Bay, Texas, became embroiled in legal proceedings with the Knights of the Ku Klux Klan. Objecting to the competition posed by the Vietnamese American shrimp boat operators, a group of white fisherman organized an anti-Vietnamese rally in February, 1981. Part of the rally included burning an effigy of a Vietnamese fisherman on a boat deck. Eventually, the US district court for the southern district of Texas found in favor of the plaintiffs, the Vietnamese Fisherman's Association, but not before the group suffered race-based humiliation and loss of income (*Vietnamese Fishermen's Association v. Knights of the Ku Klux Klan 1981*).

3 For instance, Donna Gabaccia's (1998) otherwise astute analysis of food in ethnic America fails to place any real attention on Asian America. In particular, the labor of Asian Americans in agriculture and the food service industry is virtually invisible. In a more recent work, Barbara Haber (2003) meticulously outlines how women's history in the United States can be mapped onto significant moments in US history. Asian Americans, however, are wholly absent from her analysis. A chapter titled "Cooking Behind Barbed Wire: POW's During World War II" is the only chapter focused on Americans overseas. It deals with Americans held prisoner by Japanese-occupied Philippines; essentially, Asian bodies cannot be imagined as part of "American" soil in this culinary history.

4 In a recent article about the relationship of South Asian American Studies to Asian American Studies, the co-authors are alert to the inadequacy of merely positioning South Asians at the center of critical analysis: "Revising this paradigm to correct for under-representation without critiquing its basic assumptions," they argue, "leads to the replication of the model, with new centers, and perhaps slightly altered margins" (Davé et al. 2001: 76).

5 As Chu notes, more overtly political forms of writing are less visible on the Asian American literary landscape because Asian Americans must "find a frame of reference accessible and acceptable to 'mainstream' Americans" (16). In Asian American literature, narratives about food occupy a similar position to the mother–daughter tale, or

the tale of the displaced immigrant's nostalgia. Such narratives have been viewed with suspicion because they are an appealing form of writing that appears to be ethnically affirmative and "merely" cultural. Their pointed attention to the social and cultural, with an apparent lack of "hard" political content, makes these thematic interventions "acceptable" to the mainstream.

6 Frank Chin's framework, while useful, is not wholly unproblematic. As I have argued elsewhere, the monolithic condemnation of culinary narratives also dismisses a range of Asian American texts as "fake" or "inauthentic," particularly those authored by women, because they are about food. See Mannur (forthcoming).

7 Chitra Bannerjee's personal involvement as a founding member of the Bay Area-based South Asian women's group, MAITRI, can perhaps provide an additional point of entry into her treatment of domestic abuse as a structural problem. "Maitri," meaning friendship, is a free, nonprofit organization helping South Asian women (women of Bangladeshi, Indian, Pakistani, and Sri Lankan origin or descent) with problems of domestic violence, conflict resolution, and cultural adjustment. Literature provided by MAITRI understands domestic abuse to be a problem that "cannot be solved by neglect, denial or wishful thinking" (http://www.maitri.org, April 2, 2002).

8 While I cannot fully explore here the extent of lunchroom cafeteria dynamics, this has been established as a site of conflict in race studies. See Beverly Tatum (1997).

9 Later, this piece was anthologized in the inaugural annual collection, *Best Food Writing*, edited by Holly Hughes (2000).

10 See Arjun Appadurai (1996) and Parama Roy (2002) for further discussions on nostalgia and culinary practices.

REFERENCES

Appadurai, A. (1996) *Modernity at Large: The Cultural Dimensions of Globalization.* University of Minnesota Press, Minneapolis.

Bhattacharjee, A. (1992) The habit of ex-nomination: nation, woman and the Indian immigrant bourgeoisie. *Public Culture* 5(1): 19–44.

Bladholm, L. (2000) *The Indian Grocery Store Demystified.* Renaissance Books, Los Angeles.

Chin, F. (1981) *The Chickencoop Chinaman and the Year of the Dragon.* University of Washington Press, Seattle.

Chu, P. (2000) *Assimilating Asians: Gendered Strategies of Authorship in Asian America.* Duke University Press, Durham and London.

Davé, S., Dhingra, P., Maira, S. et al. (2001) De-privileging positions: Indian Americans, South Asian Americans, and the politics of Asian American studies. *Journal of Asian American Studies* 3(1): 67–100.

Divakaruni, C. B. (1997) *Mistress of Spices.* Doubleday, London.

Eagleton, T. (1998) Edible ecriture. In: Griffiths, S. and Wallace, J. (eds.) *Consuming Passions: Food in the Age of Anxiety.* Manchester University Press, Manchester, pp. 203–8.

Gabaccia, D. (1998) *We Are What We Eat: Ethnic Food and the Making of Americans.* Harvard University Press, Cambridge.

Gans, H. J. (1979) Symbolic ethnicity: the future of ethnic groups and cultures in America. In: Sollors, W. (ed.) *Theories of Ethnicity: A Classical Reader.* New York University Press, New York, pp. 425–59.

Haber, B. (2003) *From Hardtack to Home Fries: An Uncommon History of American Cooks and Meals.* Penguin, New York.

Hughes, H. (2000) *Best Food Writing.* Avalon, New York.

Ignatieff, M. (1995) *Blood and Belonging: Journeys into the New Nationalism.* Farrar, Strauss & Giroux, New York.

Katrak, K. H. (1997) South Asian American literature. In: Cheung, K.-K. (ed.) *An Interethnic Companion to Asian American Literature.* Cambridge University Press, Cambridge, pp. 192–218.

Kim, E. (1982) *Asian American Literature.* Temple University Press, Philadelphia.

Kogawa, J. (1981) *Obasan.* Doubleday, New York and London.

Kothari, G. (1999) If you are what you eat, then what am I? *Kenyon Review* (Winter): 6–14.

Lahiri, J. (1999) *Interpreter of Maladies.* Houghton Mifflin, Boston.

Lahiri, J. (2000) Indian takeout. In Hughes, H. (ed.) *Best Food Writing.* Marlow and Company, New York, pp. 301–4.

Lee, R. (1999) *Orientals: Asian Americans in Popular Culture.* Temple University Press, Philadelphia.

Mannur, A. (forthcoming) "Peeking ducks" and "food pornographers": commodifying culinary Chinese Americanness. In: Louie, K. and Khoo, T. (eds.) *Culture, Identity, Commodity: Chinese Diasporic Literatures in English.* Hong Kong University Press, Hong Kong.

Nguyen, V. T. (2002) *Race and Resistance: Literature and Politics in Asian America.* Oxford University Press, Oxford and New York.

Prashad, V. (2000) *Karma of Brown Folk.* University of Minnesota Press, Minneapolis.

Ray, K. (1998) Meals, migration and modernity: domestic cooking and Bengali Indian ethnicity in the United States. *Amerasia Journal* 24(1): 105–27.

Roy, P. (2002) Reading communities and culinary communities: the gastropoetics of the South Asian diaspora. *positions* 10(2): 471–502.

Tatum, B. (1997) *"Why are all the Black Kids Sitting Together in the Cafeteria?" and Other Conversations about Race.* Basic Books, New York.

Vietnamese Fishermen's Association v. Knights of the Ku Klux Klan (1981) 518 F. Suppl. 993, 1010 (S.D. Texas).

Wong, S.-l. C. (1993) Big eaters, treat lovers, "food prostitutes," "food pornographers," and doughnut makers. In: Wong, S.-l. C. *Reading Asian American Literature: From Necessity to Extravagance.* Princeton University Press, Princeton.

PART 2

Identities

Foregrounding Native Nationalisms: A Critique of Antinationalist Sentiment in Asian American Studies

Candace Fujikane

As we consider the new directions in which our work in Asian American studies takes us, I want to return for a moment to the radical origins of Asian American studies in the 1969 Third World Strikes at San Francisco State College. The Third World Liberation Front (TWLF) was a coalition of African American, Asian American, Latino/a, and American Indian campus groups demanding an autonomous Ethnic Studies Program and community control over curricula and hiring. The TWLF drew critical connections between domestic civil rights struggles in the United States and international human rights struggles in imperial wars being fought in Africa, Asia, and Latin America. As an historical moment of alliance among these different campus groups and between the university and the communities beyond it, the Third World Strikes must always remind us that Asian American studies was founded on the pursuit of justice.

At the same time that the Third World Strikes were taking place, American Indians who called themselves "Indians of All Tribes" were engaged in the second occupation of Alcatraz Island in San Francisco Bay. Asserting American Indian title to the federal facility by right of discovery, American Indian activists at Alcatraz initiated the Alcatraz-Red Power Movement (ARPM) which led to 70 property takeovers in the following nine years (Johnson et al. 1997: 9). Similarly, in 1976, Hawaiians were engaged in struggles to reclaim Kahoʻolawe, an island that had been used since WWII as a site for target practice by the US military. These struggles illustrate that although American Indians and Hawaiians were allied with people of color on some civil rights issues, their primary struggle was to reclaim their ancestral lands from the United States.

Thirty years later, we must reevaluate the state of Asian American studies and the stories we tell of its origins. Where Asian Americans focus on the undeniably important alliances between peoples of color in civil rights struggles, those stories have obscured a long history of Native nationalism and the fact that Asian Americans have always been settlers in a colonial context. At this time, we cannot ignore the historical truths that Native peoples present about the US colonial state and our roles as settlers in a colonial context.

Understanding the distinction between Natives and settlers involves our own self-interrogation and reeducation. As Native scholars and activists teach us, we must think of the United States not as a democratic but as a colonial nation-state that has created the distinction between Native and settler. As settlers, we must begin to reexamine the critical frameworks we use to articulate Asian American studies. The subject of my critique is the antinationalist sentiment in Asian American studies that was first directed against the exclusions performed by American nationalism and Asian American cultural nationalism. Asian Americanist critiques of these specific forms of nationalism have ended up homogenizing other nationalist formations in ways that both indirectly and directly oppose Native nationalists engaged in struggles for national liberation. As Asian American scholars and activists committed to social and political justice, we need to hold ourselves accountable for the ways in which our settler scholarship undermines the nationalist struggles of Native peoples.

In the fall of 1998, Jonathan Okamura and I began co-editing a special issue of UCLA's *Amerasia Journal.* We started with a critical framework of race relations in Hawai'i, and it was not until Native Hawaiian nationalist and scholar Haunani-Kay Trask sent us her essay, "Settlers of Color and 'Immigrant' Hegemony: 'Locals' in Hawai'i," that we could identify the settler assumptions behind our conceptualization of our project.[1] Trask's insightful and powerful arguments showed us that our focus on *race relations* was precisely the problem. While our work sought to map out a system of racism among peoples of color in ethnically stratified Hawai'i, we were using a race-based civil rights framework that was ill-equipped for analyzing a colonial situation.[2] In effect, we were leveling the differences between Natives and non-Native peoples of color, reducing indigenous peoples to racial minorities. In our desire to locate shared critiques of racism that would provide a basis for solidarity and alliances between Natives and non-Natives, our project failed to consider the fact that in the colony of Hawai'i, "local" Asians are settlers who are part of the colonial problem.[3]

Trask had been using the term "settler" in essays published in the early 1980s, and in her 1993 collection of essays, *From a Native Daughter: Colonialism and Sovereignty in Hawai'i*, she writes:

> Modern Hawai'i, like its colonial parent the United States, is a settler society; that is,
> Hawai'i is a society in which the indigenous culture and people have been murdered,

suppressed, or marginalized for the benefit of settlers who now dominate our islands. In settler societies, the issue of civil rights is primarily an issue about how to protect settlers against each other and against the state. Injustices done against Native people, such as genocide, land dispossession, language banning, family disintegration, and cultural exploitation, are not part of this intrasettler discussion and are therefore not within the parameters of civil rights. (25)

Hawai'i's history, like that of American Indians, is a violent one of genocide and land theft. The Hawaiian population suffered a catastrophic collapse due to diseases brought by foreigners: the population went from an estimated one million Native Hawaiians in 1778 to about 40,000 in 1893, the year of the US military overthrow of the Hawaiian government. Hawai'i was annexed by the United States in 1898 as a territorial colony, and from that time to the mid-twentieth century, Hawai'i was ruled politically and economically by a white Republican settler oligarchy. In 1954, the Democratic Party takeover ushered in a new era of Asian settler political ascendancy.

Trask's essay focuses on the status of Hawai'i as a colony of the United States politically dominated by white, Japanese, and Chinese settlers. There, she critiques the ideological formulation that America is a "nation of immigrants," a master-narrative of hard work and triumph that has been adopted by a new Asian ruling class. As she argues, local Asians seek to differentiate themselves from *haole* or whites in Hawai'i when Asians, too, are settlers who benefit from the continued dispossession of Native Hawaiians. Trask writes:

Our Native people and territories have been overrun by non-Natives, including Asians. Calling themselves "local," the children of Asian settlers greatly outnumber us. They claim Hawai'i as their own, denying indigenous history, their long collaboration in our continued dispossession, and the benefits therefrom. Part of this denial is the substitution of the term "local" for "immigrant," which is, itself, a particularly celebrated American gloss for "settler." As on the continent, so in our island home. Settlers and their children recast the American tale of nationhood: Hawai'i, like the continent, is naturalized as but another telling illustration of the uniqueness of America's "nation of immigrants." (2000a: 2)

As Trask points out in her essay, indigenous peoples have the right to self-determination and self-government; minority populations do not. The United Nations Draft Declaration on the Rights of Indigenous Peoples affirms indigenous peoples' rights to self-determination, their rights to determine their political status and their economic, social, and political development (2000a: 15).

Trask's essay radically transformed the work that Okamura and I had been doing, and it provides a critical foundation for the *Amerasia Journal* issue we entitled *Whose Vision? Asian Settler Colonialism in Hawai'i*. The distinction she makes between Natives and settlers showed us that Asians in Hawai'i who now dominate the State Legislature and other state apparatuses are part of the

American colonial system. Eiko Kosasa, a sansei or third-generation Japanese settler scholar at the University of Hawai'i, follows Trask's argument by quoting Fanon: "The colonial world is a world cut in two" (Fanon 1963: 38). Kosasa explains that "[i]n colonial Hawai'i, there are two groups: Natives and settlers. Native Hawaiians are the indigenous people of the islands. It is their nation that is under US occupation; therefore, only Native Hawaiians are colonized. The rest of the population, including myself, are settlers regardless of our racial heritage" (Kosasa 1999: 1). As devastating as Asian experiences of colonialism or political persecutions were and are in Asian homelands, and as difficult as it is for Asian Americans to struggle against different forms of oppression in the United States, our very presence in Hawai'i and on the continent was made possible by a colonial process. Although Asian settlers have spent long years fighting for civil rights, the irreducible historical reality is that we have been fighting for equal access to a colonial system that Native peoples seek to dismantle. Kosasa further argues that although immigrants in Hawai'i were initially directed and educated to accept the US nation-state's interests as their own, we must take into account the historical changes that have since taken place: "We sansei and yonsei currently have the political and economic means to assist in terminating the U.S. imperial hold on the islands. As Japanese settlers, we have ascended from being collaborators in a colonial system to being enforcers and keepers of that system. Therefore, it is our obligation, our responsibility to the Native Hawaiian people and to our own community to change this unequal, colonial situation" (2000: 84). Our special issue of *Amerasia Journal* sought to make this critical intervention, and it includes both Native and Asian settler critiques of Asian settler colonialism.

While Japanese and Chinese settlers have come to dominate the political system in Hawai'i, Filipinos and other subordinated Asian groups, too, are settlers, even as the racism and discrimination they are subjected to illuminates the complex power differentials among settler groups. In his own work on colonial amnesia, Dean Saranillio argues that as Filipinos in Hawai'i struggle against intrasettler racism, they also support American colonialism in their patriotic identification with the US nation-state. Saranillio (2003) writes, "My research broadens the [*Amerasia*] journal's question of 'whose vision?' by offering another 'vision' from the standpoint of Filipino Americans, a group that lacks economic and political power, yet seeks empowerment unknowingly within a colonial state. My argument does not contend that Filipino Americans should not struggle to combat marginalization and racism; rather I argue that our current strategy of empowerment does not disrupt the colonial power structures oppressing Native Hawaiians and instead reinforces colonialism by making use of an American patriotic narrative" (5). Saranillio illustrates the ways in which Asian settlers like Filipinos who have suffered historically under US colonial rule in the Philippines share some historical commonalities with Hawaiians, but in the face of their experiences of racial profiling and discrimination in Hawai'i, Filipinos seek "empowerment" in what are actually intrasettler struggles on Native land.

As editors of *Whose Vision? Asian Settler Colonialism in Hawai'i*,[4] Okamura and I asked Asian Americans on the continent to consider their own roles as settlers. Although they do not control the same degree of political power as Asians in Hawai'i do, the presence of Asian Americans on the continent was also established through a colonial process, and Asian Americans, whose ancestral lands are in Asia, are settlers in relation to American Indians.

Indigenous peoples are differentiated from settlers by their genealogical, familial relationship with specific land bases that are ancestors to them. One is either indigenous to a particular land base or one is not. Asian Americans are undeniably settlers in the United States because we cannot claim any genealogy to the land we occupy, no matter how many lifetimes Asian settlers work on the land, or how many Asian immigrants have been killed through racist persecution and hate crimes, or how brutal the political or colonial regimes that occasioned Asians' exodus from their homelands. Certain groups are received in the United States under United Nations definitions of political refugees, but that does not change their status as settlers in Hawai'i and on the continent. The term "settler" is not about colonial intentions: most Asian settlers spend little or no time thinking about indigenous peoples. And that is precisely where the colonial problem lies. What colonial ideologies make settlers ignore indigenous peoples and the history of colonization of which we have become a part? Unwittingly or not, Asians are settlers because of our very presence on Native lands. In a colonial context, "Native" and "settler" are nonequivalent and incommensurable terms, and settlers cannot claim the rights to self-determination and self-government specific to indigenous peoples.

Not surprisingly, this critical distinction between Natives and settlers has met with considerable resistance on the part of many Asian Americans in Hawai'i and the continental United States,[5] and *Whose Vision? Asian Settler Colonialism in Hawai'i* has been subjected to disturbing critiques. Perhaps the most dangerous criticism we have received is that we are constructing "binaries" in ways that are "essentialist." I say that this criticism is dangerous because it employs colonial arguments against Native peoples in the guise of poststructuralist theory. Asian Americanists who have attacked what they see as the "essentialist motive" behind the "Native/settler" distinction reduce Native claims to identity politics.[6] As Trask argues, however, Natives struggle not for identity but for land and nation that was taken from them through the violence of colonialism: "The struggle is not for a personal or group identity but for land, government, and international status as a recognized nation. The distinction here between the personal and the national is critical. Hawaiians are not engaged in identity politics any more than the Irish of Northern Ireland or the Palestinians of occupied Palestine are engaged in identity politics. Both the Irish and the Palestinians are subjugated national groups committed to a war of national liberation" (2000a: 6). Postcolonial critics have also argued that the identity politics of the binary "colonizer/colonized" do not allow for complexities in colonial situations, yet, as Trask shows, these arguments do not address Native peoples' substantive claims to land and nation.

Although critiques of essentialized notions of subjectivity have been vitally important to our exploration of the ideological entanglements of various axes of difference, such as race, class, gender, and sexuality, such critiques become colonial when they are used *against* indigenous peoples. Asian American identity is a political category strategically essentialized for the purposes of political action, and much of the work now being done in Asian American studies has grown out of Lisa Lowe's (1996) nuanced discussion of Asian American "heterogeneity, hybridity, and multiplicity." Asian Americanists have been trained to think in poststructural terms of the "fluidity" and constructedness of racial formation, which makes it difficult for them to understand that the question of whether or not one is indigenous to a place is neither fluid nor negotiable.

What we see at the heart of these ideological arguments against the distinction between "Native" and "settler" is an antinationalist sentiment that does not take into consideration the heterogeneity of nationalisms. Asian Americanists' disabling experiences with "patriotic" American nationalisms and Asian American cultural nationalisms have often led them to assume a broadly antinationalist stance. Historically, Asian American writers and scholars have attempted to refigure racist articulations of American national identity that represent Asian Americans as "perpetual foreigners," and this desire for recognized citizenship and equal rights has led Asian Americans to important struggles for civil rights. Asian American cultural nationalism has been another related product of American national racism.[7] Frank Chin, Jeffery Paul Chan, Lawson Fusao Inada, and Shawn Wong's 1974 collection *Aiiieeeee! An Anthology of Asian-American Writers* has come to embody, for many Asian Americanists, Asian American cultural nationalism and its own performance of gendered and heteronormative exclusions.[8] Nationalist formations, however, are heterogeneous, and we need to make critical distinctions among different nationalist formations and their varying relationships to the state.

In this essay, I foreground Native nationalisms by critiquing antinationalist sentiment in the work of Asian American and cultural studies critics who actually stake their own settler claims. I begin by considering the material consequences of the failure to recognize the distinction between Natives and settlers, evident in the Supreme Court case *Rice v. Cayetano* which has resulted in a further erosion of Native rights. Extending my analysis from state politics to the academic arena, I interrogate two historical moments where Asian Americans "claim America" only to be confronted by Natives. One is a literary, phantasmatic moment that reveals the workings of the Asian American imaginary and the desire for Native peoples to legitimate Asian settler claims; the other is a literal confrontation in which a Native nationalist refuted those claims. I argue that investments in claiming America persist in the work of postcolonial and cultural studies critics like Arjun Appadurai, who casts both state and anticolonial nationalisms as necessarily violent and exclusionary only to reinstall in their place problematic narratives of "transnations" that assert an egalitarian "non-belonging." I argue that even those Asian Americanists who have tried to be supportive of Native nationalisms make settler claims, and I offer as an example my own past work in which I used the term "Local Nation" (1994) in an attempt to legitimate our settler claims to Native lands. I conclude by examining Kandice Chuh's (2001) *Imagine Otherwise: On Asian Americanist Critique*, which raises important questions for Asian Americanists at the same time that her arguments are symptomatic of a pervasive antinationalist sentiment in Asian American studies. In Chuh's own ambivalent claims to "home" in a transnational framework, I see a retreat from the hard questions Native scholars raise about our roles as Asian settlers in a colonial system.

As a fourth-generation Japanese settler in Hawai'i, I urge us to consider what our responsibilities are as Asian Americans, as settlers, to Native peoples. If critics of the term "settler" have argued that we are being divisive, that we are creating an " 'us' versus 'them' mentality," I would argue that recognizing such divisions is critical to supporting Native struggles. As Trask argues, "The position of 'ally' is certainly engaged in by many non-Natives all over the world. [...] But the most critical need for non-Native allies is in the area of support for Hawaiian self-determination. Defending Hawaiian sovereignty initiatives is only beneficial when non-Natives play the roles assigned to them by Natives. Put another way, nationalists always need support, but they must be the determining voice in the substance of that support and how, and under what circumstances, it applies" (2000a: 21). Trask and other Native nationalists make it clear that "support" does not involve settlers participating in or claiming authority over the process of Native self-determination. Kosasa further adds, "Any settler, Asian or *haole*, in a colonial situation can only represent colonial interests. We must understand the depth of our immigrant indoctrination and hence the implications of our ideological education that structures our world view in terms of settler interests" (2000: 83–4). Instead, settler support of Native struggles involves challenging our own communities and the colonial practices we engage in. Local Japanese Women for Justice has been one group in particular that has taken real risks in criticizing Japanese in Hawai'i with institutional and political power, such as Senator Daniel Inouye and the Japanese American Citizens' League (JACL).

In Asian American studies, we must make critical interventions into theories and practices that undermine the struggles of Native peoples in Hawai'i and the continent. As my colleague Cristina Bacchilega states in her own work on narratives of "legendary Hawai'i," "It matters that I self-identify as a settler. It is not guilt, but an invitation to taking responsibility for change that I want to communicate to those who, myself included, may feel unsettled by the realization that we are settlers" (Bacchilega, MS in progress). Even as we recognize the many ways we have benefited from the colonial process, the substantive issue is not guilt but the ways Asian American studies must foreground both Native nationalisms and the colonial structure of the US nation-state. Our own struggles for civil rights take place in a colonial context, and we must use a colonial framework to understand our struggles against and participation in that colonial system. And to support Native self-determination, settlers must stand *behind* Natives. As poet 'Īmaikalani Kalāhele writes to non-Hawaiians in his poem "Huli,"

> If to help us is your wish then stand behind us.
> Not to the side
> and not in front. (2002)

In Kalāhele's words, we can see that there cannot be equality between Natives and settlers in a colonial context.

I want to point now to what is at stake, what are the immediate material consequences of a refusal to recognize the distinction between Natives and settlers. The effect of ignoring such distinctions is nowhere more evident than in the US Supreme Court ruling in the *Rice v. Cayetano* case. In 1996, Harold "Freddy" Rice, a white rancher and a descendant of a member of the "missionary party" that overthrew the Hawaiian monarchy in 1893, argued that it is unconstitutional for the state to restrict voting to Hawaiians only in elections for the Office of Hawaiian Affairs (OHA). OHA is a state office charged with disbursing the monies generated from the so-called "Ceded Lands" that are held in "trust" by the State for the Hawaiian people.[9] Rice's attorneys used the Fifteenth Amendment, which prohibits states from abridging the right to vote based on race, to argue that the elections deprived Rice of his civil rights. The Supreme Court ruled in favor of Rice, forcing OHA to open its elections to non-Hawaiians. As a result of the Rice case, other lawsuits followed. *Earl Arakaki et al. v. the State of Hawai'i* (2000) claimed that the Rice decision gave non-Hawaiians the right to run for OHA trustees. The district judge ruled in favor of Arakaki, and in 2000, Charles Ota, a Japanese settler businessman and 442nd Regimental Combat Team veteran, was elected to office. Most recently, in the March 2002 lawsuit *Arakaki et al. v. Lingle*, the attorneys who filed the suit argued that OHA and the Department of Hawaiian Home Lands programs are unconstitutional because they are race-based and discriminate against non-Hawaiians.

These lawsuits illustrate precisely what happens when settlers equate themselves with Natives. In the most egregious of ironies, settlers proclaim that Native Hawaiians are depriving them of their civil rights, but they do so in order to use the argument of equal rights to take from Natives the rights guaranteed to them as indigenous peoples. The Court's construction of "justice for all" operates in the service of the state as it discursively constructs the US colonial nation-state as "our democracy" (Kennedy, "Opinion," *Rice v. Cayetano* (98-818) 528 U.S. 495, 2000). In the majority opinion, Hawaiians are viewed on the register of race as one race among others because the Court ignores the compensatory nature of

Native entitlements, acknowledged by United States Public Law 103–150 in which the US Congress apologizes to Native Hawaiians for depriving them of their right to self-determination while reaffirming its commitment to acknowledging the ramifications of the overthrow. The Court recounts the history of the overthrow only to relegate US colonialism to an ineffable past, erasing Hawaiians' present struggles for self-determination.

If the language of equal rights was wielded problematically by the US Supreme Court to elide the differences between Natives and settlers, Asian settlers were also revealing their political interests in erasing those differences. In response to the *Rice* decision, former governor Benjamin Cayetano, who is of Filipino descent, stated publicly, "I've lived in Hawai'i long enough to feel I'm Hawaiian" (aired on KITV and other Hawai'i television stations, September 19, 2000). In Hawai'i, where the word "Hawaiian" is used in reference to those of Hawaiian ancestry, such a statement in and of itself seems merely comical, but Cayetano's remark was politically motivated: he was acting on the advice of Senator Daniel Inouye by appointing non-Natives as interim OHA trustees following the ruling on the *Rice* case (Yoshinaga and Kosasa 2000: 145). We can also see Cayetano's statement as part of a larger picture of political power in Hawai'i. Mililani Trask, a Native Hawaiian nationalist and the Pacific representative to the United Nations Permanent Forum on Indigenous Issues, argues that settlers in the Asian-dominated Democratic Party have much to lose if Hawaiians' rights to land are recognized: "Hawaiians have repeatedly sought congressional legislation to correct the abuse of state wardship and address their exclusion from federal policies applicable to other classes of Native Americans. These bills have failed to pass through Congress due to opposition from Hawaii's senior senator Daniel Inouye and Hawaii's powerful Democratic Party, which benefits from a co-mingling of trust assets set aside for the 'public' and the 'Native'" (2002: 355). Hawaiians have a legal right to "Ceded" lands, yet OHA receives only 20 percent of the revenues generated by these lands. In the Asian and white settler-run state of Hawai'i, Asian settlers benefit tremendously at the expense of Native peoples.

These are some material consequences that argue for the importance of distinguishing between Natives and settlers. Beyond the arena of state politics, in Asian American studies, we can ask what psychic and material investments are revealed in resistance to the term "settler." As indigenous peoples in Hawai'i, on the continent, and around the world challenge the colonial structures that continue to oppress them, our critical frameworks in Asian American studies often become "intimate proof"[10] of our settler investments.

In the United States, anti-Asian discrimination, hate crimes, and violence have increased dramatically following the attack on the World Trade Center. If Lisa Lowe argued in 1996 that "we are witnessing a 're-racialization' of immigrants that constitutes 'the immigrant' as the most highly targeted object of a U.S. nationalist agenda" (174), the post-9/11 world has been even more gravely affected by racist legislation generated by a "patriotic" fervor that has had devastating consequences for Arabs, Muslims, South Asians, and Sikhs. Asian Americans, viewed as "perpetual foreigners," have historically been one of the groups most affected by such anti-immigrant legislation.

Citizenship and nationalism, then, have historically posed contradictions for Asian Americans. The idea of citizenship at once evokes phantasmatic desires for plenitude as well as the material realities of state violence. Lowe contends that while American national culture poses citizenship in an American liberal democracy as offering the resolution to material inequalities, citizenship does not guarantee rights precisely because racism is constitutive of the American nation-state. As Lowe argues, "these struggles have revealed that the granting of rights does not abolish the economic system that profits from racism" (26). Asians are at once necessary to the national economy as labor and "distanced" from "the terrain of national culture," and because of this, Lowe describes Asian American culture as the excess beyond narratives of American citizenship: "Because it is the purpose of American national culture to form subjects as citizens, this distance has created the conditions for the emergence of Asian American culture as an alternative cultural site, a site of cultural forms that propose, enact, and embody subjects and practices not contained by the narrative of American citizenship" (176). I find this argument about critical distancing most productive as a stance in relation to American national narratives of citizenship. I would add that this critical distancing from narratives of citizenship is particularly necessary when a nation-state is colonial.

We can both support Native claims and oppose the erosion of civil rights from a position critically distanced from an investment in US citizenship. As we struggle for the civil rights eroded by the Bush administration in the wake of 9/11, we must not lose sight of the fact that these civil rights are guaranteed by the US Constitution, what Haunani-Kay Trask describes as "the settler document that declares ownership over indigenous lands and peoples" (1993: 26). We can engage in struggles for civil rights not out of a desire for belonging to the nation but out of a recognition that discriminatory legislation affects both Natives and settlers in the US colonial system, albeit in different ways. As Native nationalists struggle for Native self-governance to be determined by Native peoples, settlers cannot afford to ignore the different kinds of violence enacted by the colonial state on Natives and settlers in the United States, like the USA PATRIOT Act, or those specifically aimed at Native peoples, like *Arakaki et. al. v. Lingle*.

I would like to turn now to an Asian American literary moment that shows us how the critique of racist American nationalism and its historical persecution of Asian immigrants turns into a narrative that attempts to justify Asian settler claims to America. Shawn Wong's 1979 novel *Homebase* traces the ghosts that haunt Rainsford Chan and his struggles to negotiate racist national ideologies that insist he can never be fully "American." Like his great grandfather who built the Central Pacific Railroad through the Sierra Nevada but was later driven back to San Francisco by anti-Chinese violence, Rainsford is constantly on the run, struggling to find a place for himself in America. Memories of his grand-father evoke the American history of the Exclusion Acts designed to restrict Chinese immigration, and these Acts become emblematic of the way in which Asian Americans have historically been excluded from full participation in an American "democracy."

The novel's indictment of American national racism, however, begins to reproduce colonial logic when Rainsford attempts to refigure that racism by claiming America for Chinese Americans who have given their lives to build the railroads that cross the American nation. The novel is, as Sau-ling Wong (1993) explains, "a clearly conscious assertion of the Chinese American's claim to the American land, as Elaine Kim (from gender concerns) and Karin Meissenburg (from historical interests) have both pointed out" (142). What is particularly revealing about this novel is that it makes these settler claims by confronting the indigenous. It is important that this novel acknowledges the colonial premise of the US nation-state, but it ends up doing so only to provide a resolution to Asian American anxieties over claiming Native land. This moment takes place on Alcatraz Island on Christmas Eve, 1969, evoking the American Indian occupa-tion of that island. Rainsford meets an American Indian man who asks him, "What are you doing here? This isn't your battle or your land" (84). This question articulates one of the most profound of Asian American anxieties: the indigenous challenge to Asian American claims to America. That anxiety, how-ever, is quickly contained by a rhetoric of equivalence. The American Indian tells Rainsford that "[m]y ancestors came from China thirty thousand years ago and settled in Acoma Pueblo," suggesting a kinship between himself and Rainsford that seemingly legitimates Rainsford's own settler claims to America (83). Wong goes so far as to narrate the American Indian offering America to Rainsford: "This is your country. Go out and make yourself at home." In the concluding lines of his narrative, Rainsford feels that he can say, "*We are old enough to haunt this land like an Indian who laid down to rest and his body became the outline of the horizon*" (95). What makes it possible for an Asian American protagonist to make such a statement? Although Rainsford's claims are responses to virulent white racism, this particular moment also illustrates the narrative means by which Asian Americans confront the indigenous in order to receive absolution, the claiming of America now fictionally "sanctioned" by Native peoples "descended from" Asians.

If this literary moment published in 1979 illustrates a settler fantasy of Asian Americans being imaginatively "offered" America by a Native, we can contrast it with an historical moment in 1997 in which Asian Americanists were literally confronted by a Native nationalist leader who refuted their settler claims to Native lands. At the 1997 Multi-Ethnic Literatures of the United States (MELUS) Conference at the University of Hawai'i, Haunani-Kay Trask delivered the keynote address in which she argued that local Asians are settlers claiming

Hawaiʻi for their own through "the back door of identity theft" (2000b).[11] Asian Americanists were troubled by her use of the term "settler," and in later conversations, they argued that Trask was reproducing state anti-immigrant racism inherent in the logic of California's Proposition 187, which prevented "illegal aliens" and their children from receiving health and social services. In fact, one Asian Americanist wrote a letter to Trask's dean complaining of her "racist" treatment of Asian Americans.

On one register, this historical moment illustrates a fundamental failure on the part of Asian Americanists to recognize that indigenous peoples cannot be equated with either the state or racial minorities. On another register, the construction of Asian Americans as "victims" of Native "racism" tells us much about the way in which Asian Americans, like the plaintiffs in the court cases threatening Native rights, see themselves as oppressed citizens of a democratic nation-state: they do not want to see the United States as a colonial nation-state, and they refuse to see themselves as beneficiaries of that colonial system. When Rainsford tells us, "My grandfather's island is Angel Island. It was there that he almost died, and that makes it his island" (S. Wong 1979: 80), his account resonates with so many other Asian American texts that narrativize the blood, sweat, and semen poured into American soil by Asian immigrants, the indeterminacy of bodily boundaries establishing, they argue, their right to claim America.

Ultimately, however, the presence of Native peoples is a reminder of that which Asian Americanists would prefer to forget: that Asian Americans can never claim America, not because of white racism, but because it is Native land. What we see in both Wong's novel and at the 1997 MELUS Conference is at once an uneasy recognition that indigenous peoples have a prior claim to America and an erasure of that claim, either through tracing Native genealogies back to Asia or by asserting the futility of Native claims in a supposedly "post"-civil rights era where Native peoples are one race among others. In both cases, Asian Americanists erase the unique political status of Native peoples in order to construct an egalitarian basis for their own civil rights claims.

If these ideological erasures of Native peoples and their rights have been taking place in the Asian American imaginary, we can examine more closely critiques of nationalism that have been indiscriminately deployed in ways that further those erasures. Asian Americanists' critiques of nationalism have been primarily derived from postcolonial discussions of Frantz Fanon's analysis of the pitfalls of national consciousness in *The Wretched of the Earth* (1963). Fanon argues that the nationalist bourgeoisie reproduces the structures of domination erected by its colonial predecessors and that "the national bourgeoisie identifies itself with the Western bourgeoisie from whom it has learned its lessons" (153). This critique extends to the "official" nationalist narratives that often reiterate colonial ideologies in the form of totalizing narratives that preclude other narratives of resistance within a nationalist movement. In Asian American studies, we have used Fanon's analyses in the important task of critiquing our own work, but we can already begin to see how Asian Americanists' focus on this particular aspect of his multidimensional analyses works against Native nationalists by implying that they are fated to reproduce colonial ideologies.

Despite the poststructural lessons we have learned about the value of hetero-geneity, one of the most persistent problems in postcolonial and Asian American studies is that poststructuralist critics themselves often homogenize nationalist formations. State nationalism, anticolonial nationalism, and cultural national-ism, each with differing objectives in relation to nation-states, each occurring in vastly different geographical, political, and epistemological sites, are portrayed as uniformly divisive and violent. As has happened all too frequently in these critiques of nationalism, much is made of nationalist violence, and less is said about the violence of the colonial state. As David Lloyd (1995: 173) argues in his essay "Nationalisms against the State," the disintegration of the former Soviet Union and of Yugoslavia has been used repeatedly as an example of the divisive-ness and violence of nationalism, which critics argue progresses inevitably from "separatism" to "ethnic cleansing." In this developmental narrative, nationalisms are represented as residual formations based on prelapsarian promises they can never fulfill. As Lloyd contends, "At the same time, and often in the same works as acknowledge its modernity, nationalism is seen as the vehicle or the stimulus for the resurgence of atavistic or pre-modern feelings and practices, at best as a nostalgic hankering after irretrievable and probably figmentary modes of society, a futile protest against inevitable cultural modernity or economic transnationality" (216). Indeed, this hostility toward nationalisms is most pronounced in postcolonial formulations of nationalism as a retrogressive *obstacle* in a developmental narrative that posits the "transnational" or the "postnational" as its *telos*.

Even as postcolonial critics articulate their concerns over the injustices that persist after nationalists have "captured the state," they are, in effect, making antinationalist arguments that are not much different in effect from those of colonial powers that seek to sustain themselves. Lloyd argues that attacks on nationalism are commensurable with colonial antagonisms towards anticolonial movements, that "current Western antinationalism has deeper historical roots and remains ideologically and formally continuous with traditional metropolitan antagonism towards anticolonial movements in the Third World" (174). Indis-criminate attacks on nationalism end up working against Native peoples engaged in anticolonial nationalist movements around the world, and we must recognize the situatedness of nationalist formations; otherwise, it is the very discourse of the "inevitable" failure of nationalism that threatens to foreclose the radical possibilities of current Native nationalist struggles.

Asian Americanists often draw from postcolonial and cultural studies critics who extol the possibilities of a "postnational" condition while engaging in critiques of nationalism similar to the ones Lloyd describes. In *Modernity at*

Large: Cultural Dimensions of Globalization (1996), Arjun Appadurai reiterates arguments concerning the violence in the "postcolony" that has been committed in the name of the nation and the ways that the nation has been "the last refuge of ethnic totalitarianism" (159). Given these reasons and increasingly mobile populations, Appadurai argues that "[w]e need to think ourselves beyond the nation" (158) by paying more attention to the role that imagination plays in creative alternatives to the nation-state: "The modern nation-state in this view grows less out of natural facts – such as language, blood, soil, and race – and more out of a quintessential cultural product, a product of the collective imagination" (161). In this framework of "deterritorialization," Appadurai envisions the United States as a "free-trade zone" for a world organized around "diasporic diversity":

> There could be a special place for America in the new, postnational order, and one that does not rely on either isolationism or global domination as its alternative basis. The United States is eminently suited to be a sort of cultural laboratory and a free-trade zone for the generation, circulation, importation, and testing of the materials for a world organized around diasporic diversity. (174)

Appadurai's contentions raise a number of concerns for me. His argument that "we must think ourselves beyond the nation" in one sweep denies the colonial history of the United States and the efforts of Native peoples to establish their own nations. In his formulation, "diasporic diversity" becomes the center while the indigenous is relegated to obscurity in the postcolonial present. Appadurai's emphasis on a "deterritorialization" that has occurred as a result of the diasporic movement of peoples and resources is particularly telling. It is this notion of "transnations of diasporic collectivities" that evokes once again, in poststructuralist form, the ideological construction of the United States as a "nation of immigrants," the difference here being that since the relationship between peoples and land is argued to be fictional, everyone equally does not belong. In this way, an egalitarian "non-belonging" clears the ground (in other words, erases the Natives) for the settler claims of "diasporic collectivities."

In an odd moment, Appadurai glosses over the fact that diasporic communities have "nations of origin" elsewhere, but indigenous peoples do not. He argues that hyphenation is reaching the point of saturation and that diasporic communities demonstrate loyalties both to their nations of origin and to America. Appadurai does not account for the indigenous in his formulation, but he compulsively lists American Indians in a pluralistic catalogue of extended, hyphenated diasporic identities: "In this scenario, the hyphenated American might have to be twice hyphenated (Asian-American-Japanese or Native-American-Senecan or African-American-Jamaican or Hispanic-American-Bolivian)" (173). At this point, the inclusion of indigenous peoples seems to be a deliberate illustration that they are no different from others in a pluralistic democracy of world travelers.

Appadurai's arguments describing the deterritorialized global flows of people do not change the substantive issue of indigenous claims to land and nation, nor do arguments that assert the colonial ambivalence that haunts the colonizer and colonized or, worse yet, assert the complicity of Native peoples in their own colonization. Even the argument that immigrants or peoples of color constitute a liminal space between colonizer and colonized does nothing to change the substantive issue of indigenous claims to land and nation.

Appadurai's emphasis on deterritorialization is, in fact, antithetical to Native worldviews. When non-Natives characterize Native Hawaiians' accounts of a genealogical, familial relationship with land as essentialist or strategically essentialist, that is itself a colonial gesture that uses Western conceptions of land as an index against which a Native consciousness is measured. In describing Hawaiians' genealogical descent from the land, Native Hawaiian nationalist, scholar, and hula practitioner Momiala Kamahele (2002) explains, "The land is our mother. Native Hawaiians call her Papahānaumoku – 'She who gives birth to lands.' As caretakers, Native Hawaiians understand that . . . she creates and ensures a living continuity between the natural world and the human world" (42). Haunani-Kay Trask further explains that it is this genealogical connection that defines the Hawaiian people: "Genealogically, we say we are descendents of Papahānaumoku (Earth Mother) and Wākea (Sky Father) who created our beautiful islands. From this land came the taro, and from the taro, our Hawaiian people. The lesson of our origins is that we are genealogically related to Hawai'i, our islands, as family" (1).

In colonial relations of power, Native conceptions of land are negated as necessarily "metaphorical" instead of literal. Kamahele draws from Fanon's analysis to argue that the US colonial power assaults the national culture of Hawaiians in order to deny their existence as a distinct people. Native Hawaiian scholar Ku'ualoha Ho'omanawanui further illustrates the ways that Native language and orature are forms of national culture that are under siege by settler scholars who dismiss Native conceptions of land: "[T]he Kanaka Maoli worldview, as espoused in our 'ōlelo makuahine (mother tongue) and our cultural traditions, is based on a very different relationship to Hawai'i than that of settlers who speak English or HCE [Hawai'i Creole English]. [. . .] These differences are also apparent in settlers' continued references to Hawai'i as a 'landscape,' 'geography,' and 'environment,' English words that connote a Western-based understanding of what land is, terms which overshadow and negate Native understandings of land as 'āina, which for Kānaka Maoli is familial" (forthcoming). What Ho'omanawanui describes here are not merely competing epistemologies but rather the epistemic and consequent material violence inflicted upon Hawaiians by settlers and the colonial state.

Asian Americanists' decontextualized and universalized critiques of nationalism presume to map out the script of "postcolonial misery" for Native nationalists precisely because of Asian Americanists' reliance on "recognizable" narratives of nationalism. These critics argue that there are no settlers in Hawaiʻi and the US continent because conditions here are not like those in Algeria or South Africa. Conditions in Hawaiʻi are different, and that is precisely the point: their argument is problematic insofar as its logic proclaims that colonial formations must be identical in order to qualify as colonial formations, and such logic precludes variations of both colonialisms and nationalisms which are products of specific material histories and economic systems. When Asian Americanists use examples of colonialism elsewhere to deny the conditions of settler colonialism in Hawaiʻi and to dismiss anticolonial Hawaiian struggles as "essentialist" and fated to fail, their arguments are indicative of their own settler interests. As Partha Chatterjee (1986) has argued, critics like Benedict Anderson take as their models for nationalisms Europe and the Americas, leaving untheorized the specific national formations in Asia and Africa: "Europe and the Americas, the only true subjects of history, have thought out on our behalf not only the script of colonial enlightenment and exploitation, but also that of our anticolonial resistance and postcolonial misery. Even our imaginations must remain forever colonized" (5). If on the one hand the argument that Hawaiians are not like nationalists in other places dangerously homogenizes nationalism, it also falsely asserts that conditions in Hawaiʻi are "not violent enough" to warrant a distinction between Natives and settlers: predictably, such settler arguments reproduce the conditions for the ongoing state violence committed against Hawaiians.

In critiquing what they see as the "retrogressive" nature of nationalism, some Asian Americanists end up infantilizing Native positions rather than recognizing the acute awareness that indigenous leaders have not only of the histories of their own struggles but also of the historical struggles of indigenous peoples around the world. Narratives in postcolonial and Asian American theory often cast such nationalist leaders as "naïve" or "theoretically uniformed." In their own critique of the persistent inability of postcolonial studies to come to terms with the indigenous, Cynthia Franklin and Laura Lyons (2003) examine such problematic narratives: "As the quotations from Bhabha, Greenblatt, and others have demonstrated, postcolonial critics often interpret any attempts to enlist or to recover parts of a pre-colonial culture as a search for a pristine past, nostalgia for lost origins, or an appeal to unreconstructed nativist authenticity. Such scholarship can attend neither to the complex politics of particular nationalist claims at specific moments in time, nor to the role of the state in denying Native lands and identity." As Franklin and Lyons point out, to respect Native epistemologies is not to romanticize them but rather to acknowledge both the inadequacies of our own theoretical frameworks in analyzing formations that emerge out of indigenous political and epistemological sites and the ways that our academic work can in fact further subjugate Native peoples.

In order to illustrate the inadequacies of our conceptions of nationalism in Asian American studies, I'd like to turn to what are now familiar arguments about the exclusionary practices of nationalists. Asian Americanists have argued

that nationalist movements demand a uniform nationalist subject that is purchased at the expense of articulations of gender or class or queer differences, and
this is indeed an important critique of Asian American cultural nationalism.
Such a critique, however, works against Native nationalists, for although femin-
isms and nationalisms are not necessarily competing political movements, it is
the way in which they are narrated over and over again as such in Asian
American studies that lead to broad attacks on nationalism, attacks that actually
serve to sustain colonial regimes.

In Hawai'i, Native women who lead nationalist struggles challenge any
easy assumption that nationalism necessarily demands a uniform nationalist
subject. Certainly, women within nationalist movements have made materially
grounded arguments about the ways that those movements succeeded in ousting
the colonial power only to preclude the participation of women in the
new nation, but these specific accounts have been decontextualized in an all
too popular narrative used in Asian American studies to proclaim the "failure"
of *all* forms of nationalism.[12] Trask's work as a nationalist leader is particularly
instructive here. Ten years after her publication of *Eros and Power: The Promise
of Feminist Theory* (1986), Trask wrote an essay on indigenous women's struggles
entitled "Feminism and Indigenous Hawaiian Nationalism" (1996), published
in the feminist journal *Signs*. There, she argues that as a nationalist, she
finds that her struggle as a Hawaiian woman is carried out within a Hawaiian
nationalist movement because colonialism has engendered the problems
specific to Hawaiian women, problems that are to be resolved within a Hawaiian
nation:

> Now, while I am, as always, an advocate of women's power and claims, my context
> is Hawaiian and not American culture, and my political work is based on Hawaiian
> self-determination. This focus includes all our people, not only our women.
> Traditional women's issues – reproductive rights, equal employment, domestic
> violence – are obviously part of the struggle for our homeland and our integrity
> as an indigenous nation. Nothing has escaped the ravages of colonization, includ-
> ing the lives of our women. But the answers to the specifics of our women's
> oppression reside in our people's collective achievement of the larger goal of
> Hawaiian self-government, not an exclusive feminist agenda. As my scope has
> enlarged over the years to encompass international linkages with indigenous
> women in the Americas, in the Pacific Basin, in the Arctic, and elsewhere, feminism
> seems more and more removed from the all-consuming struggle against our
> physical and cultural extinction as indigenous peoples. Issues specific to women
> still inform our identity as Native women leaders, but our language and our
> organizing are framed within our cultural terms, not within feminist American
> terms. (910)

Hawaiian women suffer from one of the highest rates of breast cancer, and Trask
explains that this health problem is a consequence of a capitalistic system of food

distribution and the pollution of resources by overdevelopment. She argues that "[b]ecause our disastrous health profile resulted from colonialism, our condition is not simply a 'women's issue'. [. . .] Hawaiian women's health profile is a result of colonialism and the subsequent loss of control over our islands and our lives. Thus does a 'women's issue' become a sovereignty, not a feminist, problem for us." Trask rejects American constructions of feminism that operate in service of American colonial ideologies, particularly when those constructions are used against Native nationalist movements. Trask's analysis instead illustrates the ways in which her work as a nationalist leader cannot help but engage her political concerns as a woman.

It is not my place as a settler to analyze Hawaiian nationalism. My focus here is the deeply problematic narrative settlers write out for Native nationalists. Our own reiterations of the "official histories" of nationalism often rely on developmental narratives that are unable to envision potentially richer definitions of the nation. We must realize that Native nationalists employ strategies of anticolonial resistance that are often not recognizable to us, and we must be cautious about containing the dynamic unpredictability of nationalisms within Western notions of "progress." Such a gesture tells us more about our own limitations than about nationalist movements themselves, and our sweeping generalizations about nationalisms reveal not only how well we have been educated within a colonial system, but, more disturbingly, how well we serve it.

I want to provide now a self-critique, a personal example of the ways that our use of the term "nation" to describe Asian America or its constituent groups is yet another attempt to legitimize our claiming of America. In 1994, I published an essay entitled "Between Nationalisms: Hawaii's Local Nation and Its Troubled Racial Paradise." In that essay, I argued that local Asians in Hawai'i who identify neither with Asian nation-states nor with the United States imagine themselves as an unstable "Local Nation" predicated upon anxieties over the illegitimacy of their claims to Hawai'i. Although my intent in this essay was to support Native peoples, Haunani-Kay Trask insightfully and incisively criticizes my use of the term "Local Nation." She writes,

> Ideologically, the appearance of this "local nation" is a response to a twenty-year old sovereignty movement among Hawaiians. Organized Natives, led by a young, educated class attempting to develop progressive elements among Hawaiians, as well as to create mechanisms for self-government, are quickly perceived as a threat by many Asians uneasy about their obvious benefit from the dispossession and marginalization of Natives. Arguing that Asians, too, have a nation in Hawai'i, the "local" identity tag blurs the history of Hawai'i's only indigenous people while staking a settler claim. Any complicity in the subjugation of Hawaiians is denied by the assertion that Asians, too, comprise a "nation." [. . .] Thus do these settlers deny their ascendancy was made possible by the continued national oppression of Hawaiians, particularly the theft of our lands and the crushing of our independence. (2000a: 4)

As Trask argues, I had been trying to stake a settler claim by distancing a "Local Nation" of Asians in Hawai'i from Asian Americans on the continent as well as from whites in the colony of Hawai'i. This was my attempt to create a "third space" for Asians as another category of the oppressed in Hawai'i; my use of "nation" as a metaphor sought to legitimate "Local" political struggles by equating non-Natives with Hawaiians who were working to establish a nation-state. Even the attempt to ally "Locals" with "Natives" created the illusion of a "shared" struggle without acknowledging that Asians have come to comprise that very political system that has sought to take away from Natives their rights as indigenous peoples. As I began to reread my own work through Trask's analysis, I could see how my own critical framework was predicated on settler investments.

I raise my own educational moment here because other Asian Americanists engaged in anticolonial efforts have also exhibited the same settler investments that Trask points out in my own work. I want to turn now to the importance of and problems raised by the work of Kandice Chuh. In her book *Imagine Otherwise: On Asian Americanist Critique* (2003), Chuh argues for conceiving of Asian American studies as a subjectless discourse. This argument derives from critiques of Asian American cultural nationalism of the 1970s that privileged the Asian American male subject, and Chuh contends that the uniform ethnic subject allows little room for a recognition of difference. By raising questions about what Asian American studies would look like if our use of the term "Asian American" is based not on identity politics or subjectivity but on the forms of critique themselves, Chuh argues that it is the undecidability of identity and the impossibility of any stable difference (61) that offers us the liberating potential to undermine racial essentialism. Chuh concludes that "*[u]ndecidability rather than identity* provides the grounds for unity, and identifying and contesting the forces that control intelligibility, that affiliate meanings, emerge as crucial tasks for Asian American studies. Perhaps, then, we might begin to think in terms of 'Asian American' *unification* rather than identity to frame the cultural and political collectivity that we have asked the construct of identity to do for us" (83).

Chuh argues for a subjectless discourse in order to shift Asian American studies away from a nation-based paradigm and its attendant territorialization, which has become increasingly problematic in the face of anticolonial movements such as the Hawaiian sovereignty movement. In Chuh's analysis of nation and nationalism, she critiques Asian American cultural nationalism and its privileging of race as well as American nationalism and its narratives of belonging to the American nation; neither, she argues, should form such a narrow premise for Asian American studies. She analyzes the *Rice v. Cayetano* case and makes a cogent argument about the ways that the Hawaiian sovereignty movement forces us to see that "nationalism as a framework for Asian Americanist practice, or as a framework for driving local identity formations, appears rather awkward. For, as demanded by modernity, ownership of territory legitimates nations, and nationalisms, even if unintentionally (as in cultural nationalism), can lead to territorialization in ways that can resemble the practices of colonialism itself" (138).

Chuh's work on moving Asian American studies away from territorial claims to America is particularly valuable, and I would like to push at the limits of her arguments where the indigenous appears and disappears. Despite Chuh's calls for a politics of heterogeneity, what I find troubling is that her analysis employs postcolonial criticisms that actually homogenize the heterogeneity of national-isms. Chuh's analysis makes the assumption that "nationalism" necessarily entails a certain kind of failure: its reproduction of the exclusionary logic and structure of colonialism through its demand for identification of the subject with the nation, which fails to register other forms of difference. Chuh draws uncritic-ally from work in postcolonial studies by questioning the status of the modern nation-state as an epistemological category:

> Postcolonial studies has shown that while nationalism proved a powerful framework for mounting anticolonial struggles in the Third World to achieve formal political liberation, it has not delivered on its promised "mythos of hearth and home, [which] are now the property of national elites [who] have been increasingly revealed to be corrupt, capitulationist, undemocratic, patriarchal, and homophobic" (Mufti and Shohat 1997: 3). Nation, in this regard, emerges as a fiction around which practices of liberation organize under the name of nation-alism. (127)

Chuh makes clear in her narrative frame that the subject of her critique is US nationalism and Asian Americanist reiterations of its logic, and yet this particu-lar passage delivers a critique of anticolonial struggles *elsewhere*. Nationalism, in Chuh's analysis, becomes more an abbreviation for exclusionary practices than actual struggles that occur in different places. The very representation of the inevitable failure of nationalism employs a kind of historical determinism that maintains US colonial rule.

Because of this critical reduction of nationalism, Chuh's analysis exhibits ambivalent slippages between multiple registers: a recognition that indigenous peoples are engaged in struggles for self-determination, an awareness that Asian Americans unwittingly engage in colonial practices, and a desire for a home in which all equally participate in its narration and construction. Chuh's final chapter begins to examine the ways that framing Asian American studies not within a liberal democracy but within a colonial situation forces us to rethink our relationship to the nation. Yet she disavows the territorializing that enacts colonial practices only to articulate "home" in relation to place:

> I want to suggest that Asian Americanists conceptually disown "America" the ideal, to further the work of creating home as a space relieved of states of domination. In other words, I am conceiving of home as that condition in which there is an

equality of ability to participate in negotiating and constructing the ethos of the places in which we live. (124)

The ambivalence that haunts Chuh's narrative of "home" articulates both a disavowal and a claim: the desire for an equality of participation in articulating something even as seemingly abstract as "ethos" is still premised on "the places in which we live." This desire for equality relies on American nationalist rhetoric of democracy, but differences cannot always be equated, and a reliance on equality belies Chuh's call for foregrounding differences that are often asymmetrical and incommensurable. As I have shown, the *Rice v. Cayetano* case evoked a rhetoric of "equal rights" through the Equal Protection clause of the Fourteenth Amendment in order to argue that Native entitlements "violate" non-Hawaiians' civil rights. In such a context, we can see how calls for equal participation in a colonial context become a settler claim. In places like Hawai'i, Natives will determine both the political architecture and the *ethos* of their nation; as Native nationalists remind us, that is for Native peoples to determine for themselves.

The contradiction between a desire for equality and the impossibility of equality in a colonial context leads Chuh to turn away from these difficult questions of Asian American complicity to seek a "home" in the transnational. If nation-based paradigms do not work well for Asian American studies, Chuh argues that the transnational may provide us with a better conceptual frame for Asian American studies, a transnational that marks both the flow of peoples and resources across national borders and also the "border crossings without literal movement, to a conceptual displacement of a national imaginary in order to allow for discursive and critical acknowledgment of those political and cultural practices illegible in the official discourse of the U.S. nation-state" (62). Chuh is both critical of and yet draws from Appadurai's discussion of transnations. Although she emphasizes the coercive element in a "Japanese American transnation," a product of the state's inability to imagine citizenship for Japanese Americans during WWII, she argues for the possibilities offered by a "transnational sensibility": "What strikes me as valuable about this particular iteration of this different epistemic terrain is that it identifies those subjectivities as complex and troubled, not as purely oppositional or liberating. [...] Recognition of this complexity argues for recoding 'opposition' to reflect the multiple and heterogeneous forms of oppression and resistance, the multiple and dissimilar fields of power, involved in social subjectification" (144). The transnational is an important analytic, but this particular turn to the transnational and the critique of "opposition" occur at the precise moment in Chuh's argument when Native claims demand that Asian Americans hold themselves accountable for their participation in a colonial system. The transnational, here posed as an "alternative" to the colonial, registers the ways that complicity becomes lost in "complexity." We can ask, how is the argument for complexity used to forestall an examination of the ways that we as settlers obstruct Native nationalist movements and the attainment of their goals? What kind of social action can we engage in for a justice that is neither "unstable" nor "undecidable"?

In an earlier essay entitled "Imaginary Borders" (2001), Chuh states most compellingly that "[b]y claiming ownership of U.S. national identity, Asian Americanists must also then claim responsibility for the cultural and material imperialism of this nation" (278). It is in this formulation that I see the "elsewhere" that Chuh evokes, where Asian settlers examine not only our own oppression in the United States but also the many ways we have benefited from the US colonial system, and where we seek to rectify those injustices by supporting Native peoples in their struggles for self-determination.

Throughout this essay, I have sought to illustrate the different forms that antinationalist rhetoric takes in Asian American studies. I have referred to the material consequences of our work, and if we return to the Third World Strikes and students' demands for a radical education, we do have an obligation to teach our students about the colonial present. Using the terms "Native" and "settler" affords us a new vision of the world, and we must educate both ourselves and our students about our roles as settlers in a colonial system in order to change that system. It is in calling attention to the United States as a colonial nation-state that we can more effectively work toward dismantling an American nationalism that operates under the guise of "democracy." To deterritorialize Asian settlers from the United States is not the same as rendering ourselves as "perpetual foreigners": we are instead showing how American national identity is premised on its ongoing colonial occupation of Native nations. Identifying the United States as a colonial nation-state provides a historical framework for understanding the Native/settler distinction and enables us to work toward justice for Native peoples and for ourselves.

In this essay, I have traced new directions in Asian American studies inspired by Haunani-Kay Trask's work on Asian settler colonialism. The Native and settler contributors to *Whose Vision? Asian Settler Colonialism in Hawai'i* and the substantially expanded manuscript *Asian Settler Colonialism in Hawai'i* show us that there are material consequences to our settler constructions of the world. Some of these contributors are at work on or have completed longer research projects that explore these issues in greater depth, from Eiko Kosasa's dissertation on US imperialism, settler hegemony and Japanese settlers in Hawai'i,[13] to Karen Kosasa's dissertation on art pedagogy and settler colonialism,[14] to Dean Saranillio's master's thesis on colonial amnesia and Filipino settler colonialism. These works inspire us by challenging Asian settler support of the US colonial state.

I want to end by emphasizing that in the larger picture of political justice, our struggles as Asian settlers are inseparable from the struggles of Native peoples, and our own self-interrogation can enable us to find our way to greater social and political justice, which has always been the goal of Asian American studies.

NOTES

I'd like to thank the following people who have read and commented on various versions of this essay: Cristina Bacchilega, Mark Chiang, Cynthia Franklin, Theo Gonsalves, Ruth Hsu, Eiko Kosasa, Karen Kosasa, Laura Lyons, Jonathan Okamura, Kent Ono, Dean Saranillio, Karen Su, Glen Tomita, and Ida Yoshinaga. I would especially like to thank Haunani-Kay Trask for her comments on this essay and for the many ways that she has inspired and taught me. All errors are my own.

1 I use "Hawaiian" and "Native Hawaiian" in reference to descendants of the indigenous peoples of Hawai'i.
2 For an analysis of the ethnic stratification in Hawai'i, see Jonathan Okamura (1998). For a critique of Japanese political power in Hawai'i, see Ida Yoshinaga and Eiko Kosasa (2000) and Eiko Kosasa (2000).
3 I use "local" here as a geographical marker designating ethnic groups from Hawai'i.
4 Our substantially revised issue of *Whose Vision?* is under consideration for publication as *Asian Settler Colonialism in Hawai'i*.
5 Although the continental United States is commonly referred to as the "mainland," Joe Balaz argues in the title of a poem that "Hawai'i/is da mainland to me." Hereafter I will refer to the continental United States as "the continent."
6 Criticisms of the term "settler" have not yet appeared in print, but they have surfaced at conferences and individual talks.
7 For a discussion of Asian American cultural nationalism, see Michael Omi and Howard Winant (1994).
8 See King-Kok Cheung (1990); Lisa Lowe (1996); and David L. Eng and Alice Y. Hom (1998).
9 See Melody Kapilialoha MacKenzie (1991).
10 I thank Darlene Rodrigues for this elegant phrase. See her essay, "Reimagining Ourselves: The Controversy over Lois-Ann Yamanaka's *Blu's Hanging*" (2000: 201).
11 For a discussion of different audiences' responses to Trask, see Cynthia Franklin's "Introduction" to *Navigating Islands and Continents: Conversations and Contestations in and around the Pacific* (2000).
12 For a discussion of this problem in an Irish context, see Laura Lyons (1996).
13 "Predatory Politics: U.S. Imperialism, Settler Hegemony and the Japanese in Hawai'i" (University of Hawai'i, 2004).
14 *Critical Sights/Sites: Art Pedagogy and Settler Colonialism in Hawai'i* (2002).

REFERENCES

Appadurai, A. (1996) *Modernity at Large: Cultural Dimensions of Globalization*. University of Minnesota Press, Minneapolis.
Bacchilega, C. (In progress) Legendary Hawai'i and the politics of place: narrative tradition, translation, photography and tourism. MS in progress.
Chatterjee, P. (1986) *Nationalist Thought and the Colonial World: A Derivative Discourse*. University of Minnesota Press, Minneapolis.

Cheung, K. (1990) The woman warrior versus the Chinaman Pacific: must a Chinese American critic choose between feminism and heroism? In: Hirsch, M. and Keller, E. (eds.) *Conflicts in Feminism*. Routledge, New York, pp. 234–51.

Chuh, K. (2001) Imaginary borders. In: Chuh, K. and Shimakawa, K. (eds.) *Orientations: Mapping Studies in the Asian Diaspora*. Duke University Press, Durham, pp. 277–95.

Chuh, K. (2003) *Imagine Otherwise: On Asian Americanist Critique*. Duke University Press, Durham.

Eng, D. L. and Hom, A. Y. (eds.) (1998) *Q & A: Queer in Asian America*. Temple University Press, Philadelphia.

Fanon, F. (1963) *The Wretched of the Earth*. Grove, New York.

Franklin, C. (2000) Introduction. In: Franklin, C., Hsu, R. and Kosanke, S. (eds.) *Navigating Islands and Continents: Conversations and Contestations in and around the Pacific*, special issue of *Literary Studies East and West*. University of Hawai'i College of Languages, Linguistics, and Literature, Honolulu, pp. xv–xxx.

Franklin, C. and Lyons, L. (2003) Remixing hybridity: globalization, native resistance, and cultural production in Hawai'i. *American Studies Journal* (Spring).

Fujikane, C. (1994) Between nationalisms: Hawaii's local nation and its troubled racial paradise. *Critical Mass: A Journal of Asian American Cultural Criticism* 1(2): 23–58.

Ho'omanawanui, K. (forthcoming) "This land is your land, this land was my land": Kanaka Maoli versus settler representations of 'āina in contemporary literature of Hawai'i. In: Fujikane, C. and Okamura, J. (eds.) *Asian Settler Colonialism in Hawai'i*.

Johnson, T., Champagne, D. and Nagel, J. (1997) American Indian activism and transformation: lessons from Alcatraz. In: Johnson, T., Champagne, D. and Nagel, J. (eds.) *American Indian Activism: Alcatraz to the Longest Walk*. University of Illinois Press, Chicago, pp. 9–44.

Kalāhele, 'Īmaikalani. (2002) *Kalāhele: Poetry and Art by 'Īmaikalani Kalāhele*. Kalamakū Press, Honolulu.

Kamahele, M. (2002) 'Īlio'ulaokalani: defending Native Hawaiian culture. In: Fujikane, C. and Okamura, J. (eds.) *Whose Vision? Asian Settler Colonialism in Hawai'i*. Special issue of *Amerasia Journal* 26(2): 38–65.

Kosasa, E. (1999) Review of Dana Takagi's "Forget post-colonialism! Sovereignty and self-determination in Hawai'i" posted on the Association for Asian American Studies listserv (June 24, 1999).

Kosasa, E. (2000) Ideological images: U.S. nationalism in Japanese settler photographs. In: Fujikane, C. and Okamura, J. (eds.) *Whose Vision? Asian Settler Colonialism in Hawai'i*. Special issue of *Amerasia Journal* 26(2): 66–91.

Kosasa, E. (2004) Predatory politics: U.S. imperialism, settler hegemony and the Japanese in Hawai'i. Diss. in progress, University of Hawai'i.

Kosasa, K. (2002) *Critical Sights/Sites: Art Pedagogy and Settler Colonialism in Hawai'i*. Diss. University of Rochester, New York.

Lloyd, D. (1995, 1997) Nationalisms against the state. In: Lowe, L. and Lloyd, D. (eds.) *The Politics of Culture in the Shadow of Capital*. Duke University Press, Durham, pp. 173–97.

Lowe, L. (1996) *Immigrant Acts: On Asian American Cultural Politics*. Duke University Press, Durham.

Lyons, L. (1996) Feminist articulations of the nation: the "dirty" women of Armagh and the discourse of Mother Ireland. *Genders* 24 (Summer 1996): 110–49.

MacKenzie, M. K. (1991) *Native Hawaiian Rights Handbook*. Native Hawaiian Legal Corporation, Honolulu.

Okamura, J. (1998) Social stratification. In: Hass, M. (ed.) *Multicultural Hawai'i*. Garland, New York, pp. 185–204.

Omi, M. and Winant, H. (1994) *Racial Formation in the United States: From the 1960s to the 1990s*, 2nd edn. Routledge, New York.

Rodrigues, D. (2000) Reimagining ourselves: the controversy over Lois-Ann Yamanaka's *Blu's Hanging*. In: Fujikane, C. and Okamura, J. (eds.) *Whose Vision? Asian Settler Colonialism in Hawai'i*. Special issue of *Amerasia Journal* 26(2): 195–207.

Saranillio, D. (2003) Colonial amnesia: "Filipino Americans" and the Native Hawaiian sovereignty movement. MA Thesis. University of California, Los Angeles.

Saranillio, D. (forthcoming) Colonial America: rethinking Filipino settler empowerment in the U.S. colony of Hawai'i. In: Fujikane, C. and Okamura, J. (eds.) *Asian Settler Colonialism in Hawai'i*.

Trask, H. K. (1986) *Eros and Power: The Power of Feminist Theory*. University of Pennsylvania, Philadelphia.

Trask, H. K. (1996) Feminism and indigenous Hawaiian nationalism. *Signs* 21(4): 906–16.

Trask, H. K. (1993, 1999) *From a Native Daughter: Colonialism and Sovereignty in Hawai'i*. University of Hawai'i Press, Honolulu.

Trask, H. K. (2000a) Settlers of color and "immigrant" hegemony: "locals" in Hawai'i. In: Fujikane, C. and Okamura, J. (eds.) *Whose Vision? Asian Settler Colonialism in Hawai'i*. Special issue of *Amerasia Journal* 26(2): 1–24.

Trask, H. K. (2000b) Writing in captivity: poetry in a time of de-colonization. In: Franklin, C., Hsu, R. and Kosanke, S. (eds.) *Navigating Islands and Continents: Conversations and Contestations in and around the Pacific*, special issue of *Literary Studies East and West*. University of Hawai'i College of Languages, Linguistics, and Literature, Honolulu, pp. 51–5.

Trask, M. (2002) Rice *v.* Cayetano: reaffirming the racism of Hawaii's colonial past. *Asian-Pacific Law and Policy Journal* 3(2): 352–8.

Wong, S.-l. C. (1993) *Reading Asian American Literature: From Necessity to Extravagance*. Princeton University Press, Princeton.

Wong, S. (1979) *Homebase*. Penguin, New York.

Yoshinaga, I. and Kosasa, E. (2000) Local Japanese Women for Justice (LJWJ) speak out against Daniel Inouye and the JACL. In: Fujikane, C. and Okamura, J. (eds.) *Whose Vision? Asian Settler Colonialism in Hawai'i*. Special issue of *Amerasia Journal* 26(2): 143–57.

CHAPTER FIVE

A Gay World Make-Over? An Asian American Queer Critique

Martin F. Manalansan IV

Once Upon a Time, There Was a Panel...

At the 1994 Association for Asian American Studies conference held in Ithaca, New York, a panel chaired by the late Amy Ling gathered together scholars in the emerging field of what was then called gay and lesbian studies. This panel was given the enviable task of mapping out the limits and possibilities of this field as a site for exploration within Asian American studies. A young assistant professor and two graduate students, including myself, were eventually chosen to occupy the presenter roles on the panel. During her introductory remarks, Amy Ling described the travails in setting up the panel because of the nascent nature of the body of scholarship. She also made a point to mark the occasion as a historical milestone in the field.

I do not consider the panel to be either a point of provenance or a nostalgic moment for Asian American queer studies; instead, it portrays lesbian, gay, bisexual, and transgender (LGBT)[1] scholarship's rather uneventful coming out of the research closet of Asian American studies. While most people would argue that the relative ease in establishing an LGBT research agenda for Asian American studies is due to the minoritarian and embattled position of the field itself within the academy, it also presents a rather complicated relationship between the two fields.

The inauspicious beginnings of the joint venture between the two fields may leave many to perceive a placid existence for the scholars and scholarship. At the same time, no one can disagree that the critical intervention made by queer Asian American scholarship has been to place race, sexuality, gender, and immigration at the forefront of the discussion of queer practices and identities. With critical scholarly volumes such as those edited by Russell Leong, David Eng, and Alice

Hom, to name a few, queer Asian American studies has not made its mark only in the LGBT academic debates.

However, the future of this kind of scholarship is in doubt in the face of what has been perceived as the triumphant ascendance of gays, lesbians, bisexuals, and transgendered people in mainstream life. Together with the onslaught of "positive" mass media representations of queers, critics and scholars have pointed to numerous changes in the legal landscape as evidence of this outcome, chief among these being the US Supreme Court decision against sodomy laws and the progress made toward gay marriage in Canada.

These events have not only created a celebratory moment for many LGBT Americans; they have also curiously precipitated a serious questioning about the agenda of queer studies. Based on my informal conversations with scholars and observations at recent LGBT-related conferences, I would argue that many now believe the field has become a superfluous, privileged, and elitist anachronism in the face of events that are seen to be political and social advances. In addition, there is a growing tendency to consider the discussion of racial and class issues within queer academic and political venues as unnecessarily divisive and irrelevant; another tendency is to pay lip service to racial and class issues while at the same eliding them in the discussion. In other words, the aforementioned events and discourses have rendered the future of queer studies, and, by implication, queer Asian American studies, in peril if not already obsolete.

This essay critically evaluates contemporary events and discourses around queerness. I argue against the popular view of these events as the utopic end products of a teleological narrative of progress. As such, I center the issues of race in the discussion by looking at three different genres: a television show, two gay studies books, and ethnographic interviews with Filipino gay men. In all of these texts, queers are trying to come to terms with the idea of change. In the first, the television show, change or transformation is based on a fashion "make-over."

In this essay, I deploy the "make-over" as the underlying ironic metaphor and literal process for tracking and analyzing recent scholarship and events. The transformation and changes that have occurred in the political arena can be likened to the process of a national if not global make-over – where queers are no longer subject to ugly homophobia.

In examining the relationship of LGBT studies and Asian American studies, I call for neither the mere "inclusion" of queer Asian American scholars nor the "adding on" of racial, class, and cultural differences into queer analysis. Rather, culling from the ideas of Asian American scholars and ethnographic examples from New York City, I weave a counter-narrative about the so-called "new" and somehow improved queer world. This counter-narrative presents the contemporary queer world as constituted by racist and racializing practices, xenophobic immigration laws, and the combined vilification and sexualization of the foreigner. At the same time, I sketch out a way of apprehending the changes that have occurred as a way of pointing to possible coalition work between and future paths of queer and Asian American scholarship.

Whose *Queer Eye*?

As I started re-writing this essay in the summer of 2003, what many people are calling a television and social milestone in America occurred – the premiere of the show *Queer Eye for a Straight Guy*. The show's theme and content primarily revolves around a fashion make-over of a "straight man" made possible by a group of five gay men (one of whom is a person of color). The show not only created quite a stir but also earned stratospheric ratings that encouraged the Bravo Channel, the producers of the show, to screen it almost every day. At the same time, the cast members have become minor celebrities, being featured prominently in television talk shows, newspapers, and magazines.

The show's basic narrative consists of the five gay men introducing the straight male client to trendy clothes, food, manner, and interior design. The gay men's hard work is, at least for the first five episodes, geared toward securing the approval of the straight man's wife/girlfriend. For example, in one episode, the straight man was groomed into getting a positive response from his girlfriend to his proposal of marriage.

Of course, the make-over theme did not start with the *Queer Eye* show. Fashion and interior design make-overs are at the heart of television talk shows such as *Ricki Lake* and *Oprah* and specialized feature shows like *Fashion Emergency* and *Trading Spaces*. While some shows have added a reality dimension where some "clients" or "victims" disapprove of or are aghast over the changes, the main idea is that the transformation always occurs and is completed. In most shows, however, as in the *Queer Eye*, it is crucial that the transformation is successful overall. The question remains – to what end?

What is clear is that while *Queer Eye* is funnier than most make-over shows, it contains no innovative elements, and the use of gay men as flirty and bitchy arbiters of good taste is, like in all other shows, ultimately in the maintenance and enhancement of heterosexuality. Despite the sexual innuendoes, the show is about the commodification and marketing of a particular form of cultural capital – that of an aesthetic taste that is given the label "gay" but is in the service of the "straight" man.

Cultural capital, as the show suggests, is acquired through having clothes with the "correct" fashion labels like Ralph Lauren, classy foods like foie gras, and skin and grooming products. These commodities allegedly lead to self-actualization (as a heterosexual man), happiness, and heterosexual bliss. However, the transformation is not about gay and straight per se but rather concerns the perpetuation of what has been labeled the "metrosexual" – a straight man who is fastidiously obsessed about his grooming, shelter, and manners, or, to put it in more blatant terms, a straight man who shops for and consumes high-end products. Therefore, the metrosexual and all these make-over shows are creatures of the capitalist market. Make-over shows and, by implication, gay male characters are conduits to the continued functioning of capitalist consumption.

While this is not a textual exegesis of the show, I argue that the show is neither a harmless, frivolous consumer product nor a wonderful piece of evidence of growing liberalization of attitudes towards queers. Rather, I suggest that it is necessary to read the show and other mass media products like it as a symptom of a growing political attitude and sensibility – one that insists that the queer world has undergone a make-over of sorts resulting in the creation of new "positive" legal, political, and cultural landscapes. This kind of reading unravels not only what is excluded from this popular discussion of the transformed queer world but also leads to a critical interrogation of the very process of social change itself.

New Make-Overs, Old Transformations: Looking at Stories of Closets and Stonewall

While television shows like *Will and Grace* and the *Queer Eye* are the more public examples, two recent books by prominent gay scholars – the historian John D'Emilio and the sociologist Steven Seidman – provide glaring and more troubling illustrations of this contemporary wave of celebratory views. In *The World Turned* (2002), a recent collection of essays by the eminent historian John D'Emilio, he proclaims that gays, lesbians, bisexuals, transgendered people, and other queers are experiencing a world that has moved toward a more hopeful state of affairs. As the book title suggests, the world has turned and changed radically for queers. He writes:

> Something happened in the 1990s. Something dramatic and I expect irreversible in its consequences. [...] The evidence for it comes from a host of phenomena large and small. Staid American corporations like Motorola and Chevron provide domestic partnership benefits for their gay, lesbian and bisexual employees. In Chicago, the city government has constructed rainbow towers along the main street of its chief gay neighborhood. *People* magazine puts on its cover a lesbian rock star, her lover and baby [... and so on]. (ix–x)

Then he cautions:

> I am not saying that some kind of gay utopia has arrived. The evidence to refute such a claim is as abundant as the mind-boggling changes are numerous. But profound changes can coexist with a litany of very real grievances. And since the grievances have a long history while the spectacular advances of recent years are fresh and new, forgive me if I choose to emphasize the hopeful. (x)

D'Emilio marvels at and rightly notes that the new generation of queers who grew up in the 1980s and 1990s of the post-Stonewall era, specifically the young people of today, can now see gay, lesbian, and other queer identities as part of everyday possibilities. While recognizing continuing barriers in certain sectors, D'Emilio nevertheless emphasizes the opening up of opportunities and spaces for queers in the media, on the streets and practically everywhere. However, in choosing to emphasize the "hopeful" and disregarding the "grievances," he fails to recognize the uneven and unequal nature of social change. In his chapter on Stonewall he goes even further to elide such inequalities in trying to debunk a myth that has been perpetuated around the Stonewall narratives, particularly around white gay privilege and the "misplaced resentment" of some people against the mostly white gay political and cultural establishment. D'Emilio argues:

> The assumption that privilege makes one politically suspect or somehow inadequate as an agent of social change also threatens to obscure the truth at the heart of our movement: *All* homosexuals are oppressed; gay oppression is real and vicious. It isn't necessary to shed extra tears for the plight of prosperous white gay men in order to acknowledge that if one scratches below the surface of any gay life, one will find a bottomless well of pain whose source is oppression. And gays with privilege risk their status and expose themselves to penalties when they make the leap to activism. (152)

D'Emilio creates a unitary and monolithic view of gay oppression and gay activism, and, in doing so, he dismisses the ways in which oppression as well as liberation are processes that operate and unfold disproportionately and in an asymmetrical manner. In other words, in both processes one cannot assume a level playing field. His assertion that even privileged white gay men can lead the way to gay liberation does not examine the context of the present gay political and cultural establishment where this privileged group gets to set the agenda and have their voices heard first and in a louder manner. If this is the present state of affairs for activist groups who are working for changes in the gay order of things, then what is the meaning of these changes? For whom are these changes?

In his book, *Beyond the Closet* (2002), Steven Seidman attempts to address the issue of transformation and the disparities between white queers and queers of color. He asserts that we have come a long way and that now, in so many ways for so many people, the closet is no longer the life sentence that many queers in the past have been condemned to live. He suggests that the changes can be understood in terms of the slowly disintegrating presence of the closet in many queers' lives and an increasing move from being marginal outsiders to being "out" members and citizens of the country.

Unlike D'Emilio, Seidman recognizes that the struggle for citizenship by gays and lesbians involves the complicating intersections of sexuality, race, ethnicity, and class. He makes the caveat that "race matters" (42). However, while he recognizes race as a factor, at the same time he admits to the paucity of "empirical research" on people of color and, in a long footnote, he characterized the work as "an abundance of personal testimonies or interpretive statements" (219). Therefore, he must admit to being restricted to speculations since even his own interviews with gays and lesbians of color were extremely limited. While one can take issue with his rather cavalier characterization of the body of research on queers of color, it is more important to note how race eventually falls out of his discussion to be resurrected at the end.

Race reappears in the very concluding section of Seidman's book in relation to the struggle for citizenship in a multicultural United States. Race does not enter into his discussion of Hollywood films except inasmuch as he notes that queers of color are conspicuously absent. Besides his discussion of a black woman character (played by Whoopi Goldberg) in *Boys on the Side* (1995), Seidman's analysis and solution are merely quantitative; that is, he calls for more film roles and representations of queers of color instead of considering the problem more critically by asking: What can one make of the absence of queers of color? How can race be the specter that haunts all of these films? What is the relationship of whiteness to the major legal, cultural, and social transformations in America? Seidman unsurprisingly remains silent about whiteness, much less does he consider its existence beyond the absence of "color."

I would argue that the absence of colored bodies in the films Seidman analyzes does not obliterate but rather heightens the constitutive role of race in Hollywood's cultural productions. In other words, race is not just an additive element but rather something that permeates and suffuses all cultural productions. Nevertheless, both these books and the television show *Queer Eye* illustrate the paucity of bodies and experiences of queers of color in critical and mainstream LGBT studies and representations. To address this situation, I now turn to my ethnographic interviews with Filipino queers.

Walking Through the Runways of Race and Sex: Two New York City Stories

One way to complicate the reading and critique of the contemporary moment is to juxtapose the missing elements in the three texts: the voices of queers of color. Based on my ethnographic fieldwork interviews in the late 1990s and after September 11, 2001, among Filipino and other Asian American queers, I suggest that one of the more complicating factors in the analysis of contemporary events is the ways people of color are inevitably shunted from the sites of gay mainstream political and cultural desires – the family, marriage, economic stability, and legal personhood. In other words, as the two vignettes below suggest, the reality of racial difference, the complications of immigration, and the racialized corporeal aesthetics of mainstream LGBT culture delineate a world for queers of color that can be likened to old wine in new bottles. That is, the transformations heralded in the three previous texts have affected queers of color in different, oftentimes negative, ways.

I highlight the experiences of two queer informants, Krista and Raul. In narrating their lives, I do not consider their stories in terms of the other side of the hopeful and "happy" aspects of the contemporary queer moment. At the same time, I do not suggest that the lives of these two queers as well as other queers of color amount to an endless litany of grievances, forlornness, or misery. More appropriately, their lives are struggles between pathos and pleasure and between displacement and settlement. In addition, their voices are not just a spicy exotic element mixed into a multicultural stew. Instead, what follows are voices that push the discussion along a different path, to flay open the beast called social change and complicate the ways in which change can be understood and engaged.

The first vignette is about Krista, a Filipino immigrant (M to F) transgendered[2] person. She ran a make-shift hair salon from her apartment in Jersey City and, depending on the state of her finances, would walk the streets of the Meatpacking District in Manhattan and the Journal Square Path Train Station in Jersey City as a sex worker. She had a green card but said that after September 11, 2001, she has become very wary of the police and other figures of authority. First, she said that she was still a male in her official papers. She did not have the means to do the legal paperwork to change this status and she was not sure whether she had the right to do so, especially since she was not a citizen. She said:

> It is so hard nowadays. You have to be careful even if you are legal but if you are brown or technicolored you have to be careful. Some of the other girls [sex workers] could not care less if they get arrested but you know, the police can now report you to the INS about your arrests. Someone told me that if you have had police trouble and you travel abroad, they might not let you back into the country. So look, I don't think I will be traveling anytime soon.[3]

At the same time, she was also nervous about the fact that she has had Middle Eastern clients or, as she calls them, "Arabo" or Arabs. Before September 11, she remembers seeing them hanging around the train station. They would whistle and call out to her. She said they were very macho, but also very generous. However, in the wake of the World Trade Center attacks, they have all but disappeared. To add more fear to Krista's life, she has heard that the other Filipinos who plied their wares at the train station and who have had Middle Eastern boyfriends have been questioned by the FBI and that some of them who had visa problems have been deported. She notes:

> It is a different time now. We used to get arrested and then the police will let us go. But now, they ask us who our customers are and whether we know any terrorist. But, I tell them I here for the lovin' not for the fightin' [. . .] they [the police] do

not find that funny. It is a good thing I did not have an Arabo boyfriend, otherwise, I will be in hot water.

After September 11, it has become clear that the public demand for patriotism coincided with a pernicious witch-hunt for suspicious "aliens" and unwanted immigrants. More than anything Krista's wary words about the Middle Eastern men may suggest, relationships between members of various immigrant communities and communities of color have become strained. In other words, post-9/11 has created an atmosphere of fear for immigrants and people of color that is largely different from the general mainstream uneasiness and fear. Thus, while many Americans are afraid of traveling for fear that the plane they are riding in will be hijacked, immigrants and people of color have a more complicated set of issues they have to confront, including their tenuous relationships with police and other governmental authorities like immigration officers.

I asked Krista what these frightening changes meant to her life as a queer person in relation to other more "positive" ones, particularly the public presence of gays in the mass media. She said that straight people are always fascinated with her walking as a "man trapped inside a woman's heart" and they marvel at how real she looks. She said that while gay men now grace the magazine pages and television shows, she is adamant that this development only affects white gay men who look and act in a certain way – masculine and muscular. She said she had no illusions about how the color of her skin can play a big part in how she gets treated in the bars. But at the same time, she is also cognizant of how lucky she is in certain ways to live in a city like New York where there is more "tolerance [...] but," she hastens to add, "only in specific places," meaning that there were still neighborhoods, bars, and other public places where she could get beaten up and/or harassed. She muses:

> I am sure that had I been white, I would have been able to get jobs at all these great restaurants like Lucky Cheng's and Lips [New York City theme restaurants with transvestite/transgender wait staff]. They only need a certain number of Asian and then that is it. I still have to work cutting hair and being a *puta* [whore/bitch]. If I don't do this I can't really survive. Maybe if I could look like Marilyn Monroe or Liza Minnelli, I could at least make a decent living.

Krista's fear and trepidation, as well as wariness about the gay order of things, is echoed by Raul, another Filipino immigrant. Unlike Krista, Raul is undocumented, and while he identifies as "gay," he has a lot of issues with the identity and culture that comes with the label. Raul is forty years old and, as he described himself, "homely and overweight." He said:

> Sometimes, I can't see myself in those gay shows and magazines. I have a different body, a different way of dressing up. Look at me, I live from paycheck to paycheck, do you think I can afford to go to the gym and buy those clothes?

When I asked him whether in fact his problem can be solved with a fashion make-over, he laughed and said:

> No amount of make-overs can change me. Really, unless they transplant my brain in a white man's body, there is no way it would make a difference. Like if I lost some weight and got a better salary – those will only be shallow changes. I will still confront the same big problems.

When I asked him what these big problems were, he said being undocumented or, as he terms it, "illegal" and "always in hiding." His immigration status will always make it difficult for him to assert himself and to come out of the "closet" in a big and splashy way like what he sees in the shows and magazines. He said, "As an 'illegal', you cannot be carefree. I would not even want to be photographed watching the gay pride parade. I don't want to get into any problems with the police. I might get deported."

He further asserted that following the introduction of the new stricter immigration laws, he cannot change his undocumented status even if he contracted a green card marriage. He has been undocumented for more than five years and there is no way he could alter his predicament. At the same time, Raul does not see his life as a "litany of grievances." Unlike the typical reaction to this kind of narrative, Raul sees his life not as a dismal, hopeless state of forlornness. Rather, he said:

> My life here despite being illegal is a lot better than in the Philippines because I have a job. Now, do not get me wrong, I dream of the day that I could become legal, I also don't like being looked down upon in gay bars because I am not a cute white guy, but at least I can send money back home to the Philippines and help out my parents and siblings, then I am okay.

Both Raul and Krista provide a glimpse of the other dimensions of the queer world today. Their own queer world has been prevented from reaping the benefits of new legislation and flashy media images of queer people. They live in the shadows of these seemingly revolutionary changes. While this essay is not an attempt to diminish these current developments, I would suggest that we need to frame these historic events regarding the mainstreaming of gays, lesbians, and other queers within a wider context of racial politics, worsening racist immigration practices, and the overall marginalization of peoples of color.

Living Happily Ever After in a Made-Over World...: Lessons From Asian American Studies Past and Future

The two vignettes suggest a re-consideration of the centrality of race in queer studies. If there is a crucial lesson to be learned from queer Asian American research, as Lisa Lowe (1996), David Eng (1997), Gayatri Gopinath (1996), Dana Takagi (1996), and Karin Aguilar-San Juan (1998) have long asserted, it is that the American cultural landscape hides the interconnections among sexuality, race, and nationhood. Immigration, as Lisa Lowe (1996) has suggested, unravels the tensions among racialized genderings and sexualizations of particular groups of color. Even after the so-called opening up of the gates following the Immigration and Nationality Act of 1965,[4] we find that immigration and, by implication, cultural and political citizenship in the United States have been and continue to be racialized. What does this have to do with the three texts we have been considering – the television show *Queer Eye* and the scholarly texts of queer scholars D'Emilio and Seidman?

The failure to insist on and take seriously the importance of race as a pivotal aspect of the discussion and interpretation of contemporary events of queer political and social lives has led to empty celebratory and self-congratulatory platitudes. By allowing race to fall out of the equation, such discourses render a gay world changed, transformed, and "made-over" for a select privileged few. Here, I consider privilege not to be something innate but as a status that is reified and strengthened through exclusionary discursive moves such as those discussed above. Only people with access to consumer products, cultural environments, and legal personhoods are able to be unequivocally hopeful and optimistic about this changed world. Lisa Duggan (2002) has rightly termed this condition of privilege and normalization of the queer world as "homonormativity." How then do we engage with and resist the emergence of the homonormative world?

Consider the following situation. The Anti-Violence Project, which is a multi-city effort to document and address hate or bias crimes against queers, reported that in 2002 in New York City there were dramatic increases in bias-related incidents against queer people of Middle Eastern or Arab, Latino, and South Asian descent. It is necessary to note that while September 11 is seen as a watershed event that has triggered these incidents, the issue of underreporting these situations to the police is part of the continued fear, distrust, and trepidation that queers of color in particular and people of color in general hold about the police and other government figures of authority.

The narratives of Krista and Raul demand a re-conceptualization of the contemporary moment. First, it is necessary not to see the so-called LGBT community as a monolithic and stable political body. At the same time, the new queer political agenda must work with and through the dynamic tension of differences within the community. Asian American scholars such as Lisa Lowe and Kandice Chuh have emphasized the political pitfalls of naturalizing the Asian American category; similarly, it is necessary for queer activists and scholars to perceive the category LGBT as something changing and fraught with fissures and gaps. Chuh (2003) in particular provides a sobering antidote to the intrinsic fear of internal dissent in Seidman and D'Emilio's analyses. In her book *Imagine Otherwise*, she makes productive use of the crises around Asian American studies as a field, not to dismantle it, but to show how in fact such crises, which mostly consist of internal struggles – or conflicts that D'Emilio would categorize as "grievances" – enable fruitful (re)imaginings of political and cultural goals. In other words, she suggests that such internal struggles lead not to the erosion of political will but rather to a strengthening of a particular form of ties that hinges on essential identity categories on the one hand and divergent interests and multiple hierarchies on the other. Moreover, far from rendering the joint ventures of queer studies and Asian American studies obsolete or blunted by the so-called political and cultural gains of queers, it is precisely when there is a general move toward the idea of mainstreaming that the critical edge of a queer Asian American studies is needed. Asian American queer scholars David Eng and Alice Hom (1998) have stated that it is not enough that queers of color are invited to the table; it is more important to change radically the "meal" that is to be communally shared. In other words, queers of color need to play a pivotal role in setting the political agenda and must not be relegated into mere grumbling clients. Queers of color need to set the parameters of such changes and not be the handmaidens waiting to marvel at political and cultural transformations.

The idea of "making-over" the queer world – from a world of marginalized people treated like aliens into a supposedly nurturing and more tolerant realm – needs to be examined in the face of the experiences of queer immigrants of color. As I suggested earlier, we need to question who benefits from the transformations, in what way, and to what ends. As Chandan Reddy (2003) astutely points out, not all queers are able to gain access to the benefits of marriage, family, cultural products, and legal rights. Some queers are relegated, if not totally banished, to being virtual and perpetual foreigners in these spaces and arenas. We need to get away from the seduction of transformation and the allure of the make-over, we need to examine the very premises of these changes, and we need to ask how these cosmetic changes can actually mask, if not reify, the ugly structures of oppression that they purport to erase.

NOTES

Siobhan Somerville provided the most cogent reading of this text. I am thankful for her ideas and her crucial intellectual presence. Chandan Reddy provided the inspiration for this essay with his vigilant activism and provocative ideas. I am grateful to Kent Ono for his support and generosity as well as for his astute editorial insights. I thank Dara Goldman, Matti Bunzl, C. L. Cole, David Eng, and Gayatri Gopinath for inspiring critical dialogs.

1 I use the term LGBT studies or scholarship instead of "gay and lesbian studies" to signal the transformation of this body of work to go beyond gay and lesbian issues and

identities and to signal a particular perspective that privileges a critique of hetero-normativity and the processes of normalization.

2 I use transgender here due to Krista's insistence. She said she used to be "bakla" – the Tagalog term for an effeminate cross-dresser/homosexual. She was due to undergo gender re-assignment surgery a few months after our interview in 2002.

3 Interviews were conducted in Tagalog or Taglish with Filipino informants.

4 See Luibhéid (2002) for a pioneering and excellent study on the intersection of race, sexuality, and immigration.

REFERENCES

Aguilar-San Juan, K. (1998) Going home: enacting justice in queer Asian America. In: Eng, D. and Hom, A. (eds.), pp. 25–40.

Chiang, M. (1998) Coming out into the global system: postmodern patriarchies and transnational sexualities in *The Wedding Banquet*. In Eng, D. and Hom, A. (eds.), pp. 374–96.

Chuh, K. (2003) *Imagine Otherwise: On Asian American Critique*. Duke University Press, Durham.

Cruz-Malave, A. and Manalansan, M. F. (2002) Introduction: dissident sexualities/alternative globalisms. In Cruz-Malave, A. and Manalansan, M. F. (eds.) *Queer Globalizations: Citizenship and the Afterlife of Colonialism*. New York University Press, New York, pp. 1–12.

D'Emilio, J. (2002) *The World Turned: Essays on Gay History, Politics and Culture*. Duke University Press, Durham.

Duggan, L. (2002) The new homonormativity: the sexual politics of neoliberalism. In R. Castronovo, R. and Nelson, D. D. (eds.) *Materializing Democracy*. Duke University Press, Durham, pp. 173–94.

Eng, D. (1997) Out here and over there: queerness and diaspora in Asian American Studies. *Social Text* 52–3: 31–52.

Eng, D. and Hom, A. (1998) Q&A: Notes on a Queer Asian America. In Eng, D. and Hom, A. (eds.), pp. 1–21.

Eng, D. and Hom, A. (eds.) (1998) *Q&A: Queer in Asian America*. Temple University Press, Philadelphia.

Gopinath, G. (1996) Funny boys and girls: notes on a queer South Asian planet. In: Leong, R. (ed.) *Asian American Sexualities: Dimensions of the Gay and Lesbian Experience*. Routledge, New York, pp. 119–27.

Lowe, L. (1996) *Immigrant Acts: On Asian American Cultural Politics*. Duke University Press, Durham.

Luibhéid, E. (2002) *Entry Denied: Monitoring Sexuality at the Border*. University of Minnesota Press, Minneapolis.

Reddy, C. (2003) They cannot represent themselves; they must be represented: a queer of color critique of neo-liberal citizenship and the discourse on family. Unpublished paper presented at the Association for Asian American Studies Annual Conference, San Francisco.

Seidman, S. (2002) *Beyond the Closet: The Transformation of Gay and Lesbian Life.* Routledge, New York.

Takagi, D. (1996) Maiden voyage: excursion into sexuality and identity politics in Asian America. In: Leong, R. (ed.) *Asian American Sexualities: Dimensions of the Gay and Lesbian Experience.* Routledge, New York, pp. 21–35.

CHAPTER SIX

Asian American Studies Through (Somewhat) Asian Eyes: Integrating "Mixed Race"[1] into the Asian American Discourse

Cynthia L. Nakashima

> *the people who put out that book*
> *i guess they won a lot of awards.*
> *it was a very photogenic period*
> *of California history, especially*
> *if you were a white photographer*
> *with compassion for helpless people.*
>
> *but the book would have been better,*
> *i think, or more complete, if they*
> *had put in my picture and yours, with*
> *our hakujin[2] wives, our long hair and*
> *the little signs that say, "what? me*
> *speak japanese?" and "self-determination*
> *for everyone but us." and then maybe*
> *on the very last page, a picture of*
> *our kids. they don't even look like*
> *Japanese.* (Tanaka 1980)

This poem, by Ronald Tanaka, is a powerful critique of the internment of Japanese Americans during World War II, of mainstream depictions of internment, and of the changes taking place in the Japanese American community since the war. But the first time I read it, as an undergraduate in an Asian American studies class, I hated it. It made me feel alienated – from the class, from the field, from the community. Intellectually, and even emotionally, I could understand the significance of Tanaka's feelings of anger and loss. But where did it leave me – a mixed race girl, trying to learn about my family's history, trying to learn about myself as an Asian American. As Tanaka says, I don't even look like Japanese.

Many scholars in the field of Asian American studies have established that the discipline has historically given primacy to certain versions of the Asian American experience – specifically an adult male, heterosexual, American-born, Chinese or Japanese, West Coast perspective (Lowe 1991; Takagi 1996; Spickard 2001). I would argue that we can add to this list an assumption of "mono-raciality" or "racial"/ethnic "purity." Traditional approaches to Asian American studies tend to limit the impact of the "multiracial experience" on Asian America to the confines of a "contemporary issue," i.e., Week 11 on the syllabus. In most historical accounts, the very existence of mixed race Asian Americans seems almost an impossibility,[3] and in many discussions of contemporary Asian America mixed race people are relegated to the status of inevitable (and often, as in Tanaka's poem above, doomed) byproduct of the increasing rates of interracial marriage. In fact, mixed race people usually appear in Asian American discourse as children – the children of Asian Americans, but not definitively Asian American themselves, and certainly not as empowered adults (Williams-León and Nakashima 2001).

In reality, a lot of us are all grown up, and some of us have grown up to teach and study about Asian America. Sometimes, this feels like a struggle. For example, we (meaning mixed race Asian Americanists) often marvel at the fact that the traditional approach to Asian American immigration as pre-1965 and post-1965 completely ignores the 100,000 or so "War Brides" and their mixed race families who immigrated from Asia in between these two periods (Thornton 1992; Rooks 2001; Williams-León and Nakashima 2001). While these numbers may not seem significant in the current demographic context, they meant a marked increase in the Asian American population at the time. It seems that their distance from the "center" of Asian American studies as women and children without an Asian American male as "head of household" has rendered them unimportant to the field and invisible in our collective history.

And yet, many mixed race Asian Americans have come out of Asian American and ethnic studies courses with the analytical tools, the intellectual self-confidence, and the faculty support not only to explore themselves and their families as Asian Americans, but also to embark on explorations of their mixed race identities. In fact, I would argue that the field of Mixed Race studies is a direct outgrowth of Asian American and ethnic studies, borrowing heavily from its texts, its paradigms, and its language (Williams et al. 1996).[4]

An Invitation, an Imploration

The time has come now to return the favor: Asian American studies, I invite you, as a discipline, to come and see what the mixed race discourse has to offer you in your pursuit of knowledge.

You will be surprised at how many resources exist today. There are campus organizations, community organizations, newsletters, magazines, online magazines, websites, novels, short stories, poems, autobiographies, films, dance and performance pieces, and artwork by and about people of mixed race. There is also a significant body of academic research and writing on a variety of aspects of mixed race, including many that specifically concern mixed race Asian Americans. For example, did you know that there is a complicated class typology that exists for people of mixed race in the Vietnamese American community (Valverde 2001)? Have you ever considered the ways in which mixed race Asian Americans might employ their individual and family names as signifiers of their ethnicities (Nakashima 2001)? Did you realize that the current dominant image of mixed race people as "children of the future" can be traced to mainstream depictions of Hapas in Hawai'i in the 1920s and 1930s (Rosa 2001)?[5]

To integrate mixed race perspectives would not be an act of charity on your part, but rather one of necessity. The 2000 Census, the first to allow us to check multiple boxes on the "race"/ethnicity questions, shows us that mixed race Asian Pacific Americans (APAs) make up 16.8 percent of the total APA population, the second largest subgroup after (single race)[6] Chinese (Dariotis 2003). When including mixed race people in the population, the growth rate for the entire APA population from 1990 to 2000 was 71.9 percent. Without mixed race people, it was only 46.3 percent (Lai and Arguelles 2003). As Lai and Arguelles point out, "By 2010, hapas[7] could very well be the largest [subgroup of APAs], depending on birthrate and immigration policies in the post-September 11 era" (3). Asian American studies needs to incorporate mixed race perspectives, not to be on the cutting edge but simply to remain relevant in the twenty-first century.

Furthermore, tacking the subject of mixed race (or gender, or sexuality, or class, etc.) onto the end of the discussion, whether it takes place as a course, a book, or a lecture, leaves it relatively one-dimensional and simplistic. I would replace this outdated "additive" approach with a more sophisticated integrative approach where the issues and experiences of mixed race are grappled with throughout the discussion. As others have argued before, being careful to integrate a variety of perspectives into the Asian American discourse, while messier and more complicated, allows for a much more complex and intellectually challenging representation of Asian American history, culture, identity, and community that helps us to resist the urge to "essentialize" who and what we are discussing (Lowe 1991; Takagi 1996).[8]

Consider, for example, the debate on interracial dating and marriage – a perennial favorite amongst Asian American studies students – through a mixed race perspective. Alongside an examination of the rates and the patterns and the theories and the debates, the issues of sexuality and the dynamics of gender, ask yourself and your students what the discussion itself communicates to Asian Americans of mixed race? How must it feel to have one's own family become the site of academic theorizing and public contestation? Where does all of this leave the mixed race person in terms of his or her own dating and marriage options? Indeed, integrating a mixed race worldview (not that there is just one) can and, in my opinion, should alter the entire Asian American studies discourse by disrupting the very concept of "Asian American" itself. Who and what is Asian American, and who gets to decide? What is "race" in the first place? What about ethnicity? Where did these "racial" and ethnic categories come from? Banks (2003: xi) suggests that "[t]eachers should help students to understand how racial categories have shifted over time and how established racial categories and groups have been deconstructed and new ones established". Messy and complicated, but infinitely more interesting and, ultimately, more enlightening.

Integrating Mixed Race into the Asian American Discourse

Curtiss Rooks (personal communication, 2003), a professor of Asian American studies who is himself mixed race Japanese/African American, says he has no trouble finding opportunities to integrate mixed race into his curriculum. When his students learn about early immigration, they look at the first Filipinos who came to Louisiana and their ethnically and culturally mixed families. When they study contemporary Asian American communities they learn about the women whom we call "War Brides," who can be credited as the immigration "anchors" for much of the post-1965 influx from Korea. When they consider Asian American identity, they look at models of mixed race identity alongside other psychological models.

Likewise, Professor Teresa Williams-León (personal communication, 2003), who is Japanese/European American, says that, as she has gotten more experience teaching, she has found more and more opportunities to present mixed race perspectives throughout her courses on race and ethnicity. For example, an introductory course on Asian Americans includes a look at some of the early "miscegenated" communities such as the Chinese/African Americans in Mississippi and the Sikh/Mexicans in California's Central Valley. When discussing the plantation era in Hawai'i, Fred Makino, the Hapa labor leader, is highlighted. And when considering images of Asian Americans in popular culture, celebrities such as Keanu Reeves and Tiger Woods are analyzed both as Asian Americans and as people of mixed race.

The following section offers a few more examples of ways in which to integrate the subject of mixed race into a general discussion of Asian Americans.

Early Asian immigration to the United States

While it is true that the vast majority of early immigrants from Asia were men, this does not mean that we should assume that they were all "bachelors" or that they limited themselves to relationships with women of their own ethnicity, or to women at all. Rather than making this assumption, it would be more interesting to consider the variety of ways that early immigrant men dealt with their situation and why. For example, geographic location and its accompanying social climate seems to be important – Chinese and Japanese men away from the West Coast married outside of their ethnic groups relatively frequently, as did Chinese in Hawai'i. Ethnicity and culture also seem to matter, as Filipino men dated and married women of many "racial"/ethnic groups throughout the country. In addition, social class has an impact. A true story like *On Gold Mountain* (See 1995), about a man who came to Los Angeles in the late 1800s from China and his mixed race descendants, is a good illustration of how an Asian immigrant who has achieved economic success has greater opportunities to marry, even into the dominant group. Some men had left wives and families back in Asia, some managed to bring them here, and some married Asian women who had immigrated themselves or who were native-born Americans.[9] And, of course, some chose to have relationships with other men, both inter- and intra-racially.

Taking a more in-depth approach to the issue of sex and marriage among the early Asian settlers offers a good segue into a discussion of the intense phobia against Asian male/White female relationships that was present in the anti-Asian movement, legislation, and violence (i.e. the Watsonville Riots [Takaki 1989]) during the early period. It also allows for a look at the first Asian American communities, some of which were very multiracial and multicultural like the Sikhs in the Central Valley of California (Leonard 1992), the Chinese in Mississippi (Loewen 1971) and Hawai'i, and the Filipinos in Chicago (Posadas 1989).

World War II/Japanese American internment

When discussing the relocation of Japanese Americans during World War II, it is important to mention the hundreds of mixed race people, many of whom were orphaned children, and interracially married couples who were interned. The decisions made by the War Relocation Authority about who should be locked up and why give an interesting insight into where Asian Americans fit in the dominant racial ideology of the time. For example, anyone with as little as 1/16 (one-sixteenth) Japanese ancestry was subject to relocation and internment, indicating that a "one-drop rule" of heredity was applied to Asians as well as African Americans. And, the fact that interracial families where the husband was

Japanese American were considered much more dangerous than those where the wife was Japanese American and the husband was European American offers fascinating insights into gender dynamics and assumptions about loyalty, culture, and power (Spickard 1986).

The theme of gender dynamics and interracial relationships can be continued in the discussion on World War II with a consideration of how it was the beginning of America's "Pacific Wars" and the stationing of huge numbers of American troops in Japan, Okinawa, Korea, Thailand, Viet Nam, the Philippines, Guam, and Hawai'i. US military presence in this part of the world has had an enormous impact on dominant images of Asians and Asian Americans – men and women – as well as on Asian images of Americans. The women we've come to call "War Brides" and the people we call "Amerasians" can be considered here, and they come with their own sets of immigration laws, migration patterns, and personal stories.

Asian American communities and cultures

There are many different ways to conceptualize the contemporary Asian American communities, and I think it is good to consider them all. The traditional ethnic communities such as Chinese American, Korean American, Filipino American, etcetera, continue to have meaning, as does the "panethnic" Asian Pacific American (APA) community. Like the Asian American gay/lesbian/bisexual community/ies, the mixed race Asian American community, often called the "Hapa" community, has grown considerably in the past decade or so. These kinds of "communities" vary greatly in terms of structures and institutions, geographies, affiliations, and kinds of identities and cultures. They also intersect and interact in various ways. For example, a thirty-something individual born and raised in the San Francisco Bay Area might identify with and participate in the Chinese American, pan-APA, Hapa, and gay/lesbian/bisexual communities regularly. Another individual of the same age, living in Connecticut, might find that the panethnic APA community available over the Internet offers a more viable identification than does his fifth-generation Japanese American heritage.

Although the concept of assimilation has lost a great deal of its dominance over the past few decades, it continues to hold an important place in our understanding of the evolution of ethnic cultures and communities. For many, the act of interracial marriage is still viewed as the "ultimate assimilation" and the index for loss of traditional culture and ethnic cohesion. Instead of accepting this outdated assumption without question, we should seriously consider the complex nature of culture and community. What are some of the factors that shape their evolutions? Who gets to decide who and what qualify/ies as authentic and legitimate? Demographically speaking, the Japanese American community had been decreasing in size for decades. This has been attributed to low immigration rates, low birthrates, and high outmarriage rates. And yet, the population grew from 848,000 to 1.15 million between 1990 and 2000, because people who had previously been forced to choose only one "race"/ethnicity, often checking "Other" instead, were for the first time allowed to check multiple boxes (Lai and Arguelles 2003). In fact, there seems at the present time to be a debate emerging within the Japanese American community about what direction the community's institutions should take in order to remain vital: a pan-Asian direction, where they would no longer cater specifically to Japanese Americans but to a broader "Asian American" population, or an extended Japanese American direction, where they would continue to be specific to the Japanese American community, but adopt an increasingly broad definition of who is "Japanese American" (Beeler 2003).

The idea that marrying outside of your ethnic group sends you on a straight and narrow path into the mainstream is an interesting idea to consider, and can lead to many important discussions. For example, is a mixed race person "more" or "less" Korean, for example, than a monoracial person? What if the mixed race person has a mother who immigrated to the United States from Korea and is herself fluent in Korean, whereas the monoracial person is third-generation American and can only speak a few words of Korean? What if the mixed race person has green eyes and freckles? What if the monoracial person is married to a European American? An African American? As I mentioned earlier in this essay, the first time I read Ronald Tanaka's poem, I found it to be threatening and sad. Today I appreciate it as a brilliant opportunity to discuss, openly and explicitly, a very real part of being Asian and of being mixed race in America.

Conclusion

The very act of doing Asian American studies requires us to utilize imprecise and historically troubling concepts and categories. And yet, we continue to do Asian American studies because we know that it has value. For one thing, it helps many of us makes sense of our lives and our histories and our experiences. But I agree with those in the field who argue that an understanding of Asian America that recognizes its heterogeneity is critical. It is the best defense against the dangers and the pitfalls of our "strategic essentialisms" (Lowe 1991; Ono 1995).

In this chapter, I have attempted to argue that a new direction for the field would be to recognize the enduring existence and significance of multiraciality in Asian America, and to incorporate mixed race perspectives and subjects throughout the Asian American Studies discourse. Such a revision, in my opinion, would be mutually beneficial: the field would gain greater depth and insight, a greater knowledge of who and what it is, and mixed race Asian Americans would see ourselves reflected in a context that holds great meaning for us. We would no longer be, as in the Tanaka poem, left alone on the very last page.

NOTES

1 The term "mixed race" is used here to refer to people who have families that descend from more than one of the socially constructed "racial" groups. One could argue that most of the Filipinos in this country fall into this category, as well as the majority of African Americans and Latinos, from several generations back. This being true, those involved in the recent social movement of people who identify as mixed race are more typically from families that have "mixed" in the past two or three generations.
2 "Hakujin" is a Japanese term for "White" people or people of European descent.
3 An exception to this rule is Edith Maude Eaton (1865–1914), a well-documented Eurasian journalist and fiction writer who wrote under the pen name Sui Sin Far and who is often mentioned in historical accounts of Asians in America.
4 The field of Mixed Race studies also owes much to the traditional disciplines of sociology, anthropology, psychology, history, and literature, and to the newer fields of cultural and postcolonial studies.
5 There are too many important articles and books about people of mixed race to mention all of them here, but the following is a very short list of such sources: *Mixed Race Literature*, edited by Jonathan Brennan (2002); "No Passing Zone: The Artistic and Discursive Voices of Asian-Descent Multiracials," edited by Velina Hasu Houston and Teresa Kay Williams (1997); *Rethinking 'Mixed Race'*, edited by David Parker and Miri Song (2001); *Racially Mixed People in America* (1992) and *The Multiracial Experience* (1996), both edited by Maria P. P. Root; the *Multiracial Child Resource Book*, edited by Maria P. P. Root and Matt Kelley (2003); and *The Sum of Our Parts: Mixed Heritage Asian Americans*, edited by Teresa Williams-León and Cynthia L. Nakashima (2001).
6 "Single race" refers to monoracial or "unmixed" Chinese Americans.
7 "Hapa" originated from the Hawaiian term "Hapa-Haole," which meant something like "half-foreigner" but has evolved into "half-White" (with the other "half" being Native Hawaiian). Over time, the very ethnically diverse population of the state of Hawai'i has tended to apply "Hapa" to any kind of racial/ethnic mixture. More and more, the mainland Asian American community, through cultural ties to Hawai'i, has adopted the term for mixed race Asian Americans.
8 An excellent (and impressively non-messy) example of this is the book *The New Face of Asian Pacific America: Numbers, Diversity & Change in the 21st Century*, edited by Eric Lai and Dennis Arguelles (2003). Both the subject and the voices of mixed race Asian Americans are presented throughout the text, not as an afterthought, but as a pivotal piece of the discussion.
9 Another important revision to early Asian American history would be to spend more time investigating these female pioneers from Asia, rather than approaching them as "the wives of" or the "picture brides of" immigrant men.

REFERENCES

Banks, J. A. (2003) Foreword. In: Root, M. P. P. and Kelley, M. (eds.) *Multiracial Child Resource Book: Living Complex Identities*. Mavin Foundation, Seattle, pp. x–xiii.

Beeler, M. (2003) Beyond issei: Japanese descendants forge new cultural identity. *Bay Area Living* (July 27), Living 1: 4.

Dariotis, W.-M. (2003) A community based on shared difference. In: Lai, E. and Arguelles, D. (eds.), pp. 113–21.

Lai, E. and Arguelles, D. (eds.) (2003) *The New Face of Asian Pacific America: Numbers, Diversity & Change in the 21ˢᵗ Century.* Asian Week with UCLA's Asian American Studies Center Press, San Francisco.

Leonard, K. I. (1992) *Making Ethnic Choices: California's Punjabi Mexican Americans.* Temple University Press, Philadelphia.

Loewen, J. W. (1971) *The Mississippi Chinese: Between Black and White.* Harvard University Press, Cambridge, MA.

Lowe, L. (1991) Heterogeneity, hybridity, multiplicity: marking Asian American differences. *Diaspora* 1: 24–44.

Nakashima, D. A. (2001) A rose by any other name: names, multiracial/multiethnic people, and the politics of identity. In: Williams-León, T. and Nakashima, C. L. (eds.), pp. 111–19.

Ono, K. (1995) Re/signing "Asian American": rhetorical problematics of nation. *Amerasian Journal* 21(1): 67–78.

Posadas, B. M. (1989) Mestiza girlhood: interracial families in Chicago's Filipino American community since 1925. In: Asian Women United of California (eds.) *Making Waves: An Anthology of Writings by and About Asian American Women.* Beacon Press, Boston, pp. 273–82.

Rooks, C. T. (2001) Alaska's multiracial Asian American families: not just at the margins. In: Williams-León and Nakashima, C. L. (eds.).

Rosa, J. C. (2001) "The coming of the neo-Hawaiian American race": nationalism and metaphors of the melting pot in popular accounts of mixed-race individuals. In: Williams-León, T. and Nakashima, C. L. (eds.), pp. 49–56.

See, L. (1995) *On Gold Mountain.* St. Martin's Press, New York.

Spickard, P. R. (1986) Injustice compounded: Amerasians and non-Japanese in America's concentration camps. *Journal of American Ethnic History* 5 (Spring): 5–22.

Spickard, P. R. (2001) Who is an Asian? Who is a Pacific Islander? Monoracialism, multiracial people, and Asian American communities. In: Williams-León, T. and Nakashima, C. L. (eds.), pp. 13–24.

Takagi, D. (1996) Maiden voyage: excursion into sexuality and identity politics in Asian America. In: Leong, R. (ed.) *Asian American Sexualities: Dimensions of the Gay and Lesbian Experience.* Routledge, New York, pp. 21–35.

Takaki, R. T. (1989) *Strangers from a Different Shore: A History of Asian Americans.* Little, Brown and Company, Boston.

Tanaka, R. (1980) Appendix to Executive Order. In: *Ayumi: A Japanese American Anthology.* Japanese American Anthology Committee, San Francisco, p. 240.

Thornton, M. C. (1992) The quiet immigration: foreign spouses of U.S. citizens, 1945–1985. In: Root, M. P. P. (ed.) *Racially Mixed People in America.* Sage Publications, Thousand Oaks, CA, pp. 64–76.

Valverde, K. L. C. (2001) Doing the mixed-race dance: negotiating social spaces within the multiracial Vietnamese American class typology. In: Williams-León, T. and Nakashima, C. L. (eds.), pp. 131–43.

Williams, T. K., Nakashima, C., Kitahara-Kich, G. and Daniel, G. R. (1996) Being different together in the university classroom: multiracial identity as transgressive education. In: Root, M. P. P. (ed.) *The Multiracial Experience: Racial Borders as the New Frontier.* Sage Publications, Thousand Oaks, CA, pp. 359–79.

Williams-León, T. and Nakashima, C. L. (eds.) (2001) *The Sum of Our Parts: Mixed Heritage Asian Americans.* Temple University Press, Philadelphia.

PART 3

Disciplines and Methodologies

CHAPTER SEVEN

Asian American Studies and the "Pacific Question"

J. Kehaulani Kauanui

In the Spring of 2002, I was asked to contribute an essay on Native Hawaiians to an anthology on "Asian America at dawn of 21st century." The editor explained that he was producing a book anthology called "Asian American Nation: Demographic and Cultural Change 2000 and Beyond." In the email invitation and the one-page book proposal he described it as a "public policy oriented book that examines change in the community from a demographic (i.e. Census 2000 stats) and cultural standpoint, focusing on the 1990s, and the upcoming decade." Regarding the Pacific component, he noted that he planned to include one chapter on Pacific Islanders, along with a separate chapter on Native Hawaiians that he aimed to solicit from me. The request struck me as unusual on a number of registers, not least of which was that Hawaiians would be considered separately from other Pacific Islanders.

I suggested that if his book was to include another panethnic group along with Asian Americans, such as Pacific Islanders, then it would make more sense to have Asian Americans *and* Pacific Islanders in the title rather than just "Asian American." I also asked what his intellectual rationale was for including both Pacific Islanders and Asian Americans in one book. It was not clear from his message why he would want to include work on Hawaiians and other Pacific Islanders in an anthology about Asian Americans. Indeed, I asked if he would also be including other ethnic groups who are not Asian American, such as American Indians, Latinos, and/or African Americans? And if not, why not? I also asked what he thought Hawaiians and other Pacific Islanders might have to do with his conception of "Asian American Nation." In his reply, he indicated that he had decided to change the title "to make it more inclusive" by using "Asian Pacific American" and that he would also remove the word "Nation."

None of this comforted me. Still, I thanked the editor for his reply and update on his use of the term "Asian Pacific American" but explained that I do not understand that term, or the use of it, at all and do not see it as inclusive in any positive sense. In the conflated terms "Asian Pacific American" or "Asian Pacific Islander," there is no recognition that Pacific Islanders *already* constitute a panethnic group, one requiring a very different research and policy agenda. "Asian Americans" and "Pacific Islanders" are two different panethnic groups, each with their own history, development, and problems. To merge them together has not been to the advantage of Pacific Islanders. Also, the editor's move toward Pacific "inclusion" appeared to be an afterthought, given that the original title was "Asian American Nation." The early title alone marks the deep differences one would have to account for if one was to include Pacific Islanders. For one, I cannot seriously imagine a book called "Pacific Islander nation" because most Pacific Islander histories and issues of colonialism, land, sovereignty, and political decolonization are too deep, real, and too dire to consider using the word "nation" even as a metaphor or as an umbrella covering any pan-Pacific formation. Also, given his reply, I still have no sense of the meaning and conception behind his employment of the term "Asian Pacific American" for a book that will focus on demographic and cultural change in 2000 and beyond, especially since the collection will draw heavily on Census 2000 data. Hadn't he heard about the new census categories that separated Native Hawaiians and other Pacific Islanders?

I think that any editor committed to *meaningful* Pacific inclusion would first need to adjust the book title accordingly, to read "Asian Americans *and* Pacific Islanders: Demographic and Cultural Change 2000 and Beyond." Moreover, a responsible editor would strive for *equal representation* between Asian Americans and Pacific Islanders, not just one chapter on Hawaiians and another on other Pacific Islanders. With the US context in mind, conscientious inclusion would mean including a chapter each on Hawaiians, Samoans, Chamorros (perhaps two different chapters here; one for those in or from the Commonwealth of the Northern Marianas Islands and another for those in or from Guam), Marshallese, Belauans, Tongans, and more. Regardless, the book has since been released under the title *The New Face of Asian Pacific America* (2003).[1]

These days, it is too common to find the term "Pacific" included within a range of Asian American studies scholarship. And, as a result, the terms "Asian American," "Asian Pacific Islander," "Asian/Pacific American," and "Asian Pacific American" are used irresponsibly and interchangeably, even though each arguably has a very different definition. There are also newer mutations of the terms that have resulted in comparable use of terms such as "Asian Pacifics" and "Asian Pacific Islander American." These terms are used interchangeably with little regard for the epistemological implications for the main topics addressed in the works in which they appear.[2] Moreover, most scholars that use "API" and "APA" do so when they are discussing Asian Americans (and *not* Pacific Islanders). Or, worse, the authors only use the term "Asian American" while proceeding to presume Pacific Islander inclusion within this category.

This essay attempts to map the current terrain of Asian American studies in relation to "the Pacific question." It is my attempt to disentangle Pacific Islanders from inaccurate Asian American nomenclature and to disarticulate, disaggregate, and disentangle Pacific Islander studies and Asian American studies. I explore the common misunderstanding that Pacific Islanders' challenges to inclusion within pan-Asian American rubrics are merely calls for recognizing the diversity of experience *among* Asian Americans, or that these challenges are somehow analogous to those made by scholars who are critical of the conditions and status of Filipinos and South Asians within the category of "Asian American." If we take the construction of pan-Asian ethnicity seriously, we should understand the Pacific Islander difference as *a different kind of difference.* What gets confused is that Pacific challenges to the usage of "APA" and "API" are not usually signs of investment in the category of "Asian American." My challenge to the usage of "APA" and "API," and the inclusion of the Pacific and Pacific Islanders within the category of Asian American, is not a critique of the category of "Asian American" so much as it is an investment in the concept and categories of Pacific and Pacific Islander.

I also examine the assumption that a call for critical use of the terms is a call for "inclusion." Rather, those who oppose the conflation have asked scholars not to engulf Pacific Islanders with their superficial use of the "P." But in response, one hears a dominant insistence that to reckon with the conflation would be to "exclude" Pacific Islanders – an omission that gets figured as problematic. Pacific Islanders have only been "excluded" from the subject of Asian America in much the same sense as American Indians have been. I think this comparison probably seems clearer to people. In other words, one does not see terminology like "Asian Native Americans" abound and have to wonder why Native Americans are part of that configuration. In any case, for the most part, Pacific Islanders have fought to be excluded from the Asian American category.

Moreover, there is the problem with the terms "APA" (and "API") as a gloss for Asian American *and* Pacific Americans (or Asian Americans *and* Pacific Islanders) when the acronym does not mark the *and* (as in, in addition to) and so works to have Asian *describe* Pacific. There is also a recent debate as to whether or not Pacific Islanders, as a subject of study, should become the responsibility of the Association for Asian American Studies (AAAS), as is currently being proposed in a forthcoming ballot measure, to be voted on by the entire membership.[3] Undeniably, these two are related; if the AAAS takes up the name change, it seems much less feasible to overhaul people's thinking and use of the terms "APA" and "API." Also, under the mantle of the AAAS, I think Pacific Islanders and Pacific Islander studies will both be made more invisible than ever. This entire situation is further complicated by the fact that Asian Americans and Asian Americanists seem unfamiliar with the fields of Pacific studies and Pacific Islander studies. Thus, I urge scholars to engage areas of inquiry concerning Pacific Islanders on a *comparative basis* in relation to Asian Americans, just as they might do with African American studies, Latino studies, and Native American studies.

My critique emerges from my history of fighting against the rubrics of "APA" and "API" since 1989, and from my own interventions within the context of the AAAS.[4] Besides identifying as a Pacific Islander studies scholar with ties to American studies and Anthropology (my institutional affiliations), with current work in Native studies, I also identify as a budding Asian Americanist. This interest in Asian American studies developed through my research on Hawaiian racialization during the US territorial period (1900–59) and how it differed from the ways in which Asian peoples in Hawai'i were racialized at that time.[5] To further situate myself, I should make it clear that I identify as a Pacific Islander – and, more specifically, as a mixed-blood diasporic Native Hawaiian. To me, the terms "Asian Pacific American" or "Asian Pacific Islander" seem best suited to refer to people of *mixed* Pacific Islander *and* Asian ancestry – such as a person who is Chinese and Hawaiian, and/or Chamorro and Japanese, and/or Sri Lankan and Samoan, for example. These days, I have taken to identifying myself as a *non*-Asian Pacific Islander because of the ways in which the term "Asian Pacific Islander" leaves "Asian" as the modifier describing Pacific Islander. I also do so because "Pacific Islander," even alone, is now sometimes understood as "Asian Pacific Islander," with "Asian" as the invisible or parenthetical *pre-fix*.

Who are Pacific Islanders?

It can be argued that there is a gross lack of baseline knowledge about Pacific Islanders in the United States among most Americans, not just Asian Americanists. Here, I use the term "Pacific Islander," which is inclusive of all Pacific peoples and utilized within contemporary US contexts. Peoples who constitute the panethnic Pacific Islander group are better known as Polynesians, Micronesians, Melanesians. There are problems with these terms – and their origins as categories of difference. Moreover, historically, each one is an anthropological category of racial classification. I raise them here to mark the historical distinction among these groupings and those known as Asian. And, just as Asian peoples use distinction to mark whether they are East Asian, South Asian, or Southeast Asian, so Pacific Islanders employ comparable terms such as Western Pacific, Eastern Polynesian, Western Polynesian, South Pacific, and North Pacific. The term Oceania has recently gained more currency as a way to highlight the connectivity between and among Islander groups. In other words, I am talking about those from the Pacific Basin, rather than the Pacific Rim!

Pacific Islanders are perhaps one of the most invisible panethnic groups in the United States. Prior to the 1980 Census, all Pacific Islanders, except Native Hawaiians, were completely hidden in national demographics, despite the fact that some Pacific Islanders' presence in America can be traced back to the late eighteenth century. In national demographics, Pacific Islanders have been sub-sumed into census categories such as "White, Black, and other" or "Asian-Pacific Islander." Indeed, "the term 'Asian Pacific American' emerged as a governmental term used by social agencies for their administrative convenience" (Espiritu 1992: xi). As Sucheng Chan noted two decades ago: "The differences between Asian Americans and Pacific Islanders are much greater than the similarities between them... The greatest vested interest in keeping the two groups aggre-gated are government officials and bureaucrats in funding agencies, for treating the two umbrella groups as one simplifies the work which such people have to do" (42–4). And despite recent changes in federal policy, the category "Asian Pacific Islander" persists. This is also even more complicated for Native Hawaiians who have historically, though inconsistently, been included in federal legislation on Native Americans. For example, they are included in more than 120 congressional acts dating back to 1903.

The federal Office of Management and Budget sets the race and ethnicity standards for all federal activities. In 1997, the office revised its twenty-year-old race and ethnicity standards to include Native Hawaiians as one of five categories for data collection used for federal civil rights compliance, statistical reporting, and general program and grant administration. This change also meant that Hawaiians, among other Pacific Islanders, were removed from the Asian/Pacific Islander category and given a separate category of "Native Hawaiian or Other Pacific Islander" in the 2000 US Census. The five race categories in the census are now: American Indian/Alaskan Native, Asian, White, Black/African American, and Native Hawaiians or Pacific Islanders.

It was Senator Daniel Akaka (D-HI) who organized opposition to a federal task force recommendation in July of 1997 that Native Hawaiians remain in the Asian and Pacific Islander category. In striving for the change, a working group comprised of Native Hawaiians from public and private agencies presented compelling arguments that the standards must reflect data accurately describing Native Hawaiians' social and economic situation, which has been overwhelmed by data collected for the much-larger Asian American category, where Native Hawaiian representation comprised just 3 percent. Among other goals set by Senator Akaka, the change in the revised guidelines should hopefully also heighten the federal government's sensitivity to and consideration of the political status and rights of Native Hawaiians. The same could be argued in the case of Chamorros and Samoans, at least those with ties to American Samoa. These ongoing political questions are so salient that they also complicate any easy organizing around the term "Pacific Islander American."

The new category, reflected in the 2000 Census, was supposed to be in effect as of 1997, for all new and revised record keeping or reporting requirements that include racial and/or ethnic information. Yet, very few federal agencies have modified their data collection records. This neglect poses a problem for Pacific Islanders in that our socio-economic profiles are extremely difficult to ascertain, especially since within the "Asian Pacific Islander" category, Pacific Islander data are not disaggregated from Asian American data. Still, there are some basic social profiles that should be mentioned here.

Pacific Islanders in the United States are composed of indigenous, migrant, and immigrant peoples. Those indigenous Pacific peoples under US jurisdiction include Native Hawaiians, Chamorros from Guam and the Commonwealth of the Northern Mariana Islands, and American Samoans. Issues facing these peoples are most similar to those facing American Indians and Alaska Natives. And in many cases, their migrations off-island need to be understood in the context of neocolonialism. Regarding the US Pacific Territories, Guam and American Samoa are both non-self-governing territories under Article 73 of the United Nations Charter, while the Commonwealth of the Northern Mariana Islands is said to have determined its own political status, even in light of being subject to US plenary power. Those Pacific Islanders who can be considered migrants are from the former US Trust Territories of the Pacific, now known as the Freely Associated States. These nations include the Republic of the Marshall Islands, the Federated States of Micronesia, and the Republic of Belau – recently decolonized nation-states that are geographically part of Micronesia and were formerly administered by the United States as part of the Trust Territory of the Pacific Islands, established under the United Nations Trusteeship System after World War II. Under the Compact Agreements between the United States and these Freely Associated States, citizens of those island-nations are allowed to enter the United States freely to work or to pursue education. Aside from indigenous and migrant Pacific Islanders in the United States, there are also Pacific Islander immigrants who come from other parts of the Pacific Basin – those that have no historical or political relationship to the United States, such as Tonga, Fiji, Rapa Nui, and Papua New Guinea. The 1990 census data showed that the population of immigrant Pacific Islanders was less than 15 percent of the total Pacific Island population for the US continent and Hawai'i, while data from Census 2000 have yet to be disaggregated to this degree.

According to the 2000 Census, the largest ethnic subgroups were: Native Hawaiian (401,162 respondents); Other Pacific Islander (174,912);[6] Samoan (133,281); Guamanian or Chamorro (92,611); Tongan (36,840); and Fijian (13,581).[7] Within the US nation-state, Pacific Islanders are widely dispersed – residing in all fifty states as well as the District of Columbia, and all of the US Territories. The vast majority of Native Hawaiian and Other Pacific Islanders live in the West,[8] and over half (58%) of all respondents reside in Hawai'i or California. The next highest states include Washington, Texas, New York, Florida, and Utah.

Just as in the case of other panethnic groups, the category of "Pacific Islanders" includes people of various genealogical ranks, socioeconomic backgrounds, religions, languages, histories, colors, and ethnic origins. In turn, we have our own internal issues regarding perceived and real dominance within the Pacific Islander category and among Pacific Islanders from different regions.

Panethnicity, Postmodernity, and False Analogies

In her formative work *Asian American Panethnicity*, Yen Le Espiritu uses the term "pan-ethnic group" to refer to "a politico-cultural collectivity made up of peoples of several hitherto distinct, tribal, or national origins" (2). She poses the guiding question for her book: "How, under what circumstances, and to what extent can groups of diverse national origins come together as a new, enlarged panethnic group?" Here, I am asking that we also examine the implications of this question for the conflation of two panethnic groups – Pacific Islander and Asian American – into one. What, then, is the common identity? Who is doing the submerging? Who, exactly, is assuming a common identity? And what is the basis of this alleged affinity? Even this issue of "commonality" is debated. Samoans (at least on the West Coast), for example, might find much more in common with African Americans, Hawaiians with American Indians, and Chamorros with Chicanos (e.g. Robert Underwood, former Congressman from Guam, who is Chamorro was part of the "Hispanic" Congressional Caucus as well as the "Asian Pacific" Congressional Caucus). Of course, this is dependent on any given issue at hand: education, access to housing, police brutality, land occupations, colonial displacement, and other pressing concerns.

It should also be noted that "Pacific Islander and Hawaiians" are included as "sub-components" of Asian American studies, as stated in the AAAS's statement of purpose. Why are Chinese, Japanese, Korean, and Filipino ethnicities named while the categories "Southeast Asian" and "South Asian" are left disaggregated? This is comparable to having a statement list: Hmong, Vietnamese, Cambodians, Laotians, Indians, Pakistanis, Bangladeshis, Sri Lankans, and East Asian Americans. Also, problematically, Hawaiians are included as a sub-component of Asian America named separately from the category Pacific Islanders. Moreover, the category of Pacific Islanders is hanging in this line-up, as though it is an ethnic group, rather than a disaggregated panethnic group. This amounts to de-racination and de-racialization. Since when is Pacific Islander epiphenomenal of Asian American? Just as Michael Omi and Howard Winant have argued that race as a social construct is not epiphenomenal of ethnicity, meaning that race deserves to be addressed as an analytical category of its own, so too does the category of Pacific Islander deserve its own place – *alongside* Asian Americans, African Americans, Native Americans, and Chicana/os and Latina/os, not stemming from any one of them.

Espiritu's key theoretical question "concerns the construction of larger-scale affiliations, where groups previously unrelated in culture and descent submerge their differences and assume a common identity" (3). She argues, "the term Asian American arose out of the racist discourse that constructs Asians as a homogenous group" (Espiritu 1992: 6). Now, Pacific Islanders were not included in that formation for a reason. Besides the obvious geographical distinctions,[9] I would like to suggest that it might also be because dominant American culture does not include Pacific Islanders in its orientalist exclusions. Pacific Islanders have arguably never been racialized as "Asiatic," "oriental," or "Mongolian" – nor subjected to the forms of racism brought about by that legacy. While Pacific peoples' racialization certainly has distinct long histories tied to historical and colonial experiences, one generalization can be made here: Pacific Islanders have had to contend more with persistent primitivist discourses describing us, not orientalist ones. At the very least, the distinctions between primitivism and orientalism seem tied to dominant Western perceptions of the differences between, for example, oral cultures versus literate societies and paganism versus mysticism.

A cursory comparative examination of issues of sexuality underscores my point here, as Lisa Kahaleole Hall and I have previously noted:

> Western concepts of Pacific sexuality have consistently been distorted, misrepresented, and degraded the experiences they attempted to describe. The forms this has taken are quite different from the ideologies of "emasculation" and "sexuality" imposed on Asian men and the exoticization of Asian women. Promiscuity and savagery (whether noble or bestial) were the earliest and most enduring labels applied to Pacific peoples. (Hall and Kauanui 1996: 115)

Or, as Judy Han and I have asserted elsewhere:

> It is uncommon for Samoan and Hawaiian women, for example, to be stereotyped as mysterious, meek or demure, as East Asian and Southeast Asian women often are. The eroticized images of Native Pacific Islanders are not geishas, not possessing East Asian women's perceived coyness. They are imagined to be simpler, without elaborate schemes to please men, or so goes the white male fantasy. Their appeal is in their carefree and easy going "primitiveness." (Han and Kauanui 1993: 378)

Moreover, the stereotypical passivity of Pacific Islanders is usually linked to supposed laziness and stupidity rather than to submissiveness.

Pacific Islanders challenge the superficial inclusion of the Pacific based on assertions of racial, social, political, legal, and historical differences. These are not calls for recognition of diversity of experience *among* Asian Americans. In other words, the critique is not some exercise in deconstructing the term Asian American. That it would be misunderstood as such is somewhat understandable given the recent postmodern challenges to the "subject" of Asian American studies by a variety of scholars. Yet, the Pacific challenge is quite different than these critiques.

Lane Ryo Hirabayashi and Marilyn Caballero Alquizola have written about these recent confrontations in their essay "Whither the Asian American Subject?" in which they identified a range of challenges. One example they offer is that some scholars ask if there is really any such thing as an "Asian American" subject *per se*. In other words, they ask what makes this a distinctive and viable category (169). In this logic, there is the corollary question: why are some groups included in the designation "while other groups whose experiences seem to pertain to this generic category are left out?" (169). Another example is when "scholars claim that the generalized amalgamation of the term Asian American results in essentialism and the elision of intergroup differences" such as ethnicity, class, gender, and sexuality.[10] To be clear, this is not the nature of my own critique. As Pacific Islanders comprise an entirely separate panethnic group, we also risk homogenizing our own intergroup differences along ethnic, class, gender and sexuality lines.

I think panethnicity among Pacific Islanders in the United States is nascent for several reasons. For one, our population counts are extremely low in relation to all other racial-ethnic groups. Besides, there are those on-island that are treated within American policy and dominant discourse as distinct from those who are off-island – on the continental United States. Also, the continued political struggles over the islands reckoning with a history of US neocolonialism make for pressing sovereignty claims related to nationhood status (e.g. the fight for Commonwealth status in Guam; the split among Hawaiians who are pro-federal recognition versus pro-independence) create a strong ambivalence (to say the least) toward panethnic developments. Even among those off-island, I would like to suggest here that there is a tension between those who identify with panethnic formations and those who identify more strongly as diasporic in that they identify more strongly with their respective homelands and those attendant political struggles or even community and social formations tied to their respective peoples. And here there are similarities between that sort of split and those one might find among American Indians who identify more strongly with pro-Indian or Native American politics (especially, perhaps, if they are urban Indians) than with tribal-specific politics.

A related impediment is the supposition that Pacific challenges are somehow analogous to those made by scholars who are critical of the conditions and status of Filipinos and South Asians within the category of "Asian American." Pacific Islanders face confusion from Asian American studies scholars when we ask for the "P" to be left alone; they often mishear what is being stated and assume that the Pacific challenge is akin to those advanced by Filipino and South Asian Americans (who rightly question how inclusive the Asian American category really is, pointing to the dominance of East Asian Americans within the panethnic development that tends to marginalize Filipino and South Asian Americans). Filipinos are included in "Asian American," which may or may not work to their advantage. That would seem to be an issue of categorization and status that is questionable between and among Filipinos and Asian Americans. Filipinos and South Asian critiques are important as they speak to the limits of Asian American panethnicity.

Joanne L. Rondilla has addressed what she calls "the Filipino Question in Asia and the Pacific" (2002: 56). She suggests ways of thinking about a map of the Western Pacific that would include the Philippines in a more meaningful way – as part of the Pacific Islands and as part of Asia (58). She notes that Filipinos are part of a coalition within Asian America with which they cannot affiliate wholeheartedly because their issues are often ignored and they are constantly questioning and being questioned as to whether they belong in Asian America. She asks, "Are Filipinos Asian Americans or... Pacific Islanders, and what are the implications of either formula?" Rondilla notes that not only are Filipinos counted as Asian Americans in the United States, but in fact some were "important actors in creating the idea of an Asian American panethnicity and elaborating pan-Asian American institutions" (58). During the late 1960s initiatives to create a panethnic identity in the face of being othered and orientalized, Chinese, Japanese, and Filipinos worked together to illustrate unity and recognition as Asian Americans. Pacific Islanders arguably played little or no part in this creation of an Asian American panethnic identity, even though they might very well have worked in coalition with Asian Americans on issues that may have brought them together.[11]

As Rondilla points out, the Asian American movement "was bound by the idea of yellow power" (59) that worked both as a binding force and a dividing line. She notes that Filipinos immediately rejected this idea because they felt it excluded them; they considered themselves to be brown, not yellow (59). Drawing from Ignacio's early work, Rondilla points out that during a 1972 First National Conference on Asian American Mental Health, held in San Francisco, there was a "brown Asian caucus formed to represent Filipinos, Guamanians, Hawaiians, and Samoans." Even so, each of the four groups made separate presentations. Ignacio states that this moment led to a "new ethnic thrust" in the conference which led to "the Asian American *and* Pacific Islander movements taking a major turn in its course" where the "Brown Asian *and* Pacific Islander dimension became prominent" (Ignacio 141; emphasis mine). Still, "Filipinos took part in the Asian American coalition, but as junior partners" (Rondilla 59). Here, in this Filipino "brown Asian" criticism the prominent themes are exclusion, tokenization, and marginalization. The situation of Filipinos in relation to the category of Asian American seems most analogous to the position of South Asian in relation to Asian American projects.

Examining Indian Americans, South Asian Americans and the Politics of Asian American Studies, Shilpa Davé, Pawan Dhingra, Sunaina Maira, Partha Mazumdar, Lavina Shankar, Jaideep Singh, and Rajini Srikanth have collectively offered a groundbreaking article, "De-Privileging Positions."[12] One of the many things they do is historicize the relationship of South Asian Americans to Asian

America, as well as to its official vehicle in the academy, the AAAS. They discuss the dichotomy between South and East Asian immigrants residing in the United States and argue, "This fissure stems, in part, from the physical dissimilarity between them...[and] mirrors the manner in which physical appearance distinguishes Pilipino Americans from other Asian Americans" (71–2). Elsewhere in their account, the authors also discuss other reasons for the gap, including religious differences between South Asians and other Asians that contribute to the cultural and linguistic barriers between them. Still, the emphasis in this part of their work is on marginalization and tokenization within pan-Asian coalitions. In this respect, then, the "South Asian question" seems analogous to the "Filipino question."

Perhaps, then, people hear "the Pacific question," when posed by Pacific Islanders, as a complaint about being treated as junior partners, of marginalization or holding second-class status within the coalition. This is especially telling because it seems that many Asian Americans and Asian Americanist scholars perceive Pacific Islanders as unassimilable within the rubric of "API" (e.g. "We keep inviting them, but they don't attend"). Yet, instead of dismantling the rubric, the prevailing discourse still problematically features underrepresentation, inclusion, and representation as key issues. Hence, people probably hear "the Pacific question" as a push to make the distinction between "yellow" and "brown" Asians. But I do not think that this is what is actually at stake in the Pacific Islander case. I argue that the Pacific critique is not a "brown Asian" critique – it is *a non-Asian critique*.[13] Since we are dealing with the problem of forced inclusion, Hawaiians and other Pacific Islanders generally *do not* advance critique of the Asian American category on a par with Filipinos or South Asian Americans (or Southeast Asians, for that matter).[14]

Productive Engagement, not Inclusion

There is currently a proposal to change the name of the AAAS, a change that would help to determine whether or not Pacific Islanders, as a subject of study, should be taken on by the Association. This came about at the AAAS general business meeting at the annual conference in Salt Lake City, UT, on April 26, 2002. The proposed ballot which was to be distributed in early 2004, but was not sent out due to the resolution proposal being tabled indefinitely, was to ask for a question will ask for a "yes" or "no" vote regarding the following "The Association for Asian American Studies (AAAS) shall change its name to the Association for Asian/Pacific Islander American Studies (AAPIAS)." The AAAS newsletter explained the terms of the proposal: "The back slash separates yet brings together Asian and Pacific Islander to modify American, thus distinguishing our field of study from Asian Studies or Pacific Island Studies. 'Pacific Islander' rather than 'Pacific' designates the indigenous island populations in distinction from non-indigenous people residing in the Pacific and refers to the interior of the Pacific Islands rather than the 'Pacific Rim'." Still, if the AAAS takes up the name change, it seems much less feasible to overhaul people's thinking and use of the terms "APA" and "API," which would mean that it is likely that "Asian" would still work as a modifier for "Pacific."

Oddly enough, some advocates of the Pacific inclusion make the case on the grounds of coalition politics. If coalition is the model, then what is the issue featured by that coalition? And how is it that linking two areas of study or two panethnic groups for study constitutes a coalition politic? In terms of political commitments and practices, I think any work between Asian Americans and Pacific Islanders must be based on alliances or coalitions, depending on the circumstances of any given situation, crisis, campaign, etc. I see no more ties of obligations between Asian Americans and Pacific Islanders (as groups) than I do between African Americans and Pacific Islanders, or Latinos and Pacific Islanders. I think the connections between any of these communities need to be forged, as appropriate, *issue-by-issue* in each historical moment.

Some members, including a couple of Pacific Islanders (specifically Native Hawaiian), have made the case that they support the name change as a recognition of those who are Pacific Islander scholars who do participate in the Association and that their work within, contributions to, and membership in the organization deserves to be acknowledged. But they seem to conflate their own cultural/racial/ethnic/national subject position with the scholarship and people of study (e.g. saying they want to include Pacific Islanders already based within the Association – presumably themselves – rather than making an intellectual argument about including Pacific Islander Studies *as a field*).

Should the professional assembly of the AAAS in particular be determined by the racial/ethnic-national identity/affiliation of its members rather than by their subjects of study? Asian American studies in general and the AAAS are not solely made up of Asian Americans producing scholarly work. Would the presence of African American scholars who research and write on Asian Americans within the AAAS mean that it would make sense to change the Association's name to include African Americans? I do not think so. And still, refusing that sort of name change need not preclude the development of more intellectual spaces within the Association in order to examine the histories of both African Americans and Asian Americans in a *comparative* way. Likewise, there may be fruitful intellectual linkages between Pacific Islander studies and Asian American studies (just as there may be between African American studies and Asian American studies). But that does not mean that the professional assembly of scholars within the AAAS needs to make Pacific Islander studies its responsibility. Moreover, these linkages have yet to be fully explored – and even the calls for them have been misunderstood.

For example, in preparation for the 1999 annual AAAS meeting in Philadelphia, I called for a caucus meeting for scholars to discuss the research topics related to this problematic by sending a message to the AAAS list prior to the conference date. In it, I stated: "I am interested in meeting with scholars keen to examine the relationship of Pacific Studies to Asian American Studies. Related to this proposal is [the] challenge of reckoning with (Pacific Islander and American Indian) Native contexts in which people might be writing about Asian American communities, issues and histories (e.g. Guam, Hawai'i, [and] Native North America)." Unfortunately, my suggestion was misunderstood as a call for a Pacific Islander caucus meeting! And here I had thought that the scholars within the AAAS in particular might get together to explore the region of the Pacific Islands as site of Asian immigration into the United States and Asian labor and US neocolonialism and to discuss, for example, the contentious issues and charges of Asian "settler" complicity in Pacific contexts and the labor conditions of Asian peoples in the Insular territories being exploited in the name of indigenous sovereignty. Exploring the Pacific, as a region, is necessary for developing an understanding of US imperialism and the incorporation of Asian peoples from Pacific territories, for example. And I think it is crucial that these topics be taken on for the life of the field of Asian American studies and understanding Asian American lives – not for the "inclusion" of Pacific Islanders. And this can *already* be undertaken given that the AAAS has an institutionalized board position allotted to Hawai'i and the Pacific.

At that same meeting, I chaired a session organized by Lisa Kahaleole Hall called "Where's the 'P' in 'API'?" Hall also presented a paper entitled "Which of These Things Is Not Like the Other? Pacific Islanders in Asian American Organizing and Activism." The other papers that made up this panel included "Politics of Inclusion, Tangible Strategies for Community Organizing" by Ju Hui Judy Han (who in the end was unable to attend), and Ami Mattison who presented a piece called "Asian/Pacific Specific: A Social Geography for Asian/Pacific Islander Coalitions." There, we called for the discontinued use of the "P" within Asian American projects unless the terms actually include Pacific Islanders in a comparative way or in an analysis of genuine coalitions between two different groups. And especially, then, the use of the wording is critical – as in "Asian Americans *and* Pacific Islanders" or "Pacific Islanders *and* Asian Americans," just as one would use it when looking at Asian Americans *and* Latinos or Pacific Islanders *and* Native Americans – not "APA" or "API."

Having a few Pacific Islanders within the AAAS make the case for inclusion masks the resistant absence of Pacific Islanders who are not in the organization. Moreover, in this case, the few who fight for this "inclusion" misrepresent Pacific Islander (studies) interests while they simultaneously position themselves as representatives for the larger population of Pacific Islanders or, indeed, Pacific peoples engaged in Pacific Islander studies.

Regardless of how well intentioned the proposal before the AAAS may be, if it passes, Pacific Islander studies would ultimately be subsumed under the mantle of Asian American studies, and made more invisible than ever. This is especially troubling at a time when Pacific Islanders studies is *already* emerging separately. And it is doing so building off existing and supportive Pacific presences such as the Center for Pacific Island Studies and the University of Hawai'i at Manoa, the Pacific History Association, the Association for Social Anthropology in Oceania, and thriving journals such as *The Contemporary Pacific, Pacific Studies, The Journal of Pacific History, The Journal of the Polynesian Society,* and *The Hawaiian Journal of History.*

One key development that has had an important and positive impact on the increased presence of Pacific Islander studies scholars doing work outside of area studies within US academic institutions has been the series of Pacific Studies Institutes funded by the National Endowment for the Humanities. Both the East–West Center and the University of Hawai'i Center for Pacific Islands Studies have hosted these summer programs in the last 12 years. The Institute is directed by Geoffrey White, Senior Fellow at the East–West Center and Professor of Anthropology at the University of Hawai'i. Institute faculty include Vicente Diaz (University of Michigan), Epeli Hau'ofa (University of the South Pacific), Margaret Jolly (Australian National University), J. Kehaulani Kauanui (Wesleyan University), Teresia Teaiwa (Victoria University), Albert Wendt (University of Auckland) as well as University of Hawai'i faculty. The Institute is concerned broadly with the representation of indigenous cultures and identities, particularly in relation to colonial and postcolonial histories up to the present. It is offered for scholars who may be unfamiliar with the Pacific Islands region as well as for those who already teach or conduct research in the area, including those in fields such as anthropology, art, history, literature, politics, religion, women's studies, and ethnic studies. The Institute is designed to enhance individual scholarship and broaden undergraduate teaching, and it supports up to 25 scholars for each session.

There is also the Pacific Studies Initiative (PSI) which is a joint endeavor of the East–West Center and the University of Hawai'i. The PSI sponsors a searchable website and database that make available Pacific Islands course syllabi and bibliographies.

There are also other developments on the continental United States. The University of Oregon's Center for Asian *and* Pacific Studies (my emphasis) has had a separate program in Pacific Island studies, one that is currently being revitalized. At the University of Washington, faculty on the Department of Anthropology have initiated the develop of a Pacific Islander Studies program in response to student activism among Pacific Islanders on campus whose intellectual interests are not being met by the "Asian Pacific" track in American Ethnic studies there. There is also a relatively new Pasifika-list serve, hosted by a cohort of Pacific Literature at Cornell University, which grew out of a conference at New York University, "Pacific Islands, Atlantic Worlds." That conference was sponsored by the Asian/Pacific/American Studies program which heeded challenges to the "Pacific" inclusion in its program name seriously (note that the conference itself was titled "Pacific Islands," not "Asian Pacific Islands") by exploring what good might come from a comparative focus on the Pacific.

These developments are also important given that efforts have been made to plot the intellectual and theoretical differences and investments in and between Pacific studies (as area studies) and the nascent field of Pacific Islander studies in the United States (see Diaz and Kauanui 2001). Certainly, scholars within Asian American studies should be able to relate to this move given the impetus to works that explore the connections and distinctions between Asian studies and Asian American studies (Hune 2001; Yanagisako 1995, 2002; and Palumbo-Liu 2002).

Pacific Islander studies developments are already taking place in relation to other ethnic studies fields besides Asian American studies. Indeed, meaningful attendance to the Pacific Islander absence needs to entail a new examination of existing frameworks within the field of ethnic studies. As Lisa Kahaleole Hall has theorized, there are several factors in the historical development of ethnic studies as a field that have helped to reinforce the invisibility of Pacific Islanders.

> One is the focus on paradigms of African American slavery and internal colonization of Native Americans (and sometimes Mexicans) that have been constructed in the absence of simultaneously viewing the US as a classically colonial power. Another key issue is that the important work US academics have been doing on racial formation theory has not extended toward Pacific Islanders, helping maintain a fundamental conflation and confusion of "Asian American" and "Pacific Islander" pan-ethnicities in ways which have been very detrimental to any understanding of Pacific Islander identity. (Hall 2001: 1)

But even as this history needs to be reckoned with, neither Asian Americans nor the field of Asian American studies has a responsibility to Pacific Islanders or Pacific Islander Studies, besides refraining from using our names in vain.

Lane Ryo Hirabayashi and Marilyn Caballero Alquizola's working definition of Asian American studies seems useful here: it "involves research, curriculum development, and teaching, all of which pertain to histories and contemporary concerns of Asian Americans." They also offer a working definition of the subject category of "Asian American" and describe it "a convenient designation that can be used to identify those persons of Asian descent in the United States who are interested in maintaining their diverse ethnic heritages and willing to struggle to shape their boundaries and directions" (177–8). Both of these definitions seem especially useful in developing comparable definitions for Pacific Islander (American) studies (as it involves research, curriculum development, and teaching, all of which pertain to histories and contemporary concerns of Pacific Islanders in the United States) and "Pacific Islander (Americans)" (which, likewise, is a convenient designation that can be used to identify those persons of Pacific descent in the United States).

So, why not call comparative scholarship on Pacific Islanders and Asian Americans "comparative work on Pacific Islanders and Asian Americans"? We need a comparative paradigm to re-frame these issues and topics of study. For future research, it would be useful to compare how different the fields of Asian studies and Pacific studies – as area studies programs – are in order to consider how Asian American studies and Pacific Islander studies might also be understood in relation to each other as two distinct fields of study. The visibility of Pacific Islanders and the future direction and development of Pacific Islander studies on the US continent is at stake here.

Clearly there is a need to build a Pacific Islander Studies Association. Only then could any associative partnership be considered – one that would be of *equal partners* self-determining their future respective development. It would be one thing if the AAAS resolution proposed the joining of two different institutional enterprises. At least then there would be some semblance of equality in moving forward jointly. And in such a case, we would not even be addressing inclusion, since there would be two different associations with their respective membership bodies to determine whether to link-up, on a joint-basis, or not. Then, it would not be a case of Pacific Islanders or Pacific Islander studies being accommodated, or forced, within Asian American studies or the AAAS any more than we might imagine Asian Americans being included within the category of "Pacific Islanders" or relegating Asian American studies projects to Pacific studies or Pacific Islander studies.

Conclusion

In closing, I hope to urge Asian Americanists to reflect upon the future of the field at this critical juncture. This point in time should open up more dialog about the issue of the Pacific within Asian American studies. It seems that we should also be open to further consider the political grounds of the relationship between the two. Such a moment could provide for a better understanding of this contentious situation and work to improve cultural politics for both pan-ethnic groups. Coming to terms with this relationship is more important than ever if we are to respect the terms of self-determination of the "P" and the future of Asian American projects – and whether they will work as decolonizing or colonizing entities. Asian America, and Asian American studies more specifically, has derived some power and legitimacy by not acknowledging the degree to which their own have participated in the further marginalization of Pacific Islanders – and Pacific Islander studies, through their self-promotion as both decision-maker and speaker on behalf of Pacific peoples. Indeed, it is in the disguising of both the move to be the arbitrators and the insistence on being the spokespeople, with little or no actual participation and agreement by Pacific Islanders, that has worked to provide Asian American studies with some of its distinguishing character. On the one hand, appearing to have the consent of the Pacific contingent works to give the image of Asian American studies (and Asian America at large) as being inclusive and multicultural – all while they assert, and to some degree maintain, control of Pacific cultural politics. Now is the opportunity for Asian American studies to consider its political position vis-à-vis Pacific Islanders, and the growing field of Pacific Islander studies; to rethink the field's intellectual practices and scope in such a way as to reject a politics of incorporation, and to recognize, respect, and affirm self-determination among Pacific Islanders and Pacific scholarship.

NOTES

Toward the completion of this article, I must thank those helpful friends and colleagues who have offered me important intellectual and political engagement: Lisa Kahaleole Hall (with whom I have been committed to ongoing discussions and numerous interventions regarding Pacific Islanders in relation to Asian Americans for over a decade), Glen Mimura, Adria Lyn Imada, and Khyla Russell. *Mahalo* also to Judy Ju Hui Han, Sharon Wahineka'iu LumHo, Kale Fajardo, Barbara K. Ige, and Anne Keala Kelly – all of whom have been consistently supportive of my work in this area. A very early draft of this piece was presented at the University of Illinois, Urbana-Champaign for a conference organized by Kent A. Ono, Director of Asian American Studies, called "In the Wake of a Critical Mass: New Directions in Asian American Studies," held on February 7 and 8, 2003. Thanks to all of the participants, most of whom are also contributors to this collection, who gave useful feedback. I also want to thank Henry Yu and Sefa Aina for inviting me to present this work at the Center for Asian American Studies at the University of California, Los Angeles, where they worked to make my academic visit to their campus a special occasion by insuring a Pacific Islander audience that included community members beyond the campus. Thanks also go to colleagues in the Social Science Division at Wesleyan University (where I teach) who attended my talk based on this article and provided productive insights and questions. Last but not least, I want to thank Kent Ono for inviting my contribution and for his generous editorial support and encouragement through the completion of this piece.

1 In the introduction, the authors include a short section "Why the 'P' in APA?" where they state "In the naming of this book, the term Asian Pacific America was chosen in an attempt to be as inclusive as possible while being linguistically economical. We understand the term is not universally embraced. However, we hope whatever the book arguably lacks in accurate semantics it makes up for in its content and sincerity to shedding light on the diverse characteristics, experiences and issues of all Asian American and Pacific Islander communities" (3).
2 I have also seen the terms "APA" and "API" mainly used to refer to Filipinos, or to refer to Asians from Hawai'i.
3 While producing this article, the name change debate emerged. And while this essay does not fully historicize the inclusion of the P for Pacific in the AAAS at this time, the surfacing of this issue allowed me the opportunity to voice concern within the association

as to how precisely the Pacific is a separate field. It seems to me that P within AAAS is just one example, among many, of attempted incorporation, lack of knowledge about the Pacific, and problematic power relations of Asian Americanists who argue for the "inclusion" of Pacific and Pacific Studies. Still, the historicization of the P within AAAS, an exploration of the history of the earlier name of the AAAS (which used to be the "Asian/Pacific American Studies Association"), is certainly needed in another publication site in the future, since it requires more space than I have here.

4 I should mention that I have stopped attending AAAS meetings, even while I have served on the program committee, because I fear being interpolated by those who will read my presence as a sign that I approve of the way the Pacific has been "included" or that I desire more inclusion within the institution, rather than as a sign of my scholarly interest in Asian American Studies. One day I would like to resume attendance at the AAAS meetings because of my interest in Asian American studies. I do not attend the AAAS meeting in search of Pacific offerings. For those, I attend the regular meetings of the Pacific History Association, the Association for Social Anthropology in Oceania, and the annual Center for Pacific Islands Studies conferences held at the University of Hawaiʻi, at Manoa.

5 In my ongoing work on Native Hawaiian blood quantum policy and the construction of indigeneity, I comparatively examine racial formations, with a special focus on legal racial definitions. Specifically, I trace the origins of the 50-percent blood quantum rule that continues to define "native Hawaiian." Addressing how Native Hawaiians were constructed in ways similar to and different from American Indians, my project also explores how those similarities and differences affect our understanding of miscegenation, property, and entitlement in the United States. Like the contradictory racial system defining American Indian and Black classification, the racialization of Native Hawaiians as assimilable and of Asians as perpetually "alien" would become a key component during the congressional debates which led to the passage of the Hawaiian Homes Commission Act of 1921 – the legislation which first defined Hawaiians by blood quantum. There, the presumption of indigenous assimilability was critical to the blood quantum racialization in defining "native Hawaiian." In the congressional debates, Native Hawaiian political status as US citizens was repeatedly evoked in contrast to both white American citizens and Asian "aliens." In the hearings, "Asian blood" among "part-Hawaiians" was used to discount indigeneity (see Kauanui 1999, 2002).

6 The high number of respondents selecting this "none of the above" category suggests the need for further revision of census categories.

7 For purposes of the continental United States and Hawaiʻi, 1990 Census Data show that Native Hawaiians were 58 percent of the Pacific Island population; Samoans (from American Samoa and Samoa) were 17 percent of the population and Chamorros from Guam and the Commonwealth of the Northern Marianas Islands were 13.8 percent of the population. Geographic breakdowns are not yet available for these detailed groups.

8 This includes 76.3 percent of Native Hawaiian and Other Pacific Islander *alone* respondents, and 72.9 percent of Native Hawaiian and Other Pacific Islander *in combination* respondents.

9 To some, these are not so obvious. For example, I have heard from various scholars that they account for the conflation of Asia with the Pacific, and hence "Asian Pacific," because of the geographic proximity – where lumping Oceania and Asia "makes sense."

However, these reasons seem insufficient and need examination, especially when one acknowledges that the majority of island nations are located south of the equator – hence, the "South Pacific." With proximity being a guiding force for organization principles, it would seem that we might find more constructions like "South American Pacific" since it borders more of the Pacific than does Asia. In any case, there is a need to explore the Latin Pacific, given the Spanish colonial history in both the North (e.g. Guam) and South (e.g. Rapa Nui, also known as Easter Island) Pacific. Needless to say, the geographical perspectives depend on one's location and context.

10 For discussion of the other challenges examined by these authors see Hirabayashi and Alquizola (2001: 170–1).

11 It also seems important to note that there were no appreciable numbers of Hawaiians, Chamorros, Tongans, Samoans, or other islanders in the West Coast public high schools and colleges in the 1960s and 1970s.

12 See also *A Part, Yet Apart: South Asians in Asian America* (Shankar and Srikanth 1998), a collection of essays that document the construction process of the term "South Asian" as it parallels the gradual acceptance of the term "Asian American" by peoples primarily of East and Southeast Asian ancestry. Within the context of a complex US racial terrain, there are lively debates about the extent to which South Asian Americans are (or ought to be) included within Asian America.

13 But for an example of treatment of "the Filipino question" as a non-Asian critique, see Helen C. Toribio (this volume), which especially accounts for the colonial history of the Philippines and the United States and the complexities and problems with Asian American inclusion.

14 However, not all might agree. In their essay "Pacific Islander Americans and Asian American Identity," Debbie Hippolite Wright and Paul Spickard (2002) have argued that there is ambivalence in Asian American communities and in Asian American Studies circles about the relationship between Asian Americans and Pacific Islanders Americans. They argue, "Pacific Islanders have never been central participants in the construction and performance of Asian American identity and institutions." Indeed, they claim those Pacific Islanders "have been marginal at best – guests at the Asian American table . . ." (106). Why is the absence of Pacific Islanders as central participants constituted as problematic? It could also be said that Pacific Islanders have never been central participants in the construction and performance of Native American, Chicano, Latino, nor African American identity and institutions.

REFERENCES

Chan, S. (1982) Asian American–Pacific American relations: the Asian American perspective. *Asian American and Pacific Relations, Three Studies.* Association for Asian/Pacific American Studies, Seattle.
Davé, S., Dhingra, P., Maira, S. et al. (2001) De-privileging positions: Indian Americans, South Asian Americans, and the politics of Asian American studies. *Journal of Asian American Studies* 3(1): 67–100.

Diaz, V. M. and Kauanui, J. K. (2001) Native Pacific cultural studies on the edge. In: Diaz, V. M. and Kauanui, J. K. (eds.) Special issue of *The Contemporary Pacific* 13(2): 315–41.

Hall, L. K. (2001) "Here there be dragons": Pacific Islanders and the perils of falling off the Ethnic Studies map. Paper presented at the National Association of Ethnic Studies conference, New Orleans, LA, for a special double-session: "Oceanic Interventions: Pacific Studies research, methodologies, pedagogy, and curricula within multiple cultural, theoretical, and institutional locations."

Hall, L. K. C. and Kauanui, J. K. (1994) Same-sex sexuality in Pacific literature. *Amerasia Journal.*

Hall, L. K. C. and Kauanui, J. K. (1996) Same-sex sexuality in Pacific literature. In Leong, R. (ed.) *Asian American Sexualities.* Routledge, London, pp. 113–88.

Han, J. and Kauanui, J. K. (1993) "Asian Pacific Islander": issues of representation and responsibility. *Moving the Mountains, Asian American Women's Journal.*

Hune, S. (2001) Asian American studies and Asian studies: boundaries and borderlands of ethnic studies and area studies. In: Butler, J. E. (ed.) *Color-Lines to Borderlands: The Matrix of American Ethnic Studies.* University of Washington Press, Seattle and London, pp. 227–39.

Ignacio, Lemuel F. (1976) *Asian Americans and Pacific Islanders (Is There Such an Ethnic Group?).* Pilipino Development Associates Inc., San Jose, CA.

Kauanui, J. K. (2002) The politics of blood and sovereignty in *Rice v. Cayetano. Political and Legal Anthropology Review* 25(1): 100–28.

Kauanui, J. K. (1999) "For Get" Hawaiian entitlement: configurations of land, "blood," and Americanization in the Hawaiian Homes Commission Act of 1920. *Social Text,* 59: 123–44.

Lai, E. and Arguelles, D. (eds.) (2003) *The New Face of Asian Pacific America: Numbers, Diversity & Change in the 21st Century.* Asian Week with UCLA's Asian American Studies Center Press, San Francisco.

Le Espiritu, Y. (1992) *Asian American Panethnicity. Bridging Institutions and Identities.* Temple University Press, Philadelphia, PA.

Omandam, P. (1997) Hawaiians get census category: the next census will list native Hawaiians alone, apart from Asians. *Honolulu Star-Bulletin* (October 29).

Omi, M. and Winant, H. (1994) *Racial Formation in the United States from the 1960s to the 1990s,* 2nd edn. Routledge, New York.

Palumbo-Liu, D. (2002) Modelling [sic] the nation: the Asian/American split. In: Chuh, K. and Shimakawa, K. (eds.) *Orientations: Mapping Studies in the Asian Diaspora.* Duke University Press, Durham and London, pp. 213–27.

Rondilla, J. L. (2002) The Filipino question in Asia and the Pacific: rethinking regional origins in diaspora. In: Spickard, P., Rondilla, J. L. and Wright, D. H. (eds.) *Pacific Diaspora: Island Peoples in the United States and Across the Pacific.* University of Hawaii Press, Honolulu, pp. 56–66.

Shankar, D. D. and Srikanth, R. (eds.) (1998) *A Part, Yet Apart: South Asians in Asian America.* Temple University Press, Philadelphia.

Wright, D. H. and Spickard, P. (2002) Pacific Islander Americans and Asian American identity. In: Vo, L. T. and Bonus, R. (eds.) *Contemporary Asian American Communities.* Temple University Press, Philadelphia, pp. 105–19.

Yanagisako, S. (2002) Asian Exclusion Acts. In: Miyoshi, M. and Harootunian, H. D. (eds.) *Learning Places: The Afterlives of Area Studies*. Duke University Press, Durham and London, pp. 175–89.

Yanagisako, S. (1995) Transforming orientalism: gender, nationality, and class in Asian American Studies. In: Yanagisako, S. and Delaney, C. (eds.) *Naturalizing Power: Essays in Feminist Cultural Analysis*. Routledge, New York and London, pp. 275–98.

CHAPTER EIGHT

Planet Youth: Asian American Youth Cultures, Citizenship, and Globalization

Sunaina Marr Maira

Welcome to "planet youth." This is not, as you may have anticipated, a clothing store, youth zine, or dance party. It is actually all of these, and more. Studies of youth culture have focused on the cultural productions of youth as well as on the everyday practices of youth, encompassing the worlds of family, school, work, and popular culture. The globalization of culture has also highlighted the worlding of youth culture, and potentially of youth culture studies, a turn that I will argue is significant for Asian American studies at this critical juncture in the growth of the field. Thus the notion of "planet youth," playful as it is, raises questions for the field as of youth themselves, along the lines of the oft-cited query: "What planet are *you* on?" What are our ideological investments in particular methodological and theoretical directions for Asian American studies? What worlds, communities, or areas of research seem more or less central to the field? Youth culture studies is critical for Asian American studies, not just because of its focus on a particular generation and on emerging notions of race, politics, and Asian American subjectivities that will shape the future of the field and of Asian American social movements, but also because the idea of generation and of "youthfulness" allows us to interrogate our ideas of the past and the future, of revolutionary ideals and ideological differences, and of the maturation and institutionalization of a once "youthful" field.

Yet as we draw on theories of youth to consider the development of Asian American studies itself in the conservative political climate of the last two decades, we should not let this metaphorical use obscure the very real import-ance of considering the lived experiences and cultural productions of youth themselves. Discussions of youth are charged precisely because of the symbolic weight that the category of "youth" carries. Youth culture has the burden of being the exemplary manifestation of both rebellious movements and commodified culture, of resistance and co-optation. Yet the category of "youth" is a relatively new concept and needs to be historically situated. The contemporary notion of adolescence in industrialized societies was closely tied to the post-World War II emergence of leisure industries that targeted a generation of youth that were enjoying new levels of disposable income and were between childhood education and the adult labor force. The notion of the teenager as being in this liminal phase was partly a product of these economic and social shifts, and I think this very notion of liminality, of being between childhood and adulthood, is what allows adolescence to be often perceived as a social threat, as a dramatic embodiment of the crisis that a given society is facing at a particular moment.

In a similar vein, youth culture studies has the privilege as well as the misfortune of being associated with spectacularly orthodox subjects – therefore appearing academically unconventional – thus seeming politically irrelevant. This has led to a marginalization of youth culture research even in interdisciplinary political projects such as Asian American studies, and in current work on nation and globalization that has been increasingly salient in the academy and of great relevance to the field of Asian American studies. Work on Asian American youth cultures is increasingly evident at the national conference of the Association of Asian American Studies, yet for a long time there was very little research in this area that considered the cultural practices of youth themselves. I will argue that this location on the margins is revealing – as appearances of youth culture often are – of the anxieties and desires of Asian American studies and of Asian Americanists themselves at this moment in the field. Underlying this binary of invisible and hyper-visible youth, of intellectual and political centers and margins, is a more complicated set of theoretical and institutional debates and challenges in which we are all embroiled in one way or another, regardless of our research specialization. In drawing attention to the apparent marginalization of youth culture studies in the field of Asian American studies, I am not suggesting that we all migrate to Planet Youth. My point is not to raise questions only about our objects of study, but rather to argue for a new approach to defining objects of study – whether it is youth culture or not – and to the field of Asian American studies itself.

In this chapter, I will first outline some of the limitations in existing work on Asian American youth as well as the fissures and cleavages they reveal in the field of Asian American studies. I will then discuss the need to integrate youth culture studies with research on citizenship and globalization so as to advance both areas of work, and conclude by discussing recent research where I have grappled with these issues.

Youth Culture Studies and Disciplinary Nationalisms

It is true, we Asian Americanists were all "young" once. However, the problem with either looking back on adolescence through a nostalgic haze or taking for granted a fixed temporal progression of youth to adulthood is that we risk being either too romantic or too cynical about "youth." A secret yearning to be young, or youthful, can, sometimes, underlie a projection onto youth of our own political aspirations or personal motivations. For example, one of the frequent manifestations of youth in Asian American studies is in discussions of student activists in the Asian American movement of the 1960s and 1970s. These historical portraits of the civil rights era – while not always nostalgic – often do not lend themselves to theorizing "youth culture" at a particular moment in a way that would allow students to go beyond the clichés that abound about that period and the fixed subject positions generally associated with it, or allow a new generation of academics to learn from those histories at a different moment of institutionalization of ethnic studies. At the same time, a sociological approach to youth as a fixed generational category can lead to a structuralist approach that takes for granted the ideological construction of "youth" itself. In fact, Asian American studies has assumed or even relied on the category of youth without really taking the category seriously enough, methodologically, epistemologically, or often even politically.

This brings me to the definition of "youth culture," that much-vaunted destination of commercial trendspotters and ever-youthful academics. In my view, the most incisive, and certainly the most widely influential, theory of youth culture emerged from the work of the Birmingham school of subcultural studies in the late 1970s. According to John Clarke, Stuart Hall, Tom Jefferson, and Brian Roberts in *Resistance Through Rituals* (1976), youth belong to a subculture when "there is a shared set of social rituals that define them as a group instead of a mere collection of individuals" (47). The strength of the Birmingham scholars' framework lay in their focus on youth in their everyday settings as well as embedded in a larger political or social context – an analysis that emphasized "structures, cultures, and biographies." They deliberately used the term "subculture" instead of simply "youth culture" so as to highlight a deeper structural analysis linking youth to youth industries, such as music and fashion, that had created a "teenage [consumer] market" (16). The Birmingham theorists drew on the Chicago school of sociology's work on subcultures and youth delinquency, and also on the Frankfurt school's approach to mass culture. Their intervention aimed at understanding the meanings that youth make for themselves through the use of popular culture, in the context of social transitions in Britain after World War II, particularly for working-class males. This by-now classic theory of youth subcultures drew on both semiotic and structural analyses, looking at the symbolic work of youth subculture in helping youth ideologically resolve the paradoxes they confront in different social spheres.

Of course, this theory outlines only a representational solution to the crises of youth, and critics have also argued that the Birmingham school theorists, such as Dick Hebdige (1979), over-interpreted the symbolic meanings of youth culture in terms of resistance, failing to take into account those young people who were not involved in these spectacular subcultures, and that they projected their own politics onto the youth they were studying (Cohen 1997). Feminist critics have also argued that this early work neglected the experiences of girls and young women and the more private expressions of youth subcultures (McRobbie 1991). Yet I think the Birmingham school's framework remains influential in US cultural studies because it was an early effort to take seriously the responses of youth at a collective level and to link popular culture to material forces. A cultural studies approach that aims at combining ethnographic methods with symbolic interpretation is clearly useful for Asian American studies as it moves from the largely literary-textual emphasis of the last few years to re-integrating social science research.

However, the Birmingham's school approach to studying "structures, cultures, biographies" has been transplanted to the United States, some argue, through the division of academic labor between political economy/sociology, cultural anthropology, and literary criticism. According to Lawrence Grossberg (1996), this division maps onto the linear model in communication which Stuart Hall refined as "encoding/decoding" culture by breaking it down into three steps: the analysis of processes of production, the decoding of texts, and ethnographies of consumption in specific interpretive communities. But these three dimensions are rarely considered together in youth culture studies in the United States, and critics have argued that US cultural studies, more generally, tends to neglect "the sense of culture as practice, form, and institution" and divorces "questions of power" from everyday experience (O'Connor 1996: 191).

This has to do, at least partly, with the emergence of cultural studies generally within literature or humanities departments and the ongoing resistance to interdisciplinary work more generally in the US academy, where research is still partitioned into disciplinary departments and where inter- or trans-disciplinary initiatives, such as ethnic studies or women's studies, continue to face barriers to institutionalization. This shortcoming in cultural studies is also due to the lack of incentive to collaborate across disciplines, or even simply to produce joint research. Some critics of US cultural studies have pointed out that the early working papers of the now-defunct Center for Contemporary Cultural Studies in Birmingham were generally collaborative efforts that suggested a potentially collectivist approach to academic labor. In humanities departments in the United States, there is simply no incentive for scholars to co-author research since the tenure system is based on individual publishing achievements and collaboration is not rewarded. In the social sciences and education, there is more collaborative work, but it tends to remain within the scholars' disciplinary fields. How can Asian American studies be a truly interdisciplinary field if it is shaped by the constraints of an institutional culture in which disciplinary nationalisms still rule? If programs that are meant to be interdisciplinary, such as ethnic studies or women's studies, remain tied to disciplinary frameworks, there need to be other ways in which we can learn from one another's training to build stronger methodologies and frameworks that are appropriate to complex social phenomena and multifaceted objects of study, as in Asian American studies or youth culture studies. These are some of the real logistical and structural issues in which issues of knowledge production are embedded and which shape the possibilities for a more interdisciplinary Asian American studies.

Asian American Studies: Destination Youth?

In Asian American studies, as in the US academy at large, it seems that there are three approaches to studying Asian American youth: an interpretive/cultural studies approach that focuses on cultural representations by and about youth, a developmental approach that focuses on ethnic and racial identity, and a social science approach that focuses on class mobility and academic achievement. I will not be able to provide a comprehensive review here of these growing bodies of work, but I just want to point out that "youth culture," in the sense of the actual cultural productions or everyday experiences of youth, rarely appears in each of these areas of research.

In social science research on Asian American youth, the focal paradigm tends to be that of identity development, ethnic or racial. This approach owes a debt, directly or indirectly, to the major theorist of identity and adolescence in psychology, Erik Erikson, who explicitly situated identity formation in the interaction between the individual and the cultural environment. Erikson's work allowed scientists to see adolescence as a set of culturally specific rituals, even while others argue that the notion of adolescence as a distinct period in the lifecycle is itself is a cultural construction peculiar to modern, "Western" societies.[1] However, the problem with much developmental work on ethnic identity, including work on Asian American adolescents, is that it tends to assume that ethnic identity is a linear process, detached from historical or political contexts. Stage models or typologies which have been applied to Asian American youth inevitably point to a "mature" end-point that is considered the ideal resolution of presumed "conflict" and that is implicitly tied to a particular ideological stance, but one that remains unexamined. Interview- or survey-based studies generally pay little attention to the nuanced and often-contradictory identity constructions of young people themselves, ignoring the diverse facets of self performed in everyday life and popular culture.

A promising departure from these narrow developmental approaches is the growing body of work on multiracial Asian Americans (see, for example, Williams-León and Nakashima 2001) that pushes for a more complex

understanding of ethnic identification and racialization intertwined with historical and political constructions of racialized and ethnicized bodies. This is not, of
course, to single out as exceptional a subject that is already so problematically
fetishized; not all work on multiracial identities is critical and some is squarely in
the tradition of stage models or sociological typologies of assimilation.[2] But there
is new work that challenges these approaches and uses a range of conceptual
frameworks, highlighting local contexts, identity performances, popular culture,
transnational linkages, and postcolonial histories.[3]

In the third area of work on Asian American youth, sociological studies of
second-generation and immigrant youth, the implications of the ideological
apparatus underpinning US race and ethnic politics are quite apparent, sometimes troublingly so. There has been much recent sociological research on
specific groups of immigrant and second-generation youth, yet most of this
work has focused largely on issues and indices of social and economic adaptation
of the children of immigrants and on ethnic identity typologies (Portes and
Zhou 1993; Rumbaut 1994; Zhou and Bankston 1998). This research has been
very important in providing large-scale or quantitative data on new groups of
immigrant and second-generation youth whose families have come to the United
States after 1965 from Latin America, Asia, Africa, and the Caribbean. Immigration sociologists have rightly critiqued earlier theories of unilinear assimilation,
suggesting instead a model of "segmented assimilation" that points to the
internal heterogeneity of ethnic groups. However, much of this work is still
preoccupied with the question of assimilation and has tended to neglect the
engagement of youth with popular culture and their more nuanced understandings of race, especially, and also of gender and sexuality. A promising exception
in the field of education is Stacey Lee's (1996) qualitative study of Asian American
high school youth and its analysis of Asian American youth subcultures and
notions of "model minority" students.

Most of this research assumes that young people have discrete ethnic identities
such as "Vietnamese" or "Filipino" or "Chinese," even if they are hyphenated, as
reflected in the design of studies that focus on ethnic groups in isolation and
ignore the reality of exchanges and borrowings among different groups of youth.
These complicated, even polycultural (Kelley 1999), affiliations are increasingly
apparent in youth popular culture, for young people across ethnic and class
backgrounds identify with hip hop, and white youth in different regional locations increasingly adopt markers of Latino or Asian styles. But a more troubling
assumption in some studies of immigrant and second-generation youth in the
United States is that identification with Black and Latino youth culture is
considered to be socially "maladaptive." These subcultures, often euphemistically
coded as "native-born" or "urban" youth cultures, are described as "adversarial"
and leading to "downward mobility," implying that Asian American youth are
better adapted if they identify with middle-class white American culture (Zhou
1999). Sociologists who make these claims are justified in pointing to the

undeniable disadvantages facing Asian American youth who live in poor neigh-borhoods and attend inadequate schools. However, as Eric Tang points out in an incisive critique of sociological studies of Southeast Asian immigrants, research-ers such as Alejandro Portes and Min Zhou "engage in a sweeping set of cultural and pathological assumptions about the behaviors of [. . .] the black urban poor" and portray "Asian immigrant life as a cultural, political, and economic negation of a black culture of poverty" (2000: 62, 58). This sociological literature reveals a lingering assumption about the efficacy of assimilation and culturalist stereotypes about "good" or "bad" minorities, implying that Asian immigrants succeed due to kinship networks and forms of "bounded solidarity" absent in urban "ghetto" culture (Zhou 1999: 24).

Of course, the irony is that many middle-class white American youth, even those in the suburbs, are increasingly drawn to "urban" Black and Latino youth culture. Sociologists of immigration who remain preoccupied with questions of (upward) class mobility fail to understand the ways in which these cross-ethnic or interracial affiliations may actually be adaptive for youth who find themselves marginalized within the class or racial hierarchies of the United States and feel distanced from the transplanted cultural rituals of their parents. In turning to these popular culture forms produced by youth of color in the United States, young immigrants often find vernacular theories of race and class politics in the United States that help them make sense of their own experiences and offer a sense of belonging. But social scientists would not readily understand the meanings of this engagement unless they take the trouble to ask young people what it means to them and combine survey methods with open-ended interviews or other ethnographic methods that offer insights into the desires and anxieties of youth in more subtle ways. Studies of Asian American youth would benefit greatly from more ethnographic research and more critical attention to the dialogic production of research itself, i.e., the reflexivity of the relationship between researcher and researched.

As an example of the ways in which research on Asian American youth has been framed or defined within the field of Asian American studies, the special issue of *Amerasia Journal* (1999) devoted to the second generation is revealing. This issue was later published as a volume titled *Second Generation: Ethnic Identity among Asian Americans* (Min 2002) and featured only one article from the journal issue that focuses on youth cultural production (Alsaybar 1999). While this essay takes a critical perspective on Filipino gang culture, situating it historically and also in local context, the author leaves unexamined the interest-ing antagonisms as well as expressive affiliations between young Filipino and Latino males in Southern California.[4] The politics of Asian American masculin-ity and heterosexuality also beg to be analyzed in this essay, for the author writes that Filipino American gangs are not solely composed of men because "women and gays" join them too (132). However, another essay in the published volume deftly critiques gendered and sexualized notions of virtue and citizenship in

South Asian immigrant families (Rudrappa 2002), and Yen Le Espiritu's (2002) essay on Filipino Americans provides a nuanced analysis of second-generation identity as a dynamic, nonlinear process, complementing the other chapters. The social science research published in this volume points to the importance of studies that focus on the lived experience of various groups of Asian American youth in specific contexts and that consider the complex intersections of gender, sexuality, race, class, and ethnicity.

An interdisciplinary approach to youth culture studies requires us to draw on the insights from the sociologists of immigration to situate second-generation youth and popular culture in the context of local, national, or even global processes. At the same time, we need to integrate understandings of popular culture and the nuances of subjective meaning-making into sociological or quantitative studies of youth. In order to develop a methodology for studying youth culture that would integrate "cultures, structures, biographies," we need to go beyond simply borrowing methods or themes from other disciplines into our own, essentially unchanged disciplinary approaches, whether they originate in the social sciences or humanities. Such a methodology is useful not just for youth culture studies, but for Asian American studies in general, allowing us to draw on important work in the field on both cultural representations and social practice and to speak to the historical mission of the field as an intellectual endeavor that could be a political intervention relevant to Asian American communities.

Youth Culture Studies: Global Routes?

Research on youth culture can help push the boundaries of Asian American studies if it uses an interdisciplinary approach to contribute to current debates about nationalism and globalization. The flows of people, goods, capital, and media images across national borders are embedded in, and produce, social and material inequalities that in turn drive further immigration and displacement. Youth are necessarily caught in this loop, in this movement of people and the mobilization for justice and equity, and in this cycle of production and consumption. Yet, youth culture studies in the United States has not drawn explicitly enough on critical theory and research in the areas of globalization, social movements, and citizenship, which are important currents in Asian American studies. It is important to "think youth" in these debates because many of the shifts in cultural processes that are discussed in the growing body of literature on globalization and transnationalism shape the lives of, if they are not partly produced by, young people in various local and national contexts; but there is much less focus directly on youth per se, and particularly on the ways in which young people *themselves* understand or grapple with globalization. Because of popular culture's link to global processes of production and consumption, the transnational context is often at least implicit within youth culture studies, and in fact some may argue that youth culture scholars have been studying globalization for years.[5] At the same time, though, much of this work has remained wedded to a local or national frame of reference. Even in sociological studies of youth and immigration, it seems that part of the problem in their race analyses is that there is insufficient critique of US nationalism itself, of the particular national ideologies about race, class, and ethnicity that create the notion of supposedly "adversarial" subcultures and that underlie the cultural expressions to which youth are drawn.

Much work on globalization and transnationalism has tended to focus largely or explicitly only on adults, Youth are assumed to be less fully formed social actors, or subjects less able to exert agency in the face of globalization that some scholars are, rightly, eager to document. To be sure, youth are engaged in an ongoing process of social and cognitive development and do, in fact, acquire more rights and responsibilities as they move into adulthood. However, traditional work on youth and citizenship often assumes, for example, that young citizens must be socialized into adult norms of political involvement, rather than that they are agents who may express important critiques of citizenship and nationhood, even if their rights are limited (Buckingham 2000: 13).

I began thinking more about the reasons for the disjuncture between youth culture studies and work on globalization and the need for a more adequate framework theorizing the link between the two while co-editing, with Elisabeth Soep, a collection titled *Youthscapes: Popular Culture, National Ideologies, Global Markets.* We wanted to redress the under-theorizing of youth as key players within globalization, and to go beyond the use of youth culture practices simply as handy examples to note, in passing, "monstrous" manifestations of globalization's contradictions (Comaroff and Comaroff 2001: 19) or celebratory testaments to popular culture's possibilities. However, rather than pushing for a rightful "centering" of youth culture studies in relation to an implicit "margin," we argue that youth culture studies itself has much to teach us about the production of cultural "centers" or "margins," about which bodies and which discourses are privileged, condemned, or overlooked.

We developed the notion of "youthscapes" to offer an approach that would provide an analytic and methodological link between youth culture and nationalizing or globalizing processes. "Youthscape" suggests a site that is not just geographic or temporal, but social and political as well, a "place" that is bound up with questions of power and materiality (Dirlik 2001/2002; Soja 1989). In his theory highlighting the cultural dimensions of globalization, Arjun Appadurai (1996) used the idea of a "scape" to describe dimensions of global cultural flows that are fluid and irregular, rather than fixed and finite. Ethnoscapes comprise the shifting circuits of people who animate a given social world; technoscapes draw attention to high-speed channels connecting previously distant territories; financescapes encompass new systems for accumulating and moving money;

mediascapes refer to the dispersal of images and texts; and ideoscapes embody the "imagined worlds" produced through intersections among all of the above. Youth is a social category that belongs to all five of Appadurai's categories, so we envisioned a youthscape not as a unit of analysis but, rather, as a way of thinking *about* youth culture studies, one that revitalizes discussions about youth cultures and social movements while simultaneously theorizing the political and social uses of youth.

The process of conceptualizing a site for local youth practice as embedded within national and global forces is what we mean by a "youthscape," but such an approach does not imply a formulaic analysis. Instead, it implies a reframing of a problem of conceptual disjunctures to bring together different frames of analysis, and as such is applicable to other attempts to redefine objects of study in Asian American studies, particularly for those who want to consider the importance of social movements and cultural production to Asian American studies as a field and as a political project. I will provide a brief example from my current research on Asian American youth after 9/11 to show how I am developing this approach to youth culture studies in my own work and how this study could contribute to larger questions that have taken on new urgency for Asian American studies. It is crucial that we understand the ways in which citizenship, nationalism, and social justice are understood by Asian American youth after 9/11, for this is a generation coming of age at a moment when the borders of nation and the politics of ethnicity and racialization have taken on new, highly charged meanings, as a heightened xenophobia allows for the targeting of demonized "aliens." How this generation of young people responds to the "war on terror," at home and abroad, will help us understand the shifting interracial and panethnic alliances and affiliations that have long been key to the intellectual and political formation of Asian American studies.

South Asian Muslim Immigrant Youth and Cultural Citizenship

My interest in questions about citizenship, nationalism, and youth has led, along with historical circumstances, to an ethnographic study of working-class Indian, Pakistani, and Bangladeshi immigrant students in the public high school in Cambridge, Massachusetts since fall of 2001. In the wake of the September 11, 2001, attacks and the subsequent war in Afghanistan, questions of citizenship and racialization have taken on new, urgent meanings for South Asian immigrant youth. Many South Asian Americans, Arab Americans, and Muslim Americans, or individuals who appeared "Muslim," have been victims of physical assaults and racial profiling. Cambridge is an interesting site for this research, for while media attention and community discussions of racial profiling primarily focused on South Asians in the New York/New Jersey area, there were hundreds of incidents around the country in places where South Asians have not been as visible in the public sphere or as organized, including in the Boston area.

The Cambridge public high school has an extremely diverse student body reflecting the city's changing population, with students from Latin America, the Caribbean, Africa, and Asia. Students from India, Pakistan, Bangladesh, and Afghanistan constitute the largest Muslim population in the school, followed by youth from Ethiopia, Somalia, and Morocco. The South Asian immigrant student population at the high school is predominantly working to lower-middle class, recently arrived (within the last one to five years), mostly from small towns in South Asia, and with minimal to moderate fluency in English. The majority of the Indian immigrant students are from Muslim families, most from Gujarat, and several of them are actually related to one another as their families have immigrated as part of an ongoing process of chain migration.

I found that in nearly all my conversations with these youth, as well as with their parents, the discussion would inevitably turn to citizenship, for this was an issue of deep concern to them and one that had profoundly shaped their lives and their experiences of migration. The concept of citizenship is at the heart of discussions of democracy, pluralism, and civil rights in the United States, all questions that are being debated anew after 9/11 and that are, of course, key to Asian American studies. Research on youth and citizenship is meager and generally tends to assume that young people must emulate existing adult models of "good citizenship," liberally defined, and must adjust to the status quo (Buckingham 2000: 10–11). This assumes a limited definition, too, of what constitutes the "political"; more recent work challenges these assumptions and pays attention to young people's own understandings of politics and the ways that they negotiate relationships of power in different realms of their everyday life (Bhavnani 1991: 172; Buckingham 2000: 13).

Citizenship has generally been understood in political, economic, and civic terms, but increasingly analyses focus on the notion of cultural citizenship as multiethnic societies are forced to confront questions of difference that undergird social inequity (Rosaldo 1997). Cultural citizenship – cultural belonging in the nation or the everyday experiences of inclusion and exclusion – is a critical issue for immigrant communities and minority groups for the rights and obligations of civic citizenship are mediated by race, ethnicity, gender, and sexuality (Rosaldo 1997; Miller 2001; Siu 2001; Coll 2002), as well as religion. In my research I have found that issues of economic or legal citizenship spill over into cultural citizenship and that these categories are more blurred than some theorists of cultural citizenship have perhaps acknowledged; it is important not to lose sight of the continuing salience of the traditional bases of citizenship even as they are being transformed. I am interested in the critical possibilities of cultural citizenship for galvanizing struggles for democracy and rights, particularly for young immigrants, but within the limits of technologies of subjection that are tied to both liberal multiculturalism and the inequities of global capital (Miller

2001). I think there are three ways in which South Asian immigrant youth understand and practice cultural citizenship: *flexible citizenship, multicultural or polycultural citizenship,* and *dissenting citizenship.* These three categories point to the ways in which the questions facing these youth go beyond debates about cultural rights to questions of economic, civil, and human rights, but at the same time point to the limitations of rights-based discourses.

Here, in the interest of space, I am only going to discuss the last two forms of citizenship. However, I must note that these youth all desired US citizenship as part of a long-term, family-based strategy of migration which entailed sponsoring relatives for visas and setting up transnational family businesses. This is what researchers have called "flexible citizenship," and what Aihwa Ong, specifically, suggests is descriptive of the experience of affluent Chinese migrants. Migrants increasingly use transnational links to provide political or material resources not available to them within a single nation-state (Basch et al. 1994). For these young immigrants, I realized, the very notion of citizenship was flexible and contingent, shifting with context, and they used this notion strategically to reconcile questions of national allegiance after September 11.

Multicultural/polycultural citizenship

One of the most pervasive, and also widely challenged, discourses of cultural belonging in the United States today, especially in education, is that of multiculturalism. So, not surprisingly, many of these youth talked about ideas of cultural difference and relationships with others in terms of multicultural citizenship, even if only implicitly. For most of them, it is important to emphasize that they "get along" with students from other immigrant or ethnic groups and that they have friendships that cross ethnic and racial boundaries. But it is also true that there are moments of tension among these different groups of youth. After September 11, some of the South Asian immigrant youth, particularly the Muslim boys, feel targeted as Muslims by other high school youth. Accusations such as "you're a terrorist" or "you're a bin Laden" enter into what might otherwise be just an outbreak of youthful aggression among boys, but is now part of a political discourse about Islam sanctioned by the doublespeak of George W. Bush, whose policies and rhetoric have targeted a "foreign" enemy and enemy within, despite his verbal attempts to assuage Muslim American and liberal voters. The South Asian Muslim boys and girls I spoke with have had to struggle with the impact of the "Green Scare" (Prashad 2003) on their everyday lives: Why is their religion portrayed as the enemy? Does this mean *they* are the enemy, and how can they live as such?

For Waheed, a Pakistani immigrant boy, 9/11 prompted a heightened self-consciousness about racialization that seemed, if anything, to reinforce the black–white racial polarization. He felt that African Americans were not as shattered by the 2001 attacks on the United States because, in his view, black

Americans feel alienated from the nation-state because of the legacy of slavery. While this racialized difference after 9/11 is probably more complex than Waheed suggests, what is important is that he *believes* that African Americans share his experience of marginalization within the nation. Amir, another Pakistani boy, thought African Americans were less likely to have an uncritically nationalist response to the events of 9/11 than white Americans, even though he was hesitant to extend this generalization to responses to the US war in Afghanistan. But Waheed does not completely dismiss the renewed nationalism of Americans after 9/11, saying, "The first thing is they're born here in the USA, so that's their country. [. . .] We are immigrants. [. . .] If something happens in back home, like, and someone else did, we're gonna be angry too, right?" So he is not critical of the nationalist response to what could have been cast as a human tragedy, but it is apparent that 9/11 seems to have drawn some of these youth into an understanding of citizenship that is based on racialized fissures in claims to national identity, or perhaps even a model that sees affiliation with those citizens, such as African Americans, who also seem to have a contested relationship to citizenship.

The responses of these youth seem to suggest a more critical understanding of multicultural citizenship, a potentially *polycultural citizenship*, based not on the reification of cultural difference that multiculturalism implies, but on a complex set of political affiliations and social boundary-crossings, as Robin Kelley's notion of polyculturalism suggests. This nascent polycultural citizenship is embedded in the messiness and nuances of relationships of different groups with each other and with the state, and one that allows for a political, not just cultural, resonance, based on particular historical and material conjunctures. These working-class South Asian youth sense a connection, then, with other youth of color based on their shared sense of distance from normative (white, middle-class) Americanness, even as they struggle with the challenges that Muslim identity has posed to liberal multiculturalism.

Syed Khan, an Indian immigrant who is on the Board of Religious Directors of the Islamic Center of Sharon, is the founder of Muslim Community Support Services in New England, an organization that has organized forums on issues of civil rights and offered counseling to Muslim Americans after 9/11. Khan astutely argues that the post-9/11 backlash against Muslim and Arab Americans has shown the limits of US multiculturalism, in its inability to absorb Islam as a marker of difference worth defending as cultural, or even religious, difference. Muslim Americans find that the notion of cultural pluralism has not always come to their defense because they are defined, particularly after 9/11 but also at other moments in US history such as the Iran hostage crisis and the Gulf War, as political scapegoats and *therefore* cultural aliens (Safizadeh 1999). The re-nationalization of "Americanness" after 9/11 both excludes and racializes Muslim identity, even if it is not racial at all, in the slippery sense of race in the United States. This is what Moustafa Bayoumi calls the "tragic irony" of "racial profiling" after 9/11 (2001/2002: 73).

Dissenting citizenship

Many have pointed out that the post-9/11 moment has "facilitated the consoli-
dation of a new identity category" that conflates "Arab/Muslim/Middle Eastern"
with "terrorist" and "non-citizen" (e.g. Volpp 2002). This identity category that
casts Muslim Americans outside the nation is not new, but Leti Volpp is right to
point out that a "national identity has consolidated that is both strongly patriotic
and multiracial" (2002: 1584), absorbing African Americans, East Asian Americans, and Latino(a)s. However, it seems to me that some South Asian immigrant
youth are willing to voice, even publicly, what some middle-class community
leaders have been unwilling to acknowledge. All the students I spoke to had a
thoughtful analysis of the events of 9/11 and the US bombing of Afghanistan,
speaking of it in terms of justice and human rights. Amir said to me in December,
2001: "You have to look at it in two ways. It's not right that ordinary people over
there [in Afghanistan], like you and me, just doing their work, get killed. They
don't have anything to do with [...] the attacks in New York, but they're getting
killed. And also the people in New York who got killed, that's not right either."
Jamila, a Bangladeshi girl, said, "I felt bad for those people [in Afghanistan ...]
because they don't have no proof that they actually did it, but they were all killing
all these innocent people who had nothing to do with it." Aliyah, a Gujarati
American girl who could very easily pass for Latina in large part because of her
style, chose to write the words "INDIA + MUSLIM" on her bag after 9/11. For her,
this was a gesture of defiance responding to the casting of Muslims as potentially
disloyal citizens; she said, "Just because one Muslim did it in New York, you can't
involve everybody in there, you know what I'm sayin'." This critique of the anti-
Muslim backlash was pervasive amongst the South Asian Muslim youth. Karina
said, "After September 11, they [Americans] hate the Muslims. [...] I think they
want the government to hate the Muslims, like, all Muslims are same."

After an anti-Muslim incident in the high school, the International Student
Center organized a student assembly where three of the South Asian Muslim
students delivered eloquent speeches condemning racism to an auditorium filled
with their peers. Even though these working-class youth do not have the validation
of, or time to participate in, community or political organizations, they have
become spokespersons in the public sphere willing to voice dissent. I do not want
to suggest that these youth are somehow a hidden political vanguard; not all these
youth are rushing to the microphone, and understandably some of them
are hesitant to speak about political issues in public spaces given the current
climate of surveillance and paranoia. Even those who can claim to be legal citizens
are worried about speaking out, given that we live with the USA-PATRIOT Act in
an era that feels like a new Cold War (see Chang 2002; Cole and Dempsey 2002).

Yet, even in this climate, I have found these Muslim immigrant youth to be
engaged in a practice of dissenting citizenship, a citizenship based on a critique

and affirmation of human rights that means one has to stand apart at some moments, even as one stands together with others who are often faceless, outside the borders of the nation. Dissenting citizenship is not coeval with cosmopolitanism, at least in this instance. The critique of these Muslim immigrant youth is both far more attached to regional and religious identity, and far more critical in their appraisal of US nationalism and state powers, than some liberal theorists of cosmopolitanism allow (Nussbaum 2002). The perspective of Muslim immigrant youth is very much rooted in their identities *as* Muslims, who are targeted as such by the state, and also sheds light on US national policy as a manifestation of imperial policy at this moment. Their responses conjoin warfare *within* the state to international war; it is this link between the domestic and foreign that makes this an important mode of dissent because the imperial project of the new Cold War, as in earlier times, works by obscuring the links between domestic and foreign policies.

Kathleen Moore (1999) points out that the post-9/11 curtailment of civil liberties actually continued the erosion of civil rights of immigrants that was begun by the Anti-Terrorism and Effective Death Penalty Act and the Illegal Immigration Reform and Immigrant Responsibility Act (IIRAIRA) of 1996; both of these acts narrowed the definition of the "civil community" in response to the "heightened sense of insecurity required to maintain a restructured, wartime regulatory state after the primary security target disappears. [. . .] The regulatory state perpetuates essentialized understandings of the self (as citizen) and the other (as alien) and will continue to distribute rights and therefore power hierarchically as long as a heightened sense of insecurity persists" (95).[6] The distinction between citizens/non-citizens is used in political discourse to support foreign policy and justify the military campaigns and domestic priorities of a "wartime/regulatory state" (Moore 1999). This is even more the case when the illusion of a "peacetime economy" is discarded for a nation at war as in the present moment. The "war on terror," it is important to remember, is an extension of the "war on immigrants" waged since the late 1980s and has roving and ever-expanding targets, including Latinos, Asian Americans, African Americans, and Arab Americans.

The dissent of Muslim immigrant youth is not vanguardist because it does not need to be; they are simply – but not merely – subjects of *both* the war on immigration and the war on terror. As immigrants from South Asia, they also belong to nations that have been the target of Bush's highly selective global war on terror. Their exclusion from processes of being-made as citizens and their emergent political subject-making highlight the processes of citizen-subject-making that secure consent to imperial power. The process of dissenting citizenship is not without wrinkles or contradictions, for it seems that these young immigrants implicitly understand the limits of a state-based notion of citizenship, in its economic, cultural, and political senses.

My research shows not just that the flexibility of capital evokes strategies of flexible citizenship but also that the state, of course, is flexible in its regimes of governmentality. The United States has implemented new policies for regulating workers and disciplining citizens after 9/11, from stripping due process rights from any persons deemed to be associated with "terrorism" to mass arrests of Muslim immigrant men complying with new registration requirements by the INS that target citizens by religion and national origin. This has resulted in a situation where undocumented as well as legal immigrants are terrified because of the sweeping surveillance and detention powers appropriated by the Bush–Ashcroft regime after 9/11. The loss of immigrant rights terrorizes non-citizens who are vulnerable, as some have argued, to hyper-exploitation by employers and to fear of living their lives. Yet it is important to remember that this state of emergency, this crisis of civil rights and its concomitant mode of dissenting citizenship, is not in fact exceptional (Ganguly 2001). The post-9/11 moment is not entirely new but builds on measures and forms of power already in place; this is a state of everyday life in empire.

Conclusion

This project has required the analysis of a youthscape that brings together the spatial frames of community, city, nation, and transnational relationships, and the conceptual frames of youth, citizenship, and empire. It is the links among legal, economic, and cultural citizenship that are so important for the US empire. Talking to these young people has helped me see the value of re-activating a notion of citizenship that lies between the state and an amorphously cosmopolitan "humankind," for their notion of citizenship is deeply engaged with questions of power and justice at both state and transnational scales. Contrary to John Hardt and Antonio Negri (2001), I argue that it is, in fact, imperialism that is at work, however de-centered its power, and that to link globalization to US imperialism is to understand the nature of the resurgent nationalism and everyday emergency that is life in the post-9/11 empire. While it is clear that the relations among nation, state, and capital have been transformed since earlier eras of imperialism (Aronowitz and Gautney 2003), the role of US economic and military power – increasingly tied to a unilateral foreign policy and national interests – is not to be underestimated. This is particularly apparent after the demise of Soviet communism and especially after the events of 9/11, which have led to an increasingly authoritarian exercise of US state power both at home and abroad (Marable 2003: 6). While it is obvious that imperial power no longer necessarily requires direct governance of colonized states, and the power of the state itself has generally declined (Glick Schiller and Fouron 2002), it is also evident that the power of the US state to exercise the globality of violence and globality of economy characterizes this new mode of empire, drawing on Alain Joxe's (2002) framework.

Although I share the skepticism of new theorists of empire and globalization toward a state-bound notion of citizenship, I am interested in the "decolonization of citizenship" as part of a project of radical democracy (A. Lao Montes, personal communication, 2003) that is grounded in the specific, not abstracted, struggles of ordinary people. In this, it is useful to draw on the situated examples of resistance and social movements offered by researchers in the Latino cultural citizenship project (e.g. Flores and Benmayor 1997) and connect it to the theoretical understandings of global capital and new empire in order to integrate a focus on lived experience with materialist analysis. We need an ethnography of the new empire to undergird the theories of globalization being produced and debated; a youthscapes approach, as I have argued here, could help us provide such a critical intervention. Research on youth culture continues to be important at this moment, for we need to understand what it means to come of age as subjects of empire. My research suggests that young Asian immigrants, particularly Muslim youth, are being forced to grapple with the implications of the policies of the national security state and of imperial power in their daily lives; it would be interesting to compare this to the ways in which Asian American youth who are not Muslim nor South Asian American understand civil rights and nationalism after 9/11.

The US occupation of Iraq starting in 2003 and the prospect of endless wars waged against terror, at home and abroad, suggest to me that in Asian American studies we urgently need to return to the question of empire, to produce an analysis of the current crisis and the ways in which our communities are being divided on the ground. Asian American studies is well-suited to this task, given the intimate knowledges of colonialism and empire that shape the histories of nations from which our communities originate, from India and the Philippines to Vietnam and Korea, and that are now needed to understand the current workings of imperial power. The aim of my project is to offer an ethnography of everyday life in the new empire to understand how Muslim Asian American youth are responding to this ongoing emergency. Viewing youth culture through a youthscapes approach allows for an analysis of the cultural as well as material realities of youth in local, national, and global contexts, a perspective that is critical for addressing the deeply political, and ideological, constructions of Asian American youth. Planet Youth is not only a globalized field; it is the terrain for relationships of power and struggle in which young people are inevitably immersed.

NOTES

The ethnographic research on which this chapter is based was funded by the Russell Sage Foundation and the Institute for Asian American Studies, University of Massachusetts-

Boston, and supported by my research assistants, Aaron Spevack, Palav Babaria, and Sarah Khan. I wish to thank Kent Ono for his generosity, support, and feedback and fellow organizers in the South Asian Committee on Human Rights for their courage and inspiration.

1 The anthropologist most widely known for first making this cultural constructionist argument in the US is Margaret Mead, whose *Coming of Age in Samoa* (1928) emphasized that the idea of "storm and stress" was particular to the US and that in other societies, teenage years were not necessarily as conflict-ridden because of different conceptions of the relationship of individual to community, gender, and work. Mead's work, too, has been challenged, but it is still important for its basic reminder that the notion of adolescence is an ideological construction that says as much about the society or subculture itself as it does about the trajectory of individual development. Cross-cultural research on youth by anthropologists and sociologists continues to be important, for example, the collection edited by Amit-Talai and Wulff (1995).

2 For example, some of the psychological and quantitative studies in Maria P. Root's (1992) *Racially Mixed People in America*, Sage, Newbury Park, Calif.

3 See the chapters by Mark Brinsfield, Darby Price, John Rosa, Curtiss Rooks, Loraine Van Tuyl, and Jan Weisman in Teresa Williams-León and Cynthia Nakashima (2001).

4 Accepting at face value that Filipino gangs adopted "Pinoy Pride" due to "marauding Latino cholos" (1999: 130), the article does not adequately explore the larger political context of Latino-Asian class and ethnic relations in a state that has undertaken a vigorous assault on immigrant communities and the criminalization of youth of color, nor does it sufficiently question the limits of cultural pride and interethnic violence as presumed "resistance."

5 See, for example, the valuable contributions of scholars such as Douglas Foley (1994), Juan Flores (2000), Robin Kelley (1997), Lauraine Leblanc (1999), Angela McRobbie (2000, 1999, 1994), and Tricia Rose (1994).

6 The 1996 Anti-Terrorism Act "reintroduced to federal law the principle of 'guilt by association' that had defined the McCarthy era," reintroducing "guilt by association" with groups defined by the state as "terrorist" and thus reviving the ideological exclusion of the Cold War-era McCarran–Walter Act, and giving the authority to deport non-citizens on the basis of secret evidence (Cole and Dempsey 2002: 117–26). From 1996 to 2000, the government sought to use secret evidence to detain and deport two dozen immigrants, almost all of them Muslims, but ultimately the government evidence was thrown out and the accused were released (Cole and Dempsey 2002: 127). IIRAIRA established mandatory detention of non citizens for an expanded list of criminal convictions that would make legal residents deportable for selling marijuana or drunk driving (Nguyen 2002).

REFERENCES

Alsaybar, B. D. (1999). Deconstructing deviance: Filipino American youth gangs, "party culture," and ethnic identity in Los Angeles. *Amerasia Journal* 25(1): 116–38.

Amit-Talai, V. and Wulff, H. (1995) *Youth Cultures: A Cross Cultural Perspective*. Routledge, London.

Appadurai, A. (1996) *Modernity at Large: Cultural Dimensions of Globalization.* University of Minnesota Press, Minneapolis.

Aronowitz, S. and Gautney, H. (2003) The debate about globalization: an introduction. In: Aronowitz, S. and Gautney, H. (eds.) *Implicating Empire: Globalization and Resistance in the 21st Century World Order.* Basic Books, New York, pp. xi–xxx.

Basch, L., Glick Schiller, N. and Szanton Blanc, C. (eds.) (1994) *Nations Unbound: Transnational Projects, Postcolonial Predicaments, and Deterritorialized Nation-States.* Gordon and Breach, Amsterdam.

Bayoumi, M. (2001/2002). How does it feel to be a problem? *Amerasia Journal* 27(3)/28(1): 69–77.

Bhavnani, K. K. (1991) *Talking Politics: A Psychological Framing for Views from Youth in Britain.* Cambridge University Press, Cambridge, UK.

Berlant, L. (1997) *The Queen of America goes to Washington City: Essays on Sex and Citizenship.* Duke University Press, Durham.

Buckingham, D. (2000) *The Making of Citizens: Young People, News, and Politics.* Routledge, London and New York.

Chang, N. (2002) *Silencing Political Dissent: How Post-September 11 Anti-terrorism Measures Threaten our Civil Liberties.* Seven Stories/Open Media, New York.

Clarke, J., Hall, S., Jefferson, T. and Roberts, B. (1976) Subcultures, cultures, and class. In: Hall, S. and Jefferson, T. (eds.) *Resistance through Rituals: Youth Subcultures in Post-war Britain.* Hutchinson/Centre for Contemporary Cultural Studies, University of Birmingham, London, pp. 9–79.

Clifford, J. (1998) Mixed feelings. In: Cheah, P. and Robbins, B. (eds.) *Cosmopolitics: Thinking and Feeling Beyond the Nation.* University of Minnesota, Minneapolis, pp. 362–70.

Cohen, S. (1972) *Folk Devils and Moral Panics: The Creation of the Mods and Rockers.* Basil Blackwell, Oxford, UK.

Cohen, S. (1997) Symbols of trouble. In: Gelder, K. and Thornton, S. (eds.) *The Subcultures Reader.* Routledge, London, pp. 149–62.

Cole, D. and Dempsey, J. (2002) *Terrorism and the Constitution: Sacrificing Civil Liberties in the Name of National Security.* The New Press, New York.

Coll, K. (2002) Problemas y necesidades: Latina vernaculars of citizenship and coalition-building in Chinatown, San Francisco. Paper presented at Racial (Trans)Formations: Latinos and Asians Remaking the United States, Center for the Study of Ethnicity and Race, Columbia University. March.

Comaroff, J. and Comaroff, J. (2001) Millenial capitalism: first thoughts on a second coming. In: Comaroff, J. and Comaroff, J. (eds.) *Millenial Capitalism and the Culture of Neoliberalism.* Duke University Press, Durham, pp. 1–56.

Dirlik, A. (2001/2002). Colonialism, globalization, and culture: reflections on September 11. *Amerasia Journal* 27(3)/28(1): 81–92.

Erikson, E. H. (1968, 1994 ed.) *Identity: Youth and Crisis.* W. W. Norton and Company, New York and London.

Espiritu, Y. L. (2002) The intersection of race, ethnicity, and class: the multiple identities of second-generation Filipinos. In: Min, P. G. (ed.) *Second Generation: Ethnic Identity Among Asian Americans.* Altamira (Rowman & Littlefield), Walnut Grove, CA, pp. 19–52.

Foley, D. E. (1994) *Learning Capitalist Culture: Deep in the Heart of Tejas*. University of Pennsylvania Press, Philadelphia.

Flores, J. (2000) *From Bomba to Hip Hop: Puerto Rican Culture and Latino Identity*. Columbia University Press, New York.

Flores, W. V. and Benmayor, R. (eds.) (1997) *Latino Cultural Citizenship: Claiming Identity, Space, and Rights*. Beacon Press, Boston.

Ganguly, K. (2001) *States of Exception: Everyday Life and Postcolonial Identity*. University of Minnesota Press, Minneapolis.

Glick Schiller, N. and Fouron, G. (2001) *Georges Woke Up Laughing: Long-distance Nationalism and the Search for Home*. Duke University Press, Durham.

Grossberg, L. (1996) Toward a genealogy of the state of cultural studies: the discipline of communication and the reception of cultural studies in the United States. In: Nelson, C. and Gaonkar, D. P. (eds.) *Disciplinarity and Dissent in Cultural Studies*. Routledge, New York, pp. 131–69.

Hardt, M. and Negri, A. (2001) *Empire*. Harvard University Press, Cambridge, MA.

Hebdige, D. (1979) *Subculture: The Meaning of Style*. Methuen, London.

Hondagneu-Sotelo, P. (2002) Families on the frontier: from braceros in the fields to braceras in the home. In: Suárez-Orozco, M. M. and Páez, M. M. (eds.) *Latinos Remaking America*. University of California Press, Berkeley/ David Rockefeller Center for Latin American Studies, Harvard University, Cambridge, MA, pp. 259–73.

Jameson, F. and Miyoshi, M. (eds.) (1998) *The Cultures of Globalization*. Duke University Press, Durham and London.

Joxe, A. (2002) *Empire of Disorder*. Semiotext(e), Los Angeles and New York.

Kelley, R. D. (1997) "Looking to get paid: how some black youth put culture to work." In: *Yo' Mama's Disfunktional! Fighting the Culture Wars in Urban America*. Beacon Press, Boston, pp. 43–77.

Kelley, R. D. (1999) People in me. *ColorLines* 1(3): 5–7.

Leblanc, L. (1999) *Pretty in Punk: Girls' Gender Resistance in a Boys' Subculture*. Rutgers University Press, New Brunswick, NJ.

Lee, S. (1996) *Unraveling the "Model Minority" Stereotype: Listening to Asian American Youth*. Teachers College, Columbia University, New York and London.

Lipsitz, G. (1994) *Dangerous Crossroads: Popular Music, Postmodernism, and the Poetics of Place*. Verso, London.

Lipsitz, G. (2001) *American Studies in a Moment of Danger*. University of Minnesota Press, Minneapolis.

Maira, S. and Soep, E. (eds.) (forthcoming) *Youthscapes: Popular Culture, National Ideologies, Global Markets*. University of Pennsylvania Press, Philadelphia.

Marable, M. (2003) 9/11: Racism in a Time of Terror. In: Aronowitz, S. and Gautney, H. (eds.) *Implicating Empire: Globalization and Resistance in the 21st Century World Order*. Basic Books, New York, pp. 3–14.

McRobbie, A. (1991) *Feminism and Youth Culture: From Jackie to Just Seventeen*. Macmillan, London.

McRobbie, A. (1994) New times in cultural studies. In A. McRobbie, *Postmodernism and Popular Culture*. Routledge, London, pp. 24–43.

McRobbie, A. (ed.) (1997) *Back to Reality: Social Experience and Cultural Studies*. Manchester University Press, Manchester, UK.

McRobbie, A. (1999) *In the Culture Society: Art, Fashion, and Popular Music.* Routledge, London.

Mead, M. (1928, 1961 ed.) *Coming of Age in Samoa.* William Morrow, New York.

Miller, T. (2001) *The Well-Tempered Subject: Citizenship, Culture, and the Postmodern Subject.* The Johns Hopkins University Press, Baltimore.

Min, P. G. (2002) *Second Generation: Ethnic Identity Among Asian Americans.* Altamira (Rowman & Littlefield), Walnut Creek, CA.

Moore, K. (1999) A closer look at anti-terrorism law: American Arab Anti-Discrimination Committee v. Reno and the construction of aliens' rights. In: Suleiman, M. (ed.) *Arabs in America: Building a New Future.* Temple University Press, Philadelphia, pp. 84–99.

Nguyen, T. (2002) Detained or disappeared? *ColorLines* 5(2) http://www.arc/C_lines/CLArchive/story5_2_03.html.

O'Connor, A. (1996) The problem of American cultural studies. In: Storey, J. (ed.) *What is Cultural Studies? A Reader.* Arnold, London, pp. 187–96.

Olwig, K. and Hastrup, K. (eds.) (1997) *Siting Culture: The Shifting Anthropological Subject.* Routledge, London.

Ong, A. (1999) *Flexible Citizenship: The Cultural Logics of Transnationality.* Duke University Press, Durham.

Portes, A., and Zhou, M. (1993) The new second generation: segmented assimilation and its variants among post-1965 immigrant youth. *Annals of the American Academy of Political and Social Sciences* 530: 74–98.

Prashad, V. (2003). The Green Menace: McCarthyism after 9/11. *The Subcontintental: A Journal of South Asian American Political Identity* 1(1): 65–75.

Robbins, B. (1998) Introduction, Part I: actually existing cosmopolitanism. In: Cheah, P. and Robbins, B. (eds.) *Cosmopolitics: Thinking and Feeling Beyond the Nation.* University of Minnesota, Minneapolis, pp. 1–19.

Rosaldo, R. (1997) Cultural citizenship, inequality, and multiculturalism. In: Flores, W. F. and Benmayor, R. (eds.) *Latino Cultural Citizenship: Claiming Identity, Space, and Rights.* Beacon Press, Boston, pp. 27–38.

Rose, T. (1994) *Black Noise: Rap Music and Black Culture in Contemporary America.* Wesleyan/University Press of New England, Hanover, NH.

Rudrappa, S. (2002) Disciplining desire in making the home: engendering ethnicity in Indian immigrant families. In: Min, P. G. (ed.) *Second Generation: Ethnic Identity Among Asian Americans.* Altamira (Rowman & Littlefield), Walnut Creek, CA, pp. 85–111.

Rumbaut, R. G. (1994) The crucible within: ethnic identity, self-esteem, and segmented assimilation among children of immigrants. *International Migration Review* 8(4): 748–93.

Safizadeh, F. (1999) Children of the revolution: transnational identity among young Iranians in Northern California. In: Karim, P. and Khorrami, M. M. (eds.) *A World Between: Poems, Short Stories, and Essays by Iranian-Americans.* George Braziller, New York, pp. 255–76.

Simonett, H. (2001) *Banda: Mexican Musical Life Across Borders.* Wesleyan University Press, Middletown, CT.

Siu, L. (2001) Diasporic cultural citizenship: Chineseness and belonging in Central America and Panama. *Social Text*, 19(4): 7–28.

Smith, R. C. (2002) Gender, ethnicity, and race in school and work outcomes of second-generation Mexican Americans. In: Suárez-Orozco, M. M. and Páez, M. M. (eds.) *Latinos Remaking America*. University of California Press, Berkeley/David Rockefeller Center for Latin American Studies, Harvard University, Cambridge, pp. 110–25.

Soja, E. (1989) *Postmodern Geographies: The Reassertion of Space in Critical Social Theory.* Verso, London and New York.

Tam, H. (ed.) (2001) *Progressive Politics in the Global Age.* Polity, Cambridge, UK/Blackwell, Oxford, UK.

Tannock, S. (2001) *Youth at Work: The Unionized Fast-Food and Grocery Workplace.* Temple University Press, Philadelphia.

Tang, E. (2000) Collateral damage: Southeast Asian poverty in the United States. *Social Text* 18(2): 55–79.

Vimalassery, M. (2002) Passports and pink slips. *SAMAR (South Asian Magazine for Action and Reflection)* 15: 7–8, 20.

Volpp, L. (2002) The citizen and the terrorist. *UCLA Law Review* 49: 1575–1600.

Willis, P. (1977) *Learning to Labor: How Working-Class Kids Get Working-Class Jobs.* New York, Columbia University Press.

Wilson, R. and Dissayanake, W. (eds.) (1996) *Global/Local: Cultural Production and the Transnational Imaginary.* Duke University Press, Durham.

Williams-Léon, T. and Nakashima, C. (eds.) (2001) *The Sum of Our Parts: Mixed Heritage Asian Americans.* Temple University Press, Philadelphia.

Zhou, M. (1999) The current situation of Asian American children. *Amerasia Journal* 25(1): 1–27.

Zhou, M. and Bankston, C. L. (1998) *Growing up American: How Vietnamese Children Adapt to Life in the United States.* Russell Sage Foundation, New York.

CHAPTER NINE

The Problematics of History and Location of Filipino American Studies within Asian American Studies

Helen C. Toribio

In 1999, just before a conference on Asian Americans in higher education, I asked a colleague if there was such a thing as Filipino American studies. His immediate response was "what Filipino American studies?" – this from a professor who was instrumental in creating perhaps the most comprehensive curriculum in the study of Filipinos in America in the only institution that has a college of ethnic studies. I had hoped he would answer in the affirmative and expound upon his experience and observations in developing the discipline (if it can be called a discipline), but I was not entirely surprised by his response. It was yet another illustration that the question of whether or not such a discipline even exists continues to be an issue in the Filipino American community. We both knew, as did others, of the shortcomings in this field, shortcomings that run the entire gamut, from the dearth of published research to the limited number of tenured faculty. This is not to deny the material presence of a growing body of published works, documentaries, and curricula, not to mention the proliferation of cultural productions across nearly all art forms.[1] Still, this colleague's seemingly saucy response to my question revealed an underlying frustration stemming from a need to come to terms with this field, its contents, its history, and its relationships with both community and academia. That desire to assess, reflect on, and reexamine the contents and challenges of Filipino America, however, has not provided the means by which to pursue such a project. Nevertheless, there have been several attempts to do so. For instance, during the 1990s there was a series of conferences on Filipino/Filipino American studies, which included conferences held by the Sikolohiyang Pilipino and Filipino Studies groups, both of which drew from academic circles but were not based in any specific campus or location. But these attempts were not sustainable under the very conditions that impacted their survival.

This chapter is thus a very modest attempt at problematizing Filipino American studies, and is undertaken for several reasons: First, there is no agreement among scholars who focus on the study of Filipinos in America as to a label for Filipino American studies, and as indicated by my colleague above, even its existence.[2] Second, Filipino American studies has historically had an uneasy relationship with Asian American studies, as a result of its more marginal existence relative to the fields of Chinese American and Japanese American studies which have dominated Asian American studies. Third, there are elements in Filipino American studies that make it distinct from both Chinese American and Japanese American studies and more similar to other areas in ethnic studies, such as Native American studies and La Raza studies. These elements include the histories of war between the United States and Native American tribes, Mexico, and the Philippines respectively, and the subsequent colonization of these territories.[3] Finally, there is the element of the ongoing neocolonial relationship between the Philippines and the United States that continues to influence how Filipino Americans, particularly immigrants, view and are viewed by mainstream America.

This may be no more than the ramblings of a discontented lecturer. But I hope here to at least identify some questions that may contribute to framing an approach to Filipino American studies and how the field currently challenges existing conventions in Asian American studies. At the same time, I also hope to build upon some of the theoretical works that likewise have expostulated long-standing canons in Asian American studies. More specifically, this means an approach that examines the terms Filipino/Filipino American, Asian/Asian American, and American as discursive texts, as well as an examination of the interrelationships between and among these categories.

A fundamental problem with all of these terms lies in their ambiguity. None provide a solidified definition of what they each are supposed to represent. Thus, the social movements of the 1960s served to generate productions of identities that have become a perennial project as generation after generation continue to question who they are and what it means to be American, or Asian American, or any of the more specific ethno-American designations like Filipino American. Tiresome as these questions may seem to be, especially for the more veteran scholars in ethnic studies, they highlight issues that are still current. These questions have a sustained resonance for undergraduates in Asian American studies classes as students echo a long-standing refrain to learn about themselves. The questions also continue to inform contemporary scholarship, such as Rick Bonus's (2000) study of Filipino "oriental" stores, community newspapers, and beauty pageants in southern California, each of these cultural spaces being examples of the production and re-production of identity. And in popular discourse since the declared end to the Cold War era, these questions, particularly that of what it means to be American, have been at the core of a national debate which has popularly been labeled the culture wars.[4]

Given the protraction of these questions, I confess to having developed a de-sensitized eye and ear to them. This is not to say I want to ignore them, for they reflect the continuing desire of Asian American communities for empowerment and a sense of pride.[5] But these moments of uncertainty are indicative of the dilemmas that we need to confront if a discipline like Asian American studies is to progress and remain relevant to all who rely upon it for data, analysis, and insight.

While these questions can form a starting point in the production of identities, rather than moving forward with these questions, I would like to pose a different set of questions, more fundamental than the search for meaning in labels like American, Asian American, and Filipino American. Drawing from the answer that my sassy colleague mentioned earlier about the non-existence of Filipino American studies, why do we assume that these entities exist in the first place? Why do we assume that there is an America, an Asian America, or a Filipino America within which to create a meaningful identity?

This is not the first time that this line of questioning has been followed. For example, Michel-Rolph Trouillot (1995) has posited the notion that "America does not exist," and that it is "a dream of conquest of rapture," because its history is as much about what has been "silenced" as what has been produced. On this premise, I would then postulate that if one wanted to find America, it is in Wounded Knee, Africa, Mexico, Cuba, Puerto Rico, Guam, Hawai'i, Samoa, the Philippines, and Vietnam – to name just a few places.

So, what does such an analysis mean for an Asian America? As Kent A. Ono (1995) has suggested, the term may have to be "resigned, scrapped, or disused." Ronald Takaki (1998) has noted that "there are no Asians in Asia, but a disparate array of nationalities." A popular witticism says that these disparate nationalities only become Asian once they land on the continental United States. Even then, in survey after survey (such as that undertaken by Bill Ong Hing [1994]), not all adopt the label Asian or Asian American in reference to themselves. Some maintain their distinction as Vietnamese, Taiwanese, Korean, Filipino, etc., while others specify a more regional identity – for example, the Ilokano and the Igorot in the Filipino community.

Other than its ambiguous attendance, what makes the label Asian American problematic? Here, I concur with what has already been identified by others and that is the homogenizing, essentialist, and obscurantist tendencies in narratives about the Asian American experience. The label suggests a "one-size-fits-all" standard applied to a grouping of ethnicities with shared histories of colonialism, immigration, racialization, settlement, and resistance. Needless to say, these histories are incommensurate. The dominant narratives of Asian American history, however, are Chinese exclusion and Japanese American internment – evident in contemporary literature, films, public exhibits, newsprint human interest stories, and political rhetoric. Much Asian American historiography would have us think that Asian America began in Chinatowns rather than in multiple rural and urban locations both here and in various regions throughout Asia. Nor should it be assumed that Asian America began with the process of immigration. A common gab among Filipinos, for example, says that "we are here, because you (America) went there."

I'd like to focus, then, on the Filipino American subject and to consider how it might contribute to breaking the mold of Asian American homogenization, while at the same time helping the further maturation of Asian American studies. In relation to other areas of Asian American studies, Filipino American studies, by virtue of its name, is perhaps the most indeterminate. In contrast to the designations of Korean, Chinese, Japanese, or Vietnamese, the term "Filipino" was not indigenously derived from the geographic location on which it was imposed. Thus, when one hears the word "Filipino" it does not have the same Asian cultural distinction or association. Coupled with the term "American," the label Filipino American becomes even more abstruse.

Whereas the label "Asian American" originates in the United States, this is not the case with the term "Filipino American." The 1960s appropriation of the term was at least its second incarnation. Before that, it referenced the immediate political and cultural subjugation under American rule in the aftermath of the Philippine–American War. In other words, Filipino America then was American Philippines in the early 1900s, materializing in the imposition of the English language and the wholesale appropriation of education by American teachers, the construction of American colonial architecture, and the total control of the military, among other acts of conquest, in the Philippines.

The comprehensive character of American colonialism in the Philippines, intensified by the so-called "liberation" by the United States in World War II, served to solidify colonized subjects in both nation (the Philippines) and diaspora even until now.[6] Thus, the term Filipino American is viewed by some as a redundancy (Campomanes 1992), positing the Filipino (American) as a de-nationalized subject. Illustrating this was Philippine president Gloria M. Arroyo's rush to declare the Philippines a US ally against "terrorism" in the immediate aftermath of 9/11[7] while neighboring countries in Asia were more cautious in their response to American war rhetoric. Ironically, as Arroyo hastened to place herself at Bush's side, Bush himself alienated a large group of Filipinos in America when he relieved the non-citizens from employment as airport screeners.[8]

While understandably rooted in the colonial legacies of the Philippines, this conflation of Filipino and Filipino American can have confusing consequences. For example, it makes it difficult to isolate the racist nuances in the selective denial of US citizenship to one group of World War II veterans in the Philippines, when it was granted to another (the 1st and 2nd Filipino Regiments).[9]

In contrast, others confine the definition of Filipino American within the geographic borders of the United States, delineating the Filipino American from the Filipino (Cordova 1983). Here, much precedence is placed on the so-called "bridge generation," the cohort of American-born Filipinos whose parents were among the pre-World War II manong generation. In between these extremes of bounded and denationalized Filipinos, lie other answers to the question of what is Filipino American, each with a different emphasis. Some foreground the structural conditions of racism and colonialism that inform identity formation (e.g. Espiritu 1995); others emphasize the subjective effects of social structures that manifest in alienation and anger (e.g. Revilla 1997). Still others highlight the interstitial localities that define Filipino American more as a dynamic than as a fixed state of being (e.g. Bonus 2000).

This divergence in defining Filipino America points to the variance in how Filipino America is narrated. Some are ethnographic in their approach, such as Espiritu's and Bonus's studies of Filipinos in southern California, and Okamura's (1998) study of the predominantly Ilokano settlement in Kalihi, Hawai'i. Others theorize the Filipinization of a sector of America (e.g. Strobel 2000; Mendoza 2001; Canlas 2002). Strobel, for example, has discussed the spiritual practices of Filipinos in the San Francisco Bay area, drawn from animist traditions; Canlas, in another example, reflects on the re-construction of the Filipino *poblacion* (town center) in San Francisco's South of Market area. Meanwhile, others try to provide a cross-section of the Filipino American demography, inclusive of the youth, gays and lesbians, hapas, and mail-order brides, among others (e.g. Root 1997).

Although there are scattered articles here and there, few have taken on more historical projects grounded on the American experience of Filipinos. Dorothy Fujita-Rony's (2003) publication on Filipinos in Seattle is probably the latest in a fairly short list of historical studies (e.g. Lasker 1931; DeWitt 1976, 1980; Cordova 1983; Vera Cruz 1992). This shortage of historical studies denies a fuller understanding of community development and of significant events. For example, we have yet to see a thorough historical treatment of the Kearney Street Manilatown and International Hotel in San Francisco. Conventional Asian American history says there were no Filipino ethnic enclaves before 1965 because of the migratory lifestyle of the manongs. Yet, at the same time, it has also been generally known that 40 percent of Filipinos were tied into the service economy in urban areas, creating a stationary community (Takaki 1998).

The relative absence of Filipino American historical studies is especially disturbing in relation to the history of social movements. With the exception of Philip Vera Cruz's (1992) personal accounts of his role in the United Farm Workers union, for example, we have little account of how Filipino laborers were deployed in the historic formation of a much-revered union. Even in Vera Cruz's account, there is a muffling of other voices, such as that of Larry Itliong, who had an even more instrumental role in the UFW's birth. Quieted also are the voices of collusion, the significant number of Filipino laborers who stayed with Cesar

Chavez after Itliong and Vera Cruz's departures. These rank-and-file workers represented the complexity of transnational working-class dynamics when trade union politics mixed with cultural nationalism. They were instrumental in convincing Chavez to accept the invitation by then-president Marcos to visit the Philippines in the late 1970s, much to the dismay of Vera Cruz who vehemently opposed the Philippine martial law regime and saw in it the same impulses that ran through the UFW.

The intensity of the antagonisms within the UFW, at least as far as Filipinos were concerned, was indicative of the politics of the time. The intensity resonates even now such that there remains a vacuum in historicizing this era. In the three publications on Asian Americans in the radical movements of the 1960s, one ignores the Filipino American sector altogether; a more recent one includes personal, if not sentimentalized, narratives by Filipina activists; and the third contains at least three analytical pieces on the Filipino American movement. None, however, address the interethnic antagonisms generated by the contentions over correct political lines.

Only recently does it seem that interethnic antagonisms among Asian Americans have gained more discursive attention (e.g. Kurashige and Yang Murray 2003). Although these antagonisms have always been present, I think scholarship has tended to shy away from them. It is thus more difficult to break the reproductions of myth-making, such as that which perpetuates the notion that the UFW was only an outgrowth of the Mexican American movement. And it remains unclear how the contentious Filipino and Chinese American alliance in the efforts to save the I-Hotel might have inhibited considerations of alternative strategies for housing in the wake of the I-Hotel's downfall. What is more, if there is a lesson to be drawn from the 1998 controversy over the nomination of *Blu's Hanging* for the AAAS literary award, it is on how to formulate the question which best articulates the crux of a controversy. The award became the catalyst for releasing the suppressed desire to address the issue of Filipino marginalization within the ranks of Asian American studies. I would hope that part of the questioning and challenging we take on in this second phase of Asian American studies is to create those spaces that would allow for inter- and intradisciplinary discussions on issues of marginalization and interethnic antagonisms. To ignore them would be to discard the very reason why Asian American studies came into existence in the first place.[10]

Beyond these questions of Filipino and Asian American interrelations, there remain, internal to Filipino American studies, the questions of how to handle the label and how to define the relationship between the entity the label represents and the American public at large. While the discourse has focused much on the locations of Filipino America, it has done little to address a persistent question which more often than not has become dismissive even though it is perhaps the most asked, and that is the question of the F and the P.

Conventional discourse of identity among Filipinos in America does not directly address this matter. Rather, it follows a linear history that usually begins with Spanish colonialism followed briefly by the Philippine revolution, then American colonialism, waves of immigration (ranging from two to seven depending on who defines "waves"), then a bit on social movements and activism, and/or the honor roll of who's who among Filipinos in America (e.g. Cordova, Posadas, Bautista). Presumably, knowing Filipino/Filipino American history will translate into knowing the Filipino American self, thus instilling pride and self-esteem.

Somewhere along the way, someone will always ask, so what's with the F and the P? Which one do we use? These questions do not often enter into historical discussions, resulting more in myth-making about why the P is preferable by some rather than historicizing the term Filipino (e.g. Morales 1974). Thus, the arguments go back and forth.[11] One side invokes the legislation of the "F" by the Philippine government in 1987, in the aftermath of the people's revolution in the Philippines, to reference "Filipino" (with an F) as the official designation of both the people and the language of the Philippine nation. The other side invokes the linguistic justification of the supposed absence of the F in Philippine languages, and a re-definition of the term Pilipino as the "fine chosen ones" (*pili* meaning to choose + *pino* meaning fine = *Pilipino*).

Lost in the argument is a more historical materialist approach to explicating why both letters are in simultaneous use. The use of both letters are rooted in the colonial history (by Spain and the United States – both colonizers using "F" based on the Spanish and English languages) and anticolonial history of the Philippines (e.g. the 1899 Philippine–American War and the 1960s–70s Filipino American movement in which both the "F" and "P" were used depending on the language preferred, English or Tagalog). To understand the evolution of how the term "Filipino" has been signified, writers and historians (e.g., Agoncillo 1977; Joaquin 1998) have traced its etymology from the Greek origins of the name Philip as one who loves horses, to its designation as the white Spanish elite in the Philippines, to the appropriation of the term by the Philippine *indios* for themselves to label an emerging national identity (e.g., Philippine national hero Jose Rizal). American colonialism further re-signified the term as racist sensibilities devalued the Filipino as unfit for self-government and assimilation (Schirmer 1973).

The devaluation of the term Filipino coincided with the reaffirmation of the term "American" as a white supremacist construct promoted in the print media and the world fairs of the late nineteenth and early twentieth centuries (Rydell 1984; Vergara 1995). Before the mass immigration of Filipinos to American soil, racism had already defined the Filipino as another trope for savage, monkey, and unruly child who resisted parental/colonial control.[12]

By the time the re-defined Filipino made his presence known within the United States in the 1920s, the label Filipino carried with it the definition of criminal. Racial profiling came with the recognition of the label. As Bulosan (1973, ca.1946) noted in the 1930s, "we were stopped each time these vigilant patrolmen saw us driving a car." The criminal thus had to be sanctioned with anti-miscegenation laws and immigration exclusion, while his homeland had to be disposed of as a colony, though tethered by agreements to facilitate American access to its natural resources.

If the production of identity is still paramount for Filipinos in America, particularly students in Asian American studies, it is worthwhile to explain that the co-existence of the F and the P is not antagonistic. Their use is based on a context of language, history, and location. The fact that the question always arises (in classroom discussions, for example) as to which letter is the "correct" one to use should indicate that considering this question is as legitimate as learning about Filipino immigration, the manongs, and exclusion laws. In relation to Asian American studies, the F/P question is another example of what makes Filipino American studies distinct.

Beyond its boundaries, the re-signification of Filipino America does implicate a disruption of its situation within the even more ill-defined space called Asian America, and within that contentious space called America. Given the discourse over the past 20 years – one that has questioned notions of nations, nationalities, borders, and cultural boundaries – perhaps the question that needs to be raised is no longer what it means to be American, but what America is to be. America was imagined and created out of a quest to realize a manifest destiny; its historical evolution depended upon the subjugation of conquered "others." A distinctly Filipino American perspective could contribute toward addressing the new question of what America is to be. If historical exclusion is largely responsible for the invisibility of Filipino Americans and Asian Americans more generally, that at least provides us with a starting point, a blank slate on which to write our own narratives and establish a visibility drawn from our own sensibilities.

NOTES

1 Examples of sociological and historical publications include those by Maria M. Root, Barbara Posada, Lily Mendoza, Jonathan Okamura, Leny Strobel, Rick Bonus, and Cathy Ceniza-Choy. Literary works include those published by Luis Francia, Eric Gamalinda, Marianne Villanueva, and Cecilia Manguerra-Brainard, among others. Cultural performances have proliferated among Filipino Americans, including theater by groups such as Ma-yi and Tongue-in-a-Mood; dance theater such as those by Pearl Ubungen and Alleuia Panis; music by groups such as Mahal and Bobby Banduiria; many artists in rap, hip-hop, and turn-tablism such as Q-Bert. In film there have been a number of documentaries, short and full-length feature films by directors such as Francisco Aliwalas, Rod Pulido, and Gene Cajayon. There are many more artists in visual arts, such as Manuel Ocampo and Carl Angel, in design and architecture, as well as in the culinary and martial arts.

2 For example, should "Filipino American" be scrapped and be replaced with "Filipino" to label this field? While I acknowledge that Filipino studies would be more inclusive

(since not all Filipinos in the United States consider themselves Filipino American), I also believe that a distinct Filipino American discourse is necessary to provide focus on the experience of Filipinos within the body politic of the United States.

3 Policies made by the United States regarding the Indian Wars, the 1846 war against Mexico, and the subjugation of Native Americans and Mexicans were the same policies extended to the Philippines and the colonial subjugation of Filipinos in 1899.

4 For example, during the 1992 presidential campaigns, presidential hopeful Patrick Buchanan based part of his campaign on what he declared to be a culture war. He promoted the preservation of "American values" against those who supposedly threatened them, such as immigrants (with their non-English languages) and gays and lesbians (with their non-heterosexual lifestyles).

5 Annual conferences among Asian Americans reaffirm this. These conferences run the gamut from student conferences to political conventions to meetings of historical societies within specific Asian American groups.

6 Most of the fighting during World War II in the Philippines was carried out by Filipinos, not Americans. Thus, Filipinos had already liberated most of the Philippines by the time MacArthur fulfilled his promise to return.

7 See *Philippine News* (week of September 17, 2001), and *Filipinas* magazine (October 2001 issue).

8 Information on the airport screeners from PAWIS (People's Association of Workers and Immigrants) of the San Francisco Bay Area, a coalition of community and labor groups organized in October 2001 to support immigrant airport screeners who were threatened with layoffs at the Oakland, San Francisco, and San Jose airports.

9 There were differing contexts in the granting of citizenship. The 1st and 2nd Filipino Regiments were formed in the United States and numbered 7,000 at most. Within the context of the United States, this was not a racial threat compared to the hundreds of thousands in the Philippines incorporated into the USAFFE, who were initially promised citizenship but subsequently denied.

10 See "On Strike! San Francisco State College Strike, 1968–69," by Karen Umemoto (1989). The Third World Liberation Front (TWLF) at San Francisco State College, which gave birth to Asian American studies and other ethnic studies programs in 1968, was specific in its demand to establish a school of ethnic studies and have courses taught by third-world people. Having such a school was premised on the notion of "self-determination" for each of the marginalized ethnic groups that would make up the school: Black studies, Native American studies, La Raza studies, and Asian American studies. From the beginning, however, the TWLF was riven by factionalism. Some student groups did not support the TWLF, advocating to "go-it-alone" in establishing a curriculum for their own ethnic group. Those that joined the TWLF accused one another of narrow nationalism by advocating for their own ethnic group. The Asian American student organizations themselves were not unified, as Chinese American, Japanese American, and Filipino American students organized their own respective groups. The popular slogan of "yellow power" was not one that resonated with Filipino Americans.

11 The choice of using either the "F" or the "P" is a subjective one among writers, scholars, and community advocates. Thus, while there are supporters of either argument, there are also those who prefer to allow individual choice to reign.

12 Popular newsmagazines of the time, such as *Puck* and *Judge*, produced hundreds of colored political cartoons that caricatured Filipinos (along with Hawaiians, Native Americans, Puerto Ricans, Cubans, and Samoans) as dark-skinned primitives, children, or animals.

REFERENCES

Agoncillo, T. A. (1977) *History of the Filipino People*, 5th edn. R. P. Garcia Publishing Company, Quezon City, Philippines.

Bonus, R. (2000) *Locating Filipino American Ethnicity and Cultural Politics of Space*. Temple University Press, Philadelphia.

Bulosan, C. (1973, ca.1946) *America is in the Heart*. University of Washington Press, Seattle.

Campomanes, O. V. (1992) Filipinos in the United States and their literature of exile. In: Lim, S. G.-l. and Ling, A. (eds.) *Reading the Literatures of Asian America*. Temple University Press, Philadelphia, pp. 49–78.

Canlas, M. C. (2002) *SoMa Pilipinas: Studies 2000 in Two Languages*. Arkipelago Books, San Francisco.

Cordova, F. (1983) *Filipinos, Forgotten Asian Americans: A Pictorial Essay, 1763–circa 1963*. Kendall/Hunt Publishing Company, Dubuque, IA.

DeWitt, H. A. (1976) *Anti-Filipino Movements in California: A History, Bibliography, and Study Guide*. R and E Research Associates, San Francisco.

DeWitt, H. A. (1980) *Violence in the Fields: California Filipino Farm Labor Unionization during the Great Depression*. Century Twenty One Pub., Saratoga, CA.

Espiritu, Y. L. (1995) *Filipino American Lives*. Temple University Press, Philadelphia.

Fujita-Rony, D. B. (2003) *American Workers, Colonial Power: Philippine Seattle and the Transpacific West 1919–1941*. University of California Press, Berkeley.

Hing, B. O. (1994) *Making and Remaking Asian Americans Through Immigration Policy, 1850–1990*. Stanford University Press, Stanford.

Joaquin, N. (a.k.a. Quijano de Manila) (1998) A question of identity: bringing out the invisible Filipino in history. *The Making of the Filipino Nation and Republic from Barangays, Tribes, Sultanates, and Colony*. Abueva, J. V. (ed.). University of the Philippines Press, Quezon City, Philippines.

Kurashige, L. and Yang Murray, A. (2003) *Major Problems in Asian American History: Documents and Essays*. Houghton Mifflin, Boston.

Lasker, B. (1931) *Filipino Immigration to the Continental United States and to Hawai'i*. University of Chicago Press, Chicago.

Mendoza, S. L. L. (2001) *Between the Homeland and the Diaspora: The Politics of Theorizing Filipino and Filipino American Identities: A Second Look at the Poststructuralism–Indigenization Debates*. Routledge, New York.

Morales, R. F. (1974) *Makibaka: The Pilipino American Struggle*. Mountainview Publishers, Inc., Los Angeles.

Okamura, J. Y. (1998) *Imagining the Filipino American Diaspora: Transnational Relations, Identities, and Communities*. Garland Pub., New York.

Ono, K. (1995) Re/signing "Asian American": rhetorical problematics of nation. *Amerasia Journal* 21(1–2): 67–78.

Revilla, L.A. (1997) Filipino American identity: transcending the crisis. In: Root, M. P. P. (ed.).

Root, M. P. P. (ed.) (1997) *Filipino Americans: Transformation and Identity.* Sage Publications, Thousand Oaks, CA.

Rydell, R. W. (1984) *All the World's a Fair: Visions of Empire at American International Expositions 1876–1916.* University of Chicago Press, Chicago.

Schirmer, D. B. (1972) *Republic or Empire: American Resistance to the Philippine War.* Schenkman Pub. Co., Cambridge, MA.

Strobel, L. M. (2001) *Coming Full Circle: The Process of Decolonization Among Post 1965 Filipino Americans.* Giraffe Books, Quezon City, Philippines.

Takaki, R. T. (1998) *Strangers from a Different Shore: A History of Asian Americans,* updated and rev. edn. Little, Brown and Company, Boston.

Trouillot, M.-R. (1995) *Silencing the Past: Power and the Production of History.* Beacon Press, Boston.

Umemoto, K. (1989) On strike! San Francisco State College strike, 1968–69. *Amerasia Journal* 15(1): 3–41.

Vera Cruz, P. (1992) *Philip Vera Cruz.* Scharlin, C. and Villanueva, L. (eds.). UCLA Labor Center and Asian American Studies Center, Los Angeles.

Vergara, B. M., Jr. (1995) *Displaying Filipinos: Photography and Colonialism in Early 20th Century Philippines.* University of the Philippines Press, Quezon City, Philippines.

CHAPTER TEN

Rethinking Asian American Agency: Understanding the Complexity of Race and Citizenship in America

Taro Iwata

As has been demonstrated by the essays in this volume, scholars have begun to contest the basic principle of traditional Asian American studies orthodoxy that assumes victimhood of Asian immigrants/Asian Americans, and its flip-side which celebrates the oppositional agency of a supposedly united Asian America. Therefore, we are faced with two crucial questions: What will be the effect of this questioning of traditional assumptions in Asian American studies? And how should we understand and approach the potentially divisive issue of historical conflicts among Asian American groups?

In this chapter, I argue that a comparative framework of ethnic histories, especially the relationships among Asian American groups and other groups of color, may offer a solution to the ongoing reevaluation of Asian American victimhood and panethnicity. This type of scholarship has the potential to help us correctly understand both the collusive and the conflictive origins of Asian American panethnic identity and thus to enable us to situate in a larger framework seemingly problematic attempts by one Asian American group to undermine another Asian American group, or other groups of color. More importantly, this comparative approach offers a nuanced understanding of race and citizenship in America. Therefore, this chapter will call on historians to undertake more comparative research of relationships among and between different Asian American groups, as well as with other groups of color. In order to demonstrate the potential of such analyses to advance the field of Asian American studies, in the next section I will briefly review and critique the recent emergence of this type of scholarship. Then I will use my own case study on the relationship between Native Hawaiians and Japanese immigrants/

Japanese Americans in prewar Hawai'i to pinpoint theoretical challenges in conceptualizing a study of this kind. Finally, I will discuss how comparative approaches can improve our understanding of existing and historical dimensions of power in Asian America.

The Rise of Comparative Ethnic Histories

Over the past two decades a stimulating body of comparative ethnic histories has emerged in the field of Asian American studies. This kind of research first appeared in the 1960s and 1970s when the first phase of Asian American studies emphasized the victimization of Asian Americans. Most notable among this scholarship is the work of Roger Daniels.[1] However, in the 1980s a new group of mostly Asian American scholars started to react to these earlier notions of victimhood by celebrating Asian American agency, often by idealizing Asian American panethnicity against white racism. Then in the 1990s, a younger generation of historians began to struggle in order to understand the undeniable actions of Asian American groups to undermine each other, or other racial groups. Comparative approaches to ethnic histories of Asian Americans therefore emerged in part as responses to the earlier discourses of victimization and romanticized Asian American unity.

Unlike traditional Asian American historical analysis, these studies either compare Asian Americans with other groups of color (for example, Native Americans and Native Hawaiians) or contrast two or more Asian American groups to illuminate or allude to power imbalances among those groups. By touching on competitions among groups of color, this body of literature potentially leads to the rethinking of issues of Asian American solidarity and agency. The emergent historiography includes Ronald Takaki's monumental *Pau Hana: Plantation Life and Labor in Hawaii* (1983), and his *Strangers from a Different Shore: A History of Asian Americans* (1989), Chris Friday's *Organizing Asian American Labor: The Pacific Coast Canned-Salmon Industry, 1870–1942* (1994), and "Competing Communities at Work: Asian Americans, European Americans, and Native Alaskans in the Salmon Canneries of the Pacific Northwest" (1999); Gail Nomura's "Within the Law: The Establishment of Filipino Leasing Rights on the Yakima Indian Reservation" (1994), and her upcoming book, *Contested Terrain: Japanese Americans on the Yakima Indian Reservation*. We might also consider Daniel Liestman's "Horizontal InterEthnic Relations: Chinese and American Indians in the Nineteenth Century American West" (1999); Tomás Almaguer's "Racial Domination and Class Conflict in Capitalist Agriculture: The 1903 Oxnard Sugar Beet Workers' Strike" (1984), which discusses Japanese–Mexican cooperation on labor issues; and Eiichiro Azuma's "Interethnic Conflict Under Racial Subordination: Japanese Immigrants and Their Asian Neighbors in Walnut Grove, California, 1908–1941" (1994) and "Racial Struggle, Immigrant

Nationalism, and Ethnic Identity: Japanese and Filipinos in the California Delta, 1930–1941" (1998). Although written outside the field of history, Yen Le Espiritu's *Asian American Panethnicity: Bridging Institutions and Identities* (1992) is also worth mentioning here.[2]

How do these works deal with the issue of Asian American agency, and what are their strengths and weaknesses? Let us analyze some particular examples. One problem inherent in a comparative ethnic study of Asian Americans that tends to obscure rather than to elucidate issues is some historians' well-meaning sensitivity to Asian American unity. For instance, Takaki (1983) focused on the 1920 sugar strike on the island of Oʻahu, Hawaiʻi, in which over 4,000 Japanese plantation laborers joined 2,000 Filipino colleagues already striking for a higher wage to compensate for the skyrocketing post-World War I inflation. Takaki does note that Native Hawaiians, Chinese, and Koreans were hired by sugar planters as strikebreakers, thereby alluding to potentially conflicting interests of groups of color in prewar Hawaiʻi. However, his narrative tends to focus on and celebrate Asian American agency and pan-Asian American alliance. According to Takaki:

> Men and women of different ethnicities, remembering how they had lived and labored together on the plantations, now fought together to reach the same goal [...] Feeling a new sense of cooperation and unity that transcended ethnic boundaries, the leaders of the Japanese Federation of Labor questioned the validity of "blood unionism" and the existence of two separate labor unions, one for the Japanese and another for the Filipinos, and suggested the consolidation of the two federations into one union. (1983: 174)

Other historians dispute this interpretation for lack of evidence. Masayo Umezawa Duus (1999), for example, offers many proofs that Filipino-Japanese cooperation during the strike was only strategic, and lacked consistency. As she notes, "[Filipino strike leader Pablo] Manlapit's decision [on February 8, 1920, eight days after the Japanese joined the striking Filipinos] to call off the strike deepened the Japanese laborers' contempt for the Filipinos and widened the rift between them. The Federation of Japanese Labor continued to provide the Filipinos with monetary assistance, but they no longer trusted or relied on them" (78). It follows, as Moon-Kie Jung (2002) argues, that the existing scholarship on prewar Hawaiʻi produced "an inadequate grasp of the racial inequality and division between Japanese and Filipino workers" due to "an anachronistic deployment of a pan-Asian racial category and an attenuated conceptualization of racism" (77).

Azuma's work (1994), on the other hand, stands out as a study of interethnic conflict among various Asian American groups. He examines how and why Japanese immigrants and their US-citizen children in prewar Walnut Grove, California, perceived and dealt with their Chinese, East Indian, and Filipino neighbors as potential or real competitors. During this era many Japanese believed that the Chinese would not only jeopardize the Japanese economic base, but would also socially damage a positive image of the Japanese in California, which these issei (first-generation Japanese immigrants) believed existed. Other Asian immigrants were seen as threats to Japanese employment and economic prosperity. For example, as an indirect means to control the Chinese "threat" to farm employment, some Japanese immigrants helped local police control Chinese gambling houses in the 1900s, and in 1920 marched throughout Chinatown, chanting anti-Chinese slogans. In the mid-1910s, the Japanese successfully drove many of their East Indian competitors out of the asparagus fields in the California Delta. Japanese immigrants also vilified Filipino men as a "menace" to Japanese racial purity, fearing that Filipino men might prey upon Japanese women, because of the dearth of Filipino women in the area. Azuma's work is exceptional, because it focuses on the attempts by Japanese immigrants and Japanese Americans to undermine other Asians.[3]

It should be noted, however, that Azuma sees the political and economic structures of white domination as the ultimate cause of fierce intra-Asian immigrant competitions and Japanese actions to damage other Asians' interests. At one point Azuma does acknowledge external and transnational factors such as the racial prejudice the Japanese brought from their homeland and existing Japanese–Chinese antagonisms in Asia (and beyond) from this period. Nevertheless, he represents white racism as the most important cause for problematic Japanese agency. In his words, "the Issei had virtually no control over their own destiny" and thus were at the mercy of white landowners, who had the options of hiring fieldhands from other Asian groups (1994: 47). Therefore, he suggests that the Japanese (and, for that matter, other Asian immigrants) had no choice other than to undermine each other in order to survive fierce economic competition. In this way, Azuma does acknowledge the competitions between Asian American groups that Takaki glossed over, but, in the end, he inadvertently reinforces an older explanation of white domination. This emphasis on white racism, a source of unity and contemporary empowerment, shifts much of Asian American individuals' responsibilities for their problematic actions to dominant whites. As a result, it paradoxically deprives Asian immigrants and Asian Americans of their agency – both good and bad.

Chris Friday's works (1994, 1999) may be situated somewhere in between the approaches taken by Azuma and Takaki. Friday openly acknowledges competitions and hostilities over canneries employment among Native Alaskans, Chinese, Japanese, Filipino, Koreans, Native Hawaiians, American Indians, Mexicans, and African Americans, among others, in the prewar Alaska labor market. Using much space in his works to discuss the details of these groups' conflicting interests, Friday confronts efforts among these groups to undermine each other. But for Friday, the struggles he identifies represent the beginning of a process in which previously competing groups of color transcend ethnic hostilities and adopt a new, shared laborer identity. In fact, three major Asian groups – Chinese,

Japanese, and Filipinos – successfully formed a strong interethnic labor alliance in the 1930s and 1940s, which materialized and lasted despite the worsening of the Sino-Japanese War. Friday's scholarship is informed in part by the tendency in classic labor history to privilege class over race, and thus highlights the formation of an interethnic worker identity instead of Asian American panethnicity. Nonetheless, he offers a useful model for comparative approaches on Asian American history that enables a more flexible understanding of interethnic tensions and alliances.

As we have seen, the existing comparative ethnic histories of Asian American relations among themselves and other groups of color have the potential to open our eyes to new and stimulating issues within the field of Asian American studies. Chief among these are issues of power in previously understudied relationships among Asian Americans and also among different groups of color. I also wish to show that as innovative as the new type of scholarship might be, it also tends to remain ambivalent with regard to a pair of issues: problematic Asian American agency and Asian American unity. These issues in fact constitute two sides of the same coin, because there seems to be an apprehension among many Asian Americanists that the basis of intra-Asian American cooperation might be jeopardized if scholars focus on the history of conflicts among Asian Americans. In any case, one might still locate these issues within these studies by reading between the lines in order to explore: (1) relationships among different groups of color with potentially conflicting interests; (2) cases in which victims of racism can themselves benefit from white domination, from which they simultaneously suffer; and (3) how notions of race and citizenship developed in multiethnic settings, in often surprising and fascinating ways.

With the recent trend to reject essentialist interpretations of history (i.e., seeing whites only as victimizers and groups of color only as victims), comparative ethnic histories of Asian Americans offer new opportunities to more closely examine both colluding and contested factors in the development of Asian American panethnicity. This, I argue, will in turn lead to a more subtle understanding of the existing diversity of various Asian American groups, and also of the structure of white domination. For instance, it must be recognized that these groups of color shared many common experiences as victims of white racism, but at the same time they might have many stakes in white racism. More importantly, comparative ethnic histories would enable us to address an understudied topic in the field. For example, we may better understand how, despite some initial and current intra-Asian American group conflicts, a significant Asian American identity and solidarity evolved. Flexible interpretations of comparative scholarship would allow us to build on the current Asian American studies efforts to resist essentialism, and to be more inclusive and diverse. In this way, the comparative approach to Asian America helps us to avoid the tendency toward simplistic conceptualizations of power in single ethnic scholarship.

Simultaneously, comparative *race* studies, which are emerging in various sub-fields of history, may also be undertaken.

In fact, a comparative ethnic assessment of Asian America may be used to strengthen the ties between the fields of Asian American studies and ethnic studies at large. For example, there has been a rapid and solid build-up of a body of literature examining the historical relationships between Native Americans and African Americans. This body of work includes Daniel Littlefield's *The Cherokee Freedman: From Emancipation to American Citizenship* (1978); Donald Grinde and Quintard Taylor's "Red vs. Black: Conflict and Accommodation in the Post Civil War Indian Territory, 1865–1907" (1984); Katja May's *African Americans and Native Americans in Creek and Cherokee Nations, 1830s to 1920s: Collision and Collusion* (1996); and Circe Sturm's "Blood Politics, Racial Classification, and Cherokee National Identity" (2002). These studies, with their analyses of both conflicts and cooperation between American Indians and blacks, provide a model for comparative studies of groups of color. Since the comparative relational histories of Native Americans and African Americans have for some time debated and theorized on the issue of America's indigenous peoples and African Americans – many of whom were slaves or ex-slaves – trying to undermine each other, similar studies on Asian American relations could benefit from exchanges with this fast-developing scholarship. Comparative race histories of Asian Americans, African Americans, and Native Americans would together shed light on the issues of agency and white domination, and therefore advance not only Asian American studies but also the larger field of ethnic studies.[4]

Such approaches to Asian America may cross nation-state boundaries, and thus enter into transnational debates. Currently, my own scholarship compares how Japanese immigrants related to local populations in two multiracial, multiethnic locations: Hawai'i, where the Japanese were racialized and discriminated against, and Manchuria (the northeastern region of China), where the Japanese were colonial masters, in the same prewar period. The duality of prewar Japanese immigrant statuses – simultaneously victims in one location and victimizers in another – not only provides a crucial example to challenge die-hard, singular notions of power and domination, but also offers a fresh opportunity to illuminate the geopolitical dimensions of race/ethnicity and citizenship in historical and sociological contexts. The possibilities for this type of research are infinite. One may build upon studies of Chinese and East Indian diaspora to investigate Chinese/Indian relationships with other groups of color in multiracial locations, such as Chicago, London, and Nairobi; or one may compare how Filipino immigrants dealt with Native Americans in Washington's Yakima Indian Reservations, Native Hawaiians in Hawai'i, and Native Alaskans in Alaska in the prewar period. Yet another possibility is to analyze interactions between Mexican Americans and different Asian American groups in the US–Mexican borderlands.

To be sure, there are certain drawbacks to this comparative ethnic approach. An obvious danger is lopsidedness. Depending on the historian's linguistic and research ability, as well as the scope of coverage and the availability of sources, the discussion of one group may become thinner than that of another. Furthermore, theoretical contributions of comparative ethnic studies may be negatively affected by the insufficient conceptualization of the overall framework. But, if done correctly, I maintain that this type of scholarship will enable us to see what we tend to overlook in single-ethnicity, single-race studies. In the next section, I will use my own work to discuss some of the challenges of writing comparative histories.

Challenges in Writing Comparative Ethnic Histories

I experienced both technical and theoretical difficulties in undertaking my work-in-progress, tentatively entitled "Race and Citizenship as American Geopolitics: Japanese and Native Hawaiians in Hawai'i, 1900–1941." This research compares political, economic, and social strategies of Japanese immigrants, Japanese Americans (nisei), and Native Hawaiians in a multiracial, multiethnic setting where these groups coexisted with whites, Chinese, Filipino, Koreans, Portuguese, and Puerto Ricans. A major goal of this project is to analyze the relationship between indigenous Hawaiians and Japanese immigrants/nisei. The technical challenges I encountered include difficulty in contextualizing the actions of only three groups – Japanese immigrants, Japanese Americans, and Native Hawaiians – when there were so many other groups present on the islands. I also found it difficult to cover a sufficient time span so that readers could grasp seemingly ironic and contradictory workings of American citizenship, both of which occurred in the prewar period. I tried to deal with the first issue by establishing the primacy of the Japanese and Native Hawaiian groups in the islands during this period, and by addressing the other groups wherever and whenever they had significant impact on the Japanese–Hawaiian relationship, and on the politics and society of Hawai'i as a whole. I tried to solve the second issue by extending the coverage of my study to the first four decades of the twentieth century, two of which saw a relative political rise of Native Hawaiians at the cost of the political emasculation of Japanese and other Asian immigrants (1900 to mid-1920s), and one in which Japanese Americans rose politically, largely at the cost of Native Hawaiians (1930–1941).

Theoretical difficulties, however, were far more challenging. They included finding convincing frameworks to explain why two groups of color, both victims of white racism, tried to undermine each other, rather than to cooperate to resist white domination. Also, how could Native Hawaiians, who made conscious efforts to undermine the Japanese, be disempowered in large part by their former victims? How did the structure of white domination figure into the relationship between Native Hawaiians and Japanese immigrants/Japanese Americans? In order to address these issues, I first had to pinpoint the factors that mediated the relationship between the Hawaiians and the Japanese, as well as between Native Hawaiians and whites. This also required a reassessment of existing scholarship on how the Japanese related to whites in Hawai'i. This was not an easy task; there seemed to be so many mediating factors – from business competition, to intermarriage, to justice – and I had to locate the most important ones from them. What proved even more difficult was to shift my focus from white racism to "problematic" behaviors of groups of color. Would it not compromise my argument about the primacy of white domination? In the end, I took that risk. By focusing on the seemingly problematic agency of Native Hawaiians and the Japanese, I tried to strengthen my argument about white dominance, suggesting that white racism derives much of its strength from the investment of peoples of color in the structure of white domination. What did I select to include in my narrative of modern Hawaiian history to achieve this end? In the following paragraphs, I will discuss a small fraction of my overall historical narrative. Readers will notice that I tried not to shift Japanese and Native Hawaiian responsibilities to white racism, but at the same time made connections between "problematic" actions of these groups of color and the larger factors in white domination, i.e., law, citizenship, and US geopolitical interest.

The indigenous Kingdom of Hawai'i has been the site of a constant power struggle since its first Western contact in 1778, especially over the issue of non-native land ownership. After the legalization of private land ownership in 1848, the kingdom's economy became increasingly reliant on sugar plantations, which were operated by a handful of white missionaries and their descendants. These planters purchased vast amounts of land, previously held communally by Native Hawaiians, and became increasingly dominant in the kingdom's politics. Meanwhile, the islands' Chinese and Japanese populations increased rapidly during this period, as the white planters began relying on Asian laborers to replace Native Hawaiian fieldworkers. This laid the foundation for political and economic competitions among Native Hawaiians, Asians, and whites in the next century. At the same time, many of the plantation operators started to advocate the annexation of the indigenous kingdom to the United States in order to obtain better market conditions for their product, and to eliminate political risk in their profitable mega-business. The white annexationists' interests were closely aligned with the increasing US geopolitical interest in the Pacific and Asia. The political tension in the kingdom eventually culminated in the 1893 overthrow of Queen Lili'uokalani and the establishment the following year of the white-controlled Republic of Hawai'i. The United States eventually annexed the islands in 1898, ignoring petitions opposing annexation that were signed by more than half of the Native Hawaiian population. In 1900, Hawai'i became an incorporated territory of the United States, effectively ending Native Hawaiians' anti-annexation, pro-independence struggles.

Hawai'i's new status as an integral part of the United States had a significant impact on the citizenship status of Native Hawaiians, Japanese immigrants, and their descendants. One of the most important changes was the extension of the US Constitution to this incorporated territory (and not to the Philippines, an unincorporated territory). As a result, the Hawai'i-born descendants of Asian immigrants automatically became US citizens, based on the *jus soli* principle (acquisition of citizenship at birth) in the Fourteenth Amendment. However, their parents, not being "free white persons" within the meaning of US naturalization laws, were ineligible to become American citizens. Meanwhile, Native Hawaiians, formerly ineligible to naturalize as US citizens, were suddenly declared citizens because a federal law that stipulated that citizens of the Republic of Hawai'i – the vast majority of them Native Hawaiians – were now US citizens. In this way, Native Hawaiians were empowered overnight, holding the majority of registered votes.

Therefore, the Territory of Hawai'i at the turn of the century became a fascinating outpost of the expanding US "empire," where a small minority of whites maintained ultimate political power, with Native Hawaiians controlling many elected and appointed government jobs. Asian immigrant laborers – more than the majority of the total population – were thus deprived of a means of political participation. Since much of the Asian American community was still below voting age, whites and Native Hawaiians were able to dominate territorial politics. During the first two decades of the twentieth century, Native Hawaiians formed a strategic alliance with whites to suppress the potential rise of Asians in the island economy and politics. Together with white legislators, Native Hawaiian politicians helped pass the 1903 Citizenship Labor Act, which excluded those who were ineligible to naturalize – namely Asians – from government jobs.

However, this initial empowerment of Native Hawaiians was short-lived. As the population of second-generation, US-citizen Asians rose dramatically, along with that of the newcomers from the continental United States (many of them military personnel who were sent to the islands in order to fortify the territory against potential Japanese geopolitical threat), Native Hawaiians surrendered much of their political influence, and in 1922 they lost their majority voter status. As an increasing number of Asian Americans reached voting age in the 1920s and 1930s, Japanese Americans began to be elected and appointed to offices, gradually replacing Native Hawaiians. In this way, US citizenship, which had initially empowered Native Hawaiians, later worked to disempower them. Strangely, it was during this prewar era when a part of the basis for local identity – a social alliance of groups of color defined against whites – was formulated. Most notably, after the 1931 Massie case, in which Native Hawaiians and Asian Americans were accused of an alleged rape of a white woman, Native Hawaiians and Asian Americans started to share a common sense of injustice and victimhood at the hands of whites. Local identity began to emerge in the late 1960s along with the rise of Asian American identity on the continental United States. What made this identity unique is that the Native Hawaiians implicitly extended legitimacy to the Asian American presence in the islands by agreeing to participate in this panethnicity. However, this local identity has been merely a strategic alliance for Native Hawaiians. In the early 1970s, Native Hawaiians launched an independent Native Hawaiian movement that excluded both Asians and whites, sharply focusing on their claims to the land of Hawai'i as well as Hawaiian nationhood. To this day, Native Hawaiians use both of these strategies – one that positions them as non-white US citizens along with Asian Americans, and another that positions the native people as a nation, and as having exclusive claims to the land and sovereignty of Hawai'i against non-indigenous peoples, including Asian Americans.

Victimhood and Power

As we have seen, historical disempowerment and victimization of groups of color can differ drastically, which makes it difficult simply to categorize those groups as sharing a victim status resulting from white racism. Then, how should historians address this issue? I propose that we shift some of our focus from white racism and domination to recognizing diverse and inherent interests of groups of color, some of which might exist outside the framework of white domination. Without such a paradigm shift, I argue, it would become very difficult to understand fully why groups of color at times tried to undermine each other, rather than to cooperate. To move part of our focus away from white domination may not be easy, since we have long assumed that the power imbalance between whites and peoples of color in substantial part shaped experiences of these groups. Here, I am not disputing this assumption, which I believe is still very valid. But it should not be the only explanation. Likewise, unless we confront the problematic agency of Asian Americans, we would not be able to fully grasp the development of Asian American identity, and, more importantly, the structure of white domination.

Here, it might be useful to analyze dimensions of power in the Asian American community. Based on my analysis in this chapter, I argue that the notions of power for Asian Americans have always been double-sided: historical victimization, and paradoxical empowerment from the construction of Asian American history as one of disempowerment. In addition, earlier limitations on citizenship privilege, social mobility, and economic opportunities served as an important basis for developing a shared Asian American identity as common victims of white racism. According to Michael Omi (1997: 17):

> Prior to the late 1960s...there were no people who identified as "Asian Americans." In the wake of the civil rights movement, distinct Asian ethnic groups, primarily Chinese, Japanese, Filipino and Korean Americans, began to frame and assert their "common identity" as Asian Americans...The panethnic organization of Asian Americans involved the muting of profound cultural and linguistic

differences and significant historical antagonisms, which existed among the distinct nationalities and ethnic groups of Asian origin. In spite of diversity and difference, Asian American activists found the political label a crucial rallying point for raising political consciousness about the problems in Asian ethnic communities and in asserting demands on political institutions.

The prior exclusions became the foundation of Asian American demands for political, social, and economic equality, as well as compensation. This strategy has in general worked well to empower Asian Americans. It was especially effective in combating violence against Asian Americans, winning reparations for Japanese internment, obtaining funding for Asian American social services, and establishing Asian American Studies programs at many US universities, among other achievements. Moreover, according to Espiritu (1992: 161), this panethnicity was an Asian American way to express agency, to reclaim "Asian America," which was originally an arbitrary imposition by the dominant group. She suggests that effectiveness and potential benefits of Asian American panethnicity derives from its collective bargaining position against the dominant group:

> Pan-Asian unity is necessary if Asian Americans are to contest systems of racism and inequality in American society – systems that seek to exclude, marginalize, and homogenize them. Given the external pressures and the benefits it promises, panethnicity, in contrast to [single] ethnic particularism or assimilation, may well define the future of ethnicity for other racial minority groups in the United States as well. (175)

Therefore, for Espiritu, pan-Asian American identity, which is based on collective disempowerment, would remain a major source of power for Asian Americans in the future, even though Asian America is increasingly marked by heterogeneity and hybridity.[5]

However, traditional Asian American panethnic empowerment strategy has been facing serious challenges since the early 1990s. As other racial and ethnic groups began to question the long-assumed victim status of Asian Americans, the traditional notions of power in Asian America were to a degree destabilized. Most visible examples include the conflicts between African American and Korean immigrants/Korean Americans in several large US cities, and the Native Hawaiian accusations of "Asian settler colonialism" in Hawai'i. During the 1990s, especially following the 1992 Los Angeles rebellions, many African Americans viewed Koreans as being "on the other side" with whites.[6] By contrast, the Koreans preferred to represent themselves as a scapegoat in-between whites and blacks. In adopting this representation, Korean Americans are, like their African American neighbors, victims of white racism and African American misunderstanding, and thus to a large extent helpless. This kind of rhetoric has been used often to neutralize black criticisms, but seems to have failed to convince African Americans.[7]

Meanwhile, in Hawai'i, the rise of the Native Hawaiian sovereignty movement in the early 1990s threatened Asian American victimhood in two ways: first, some Native Hawaiians equated Asian Americans with whites as colonial settlers, and, secondly, the native movement's emphasis on the indigenous people's exclusive claims to the lands and sovereignty of Hawai'i destabilized the foundation of the existing local identity – the exclusion of the *haole* or whites by Asian Americans and Native Hawaiians as common victims of white racism.[8] Although the development in the islands did not affect Asian American panethnicity on the continental United States, it nevertheless showed, along with the black questioning of Asian American victimhood, the limitations of the traditional empowerment strategy of Asian Americans.

Can existing Asian American panethnicity fully address the challenges from African Americans and Native Hawaiians? To be sure, the panethnic notion is open to many theoretical contradictions. For example, Espiritu acknowledges the existing divisions among Asian Americans in a detailed manner (i.e., Filipino American attempts to privilege Filipino identity over Asian American panethnic identity). However, Espiritu does not seem to have anticipated the questioning of Asian American victimhood. Likewise, many Asian Americanists and Asian Americans do not appear to have been theoretically prepared to meet the challenges. In this sense, the assumption of victimization of Asian Americans has grown somewhat rigid, and unable to address new issues, especially those which are framed in poststructuralist ways. The traditional dimension of power of Asian Americans, therefore, requires rethinking and reinterpretation. One possible solution may be to move our analysis away from white racism.

Conclusion

Shifting attention away from white racism in comparative ethnic histories is a strategic move that leads ultimately to a renewed and more complete refocus on white domination. In that sense, the paradigm shift will allow us to see complexity in simplicity (i.e., white racism), and vice versa. In this scheme, the structure of white domination is not perceived as a dichotomous relationship between whites and non-whites, but as a complex web of distinct and shifting interests among communities of people, which are in large part formed by definitions of race and citizenship at the time. This approach enables us to see Asian Americans for who they really were – both victims and potential victimizers – and at the same time to explore how groups of color were at times responsible for the reinforcement of white racism. In the words of the Asian American legal scholar Frank H. Wu (2003: 9):

> Interracial conflict among people of color is a complicated problem, with much blame to be shared. Asian Americans have been both perpetrators and victims,

sometimes simultaneously so, rendering the terms "perpetrator" and "victim" less useful than inflammatory by giving up pragmatism for blame. At the very least, Asian Americans should concede responsibility for some of the problems...

But then, at what cost? To confront Asian American "complicity," I argue, would in turn paradoxically empower us with a more accurate and healthy understanding of Asian America – both imagined and real. Furthermore, exploring struggles among groups of color produces the opportunity to uncover the ways in which their efforts to acquire full citizenship privileges enjoyed by whites was central to those conflicts. In this way, the primacy of white domination in Asian American history is reconfirmed, and at the same time, the complexity of race and citizenship in America would be illuminated.

On a related issue, rather than to rely solely on the traditional "divide and rule" theory to explain aspects of white domination, one may also consider the distinct interests of groups of color. In fact, how can one divide what was not necessarily one in the beginning? This new approach offers a strategic focus away from imagined, ahistorical Asian American panethnicity in order to rediscover the ways in which Asian Americans left behind some of their conflicting interests. In other words, in comparative ethnic histories, we can examine the processes of becoming Asian American, or, more precisely, overcoming initial conflicting interests. This process, in turn, enables us to better explain the preeminence of white domination. It should be noted that there were at times significant levels of cooperation and solidarity against whites among Asian Americans, and between Asian Americans and other groups of color. I am suggesting that we study collision to understand collusion, and vice versa.

In this sense, a reinterpretation of existing comparative Asian American histories, such as those carried out by Ronald Takaki, Chris Friday, and Eiichiro Azuma, offers us opportunities to address intricate dimensions of power in Asian America. Takaki's work shows how Japanese and Filipino immigrant laborers in Hawai'i in 1920 used their common victimhood to forge a strategic alliance against white racism, but in the end failed. When we shift our attention from white domination, we can transcend Takaki's well-meaning focus on Asian American unity. As a result, we would be able to notice how the Japanese–Filipino panethnic cooperation was founded on independent and at times contradictory interests of these groups. Friday's works about pan-Asian labor alliance in the 1930s and 1940s in Alaska shows the intersections of class and panethnicity, both of which may be based on shared experiences of victimization. His works are informed by a tendency to privilege class over race/ethnicity, and in that sense are incompatible with the basic tenets of Asian American studies. Nevertheless, they offer a model for comparative ethnic histories of Asian Americans, in which initial intra-Asian immigrant conflicts can be interpreted as an important basis for the overall development process of a pan-Asian American alliance. Azuma's article, which focuses on Japanese immigrants' efforts to undermine other Asian groups in California in the prewar period, also provides a model for comparative scholarship. By analyzing non-dichotomous aspects of power within several Asian immigrant communities, Azuma's work point to the possibilities of new conceptual frameworks in Asian American histories.

In conclusion, I advocate undertaking a more comparative ethnic historical approach to Asian America, and engaging in exchanges with other similar scholarship on, for example, the relationship between Native Americans and African Americans. This approach will enable us to reach a fuller understanding of our agency, our Asian American identity, and our place in America. On a final note, shifting our focus from white domination does not mean that comparative ethnic histories will let white racism off the hook. Quite the contrary. Confronting our ancestors' problematic agency will put them on the same moral footing with the dominant group, which will in turn empower the ancestors. The study of Asian America should empower, rather than languishing in an agency-free victimhood.[9]

If previous victimization was our major source of power in Asian America in the past thirty years, and now that part of this victim status is starting to be questioned, it is time that we move on. Furthermore, facing our own agency, both good and bad, is the best way to overcome the model minority myth of Asian Americans. When we do, we will no longer need overcompensating Asian American media works such as *Better Luck Tomorrow* (2003) – Asian American youth characters in this MTV film are criminals and murderers in order to dispel the model minority image. Asian Americans, after all, have always been engaged in problematic actions in their history.

NOTES

1 This kind of white scholars' advocacy of peoples of color's victimhood – such as that of Daniels – is criticized for downplaying those peoples' agency. As Christine Clark, education professor at New Mexico State University and co-editor of *Becoming and Unbecoming White* (Westport, CT: Bergin & Garvey, 1999), said in an interview, some whites view themselves as "saviors," and they "only feel comfortable if they are working with people of color with a victim-focused identity. That takes agency away from people of color" (Rodriguez, 1999).
2 Some journalistic essays – such as AnnaMarie Vu's "Is Asian American Pan-Ethnicity Realistic?" (April 2003): 6–7 – are also useful as interpretive aids for Asian American comparative ethnic histories.
3 Azuma seems to share an awareness of problematic Asian American agency with his mentor, the late Yuji Ichioka. Ichioka, in his 1997 *Amerasia* article entitled "The Meaning of Loyalty: The Case of Kazumaro Buddy Uno," wrote about a nisei named Buddy Uno who worked for and naïvely supported Japanese military during World War II, and as a consequence had been seen in the Japanese American community as a traitor and a "disloyal nisei." For Ichioka, Uno's loyalty to Japan should not be

considered problematic, since the dominant group rejected the notion of loyal nisei in the first place. According to the historian:

> Since he was on the Japanese side during the Pacific War, Uno has been banished into historical oblivion as a *persona non grata*. His case raises a fundamental historical question. What is the meaning of loyalty in a racist society? Speaking specifically in terms of Japanese-Americans, how can white America justifiably classify any Nisei as disloyal when it itself refused to accept the Nisei as Americans? Rephrased in another way, how can the category of a disloyal Nisei have any meaning in a society which overwhelmingly rejected the Nisei on racial grounds? If we place Uno, with all of his faults, within the framework of these questions, there is no justification for treating him as a disloyal Nisei and keeping him beyond the pale of Japanese-American history. That history cannot and must not be an exclusive one of so-called loyal Japanese-Americans. In order to fully comprehend the Nisei generation in all its complexities, it must become inclusive. And that entails bringing Kazumaro Buddy Uno back within the pale and granting him – and other Nisei like him – a rightful place in Japanese-American history. (62–3)

In this way, Ichioka's study of nisei's diversity and problematic agency stayed within the traditional Asian American studies paradigm of disempowerment and victimhood. For more on nisei's agency during prewar and Pacific War periods, see Stephan (1997).

4 Foley (1997) and Leiker (2002) might be included in this category.
5 See, for example, Lee (1994: 188).
6 For arguments that position Asian immigrants and Asian Americans on the side of whites against African Americans, see, for example, Warren and Twine (1997). In fact, a large number of Asian Americans, like many whites, seem to feel that affirmative action and social welfare programs give unfair advantages for African Americans. As legal scholar Keith Aoki noted: "Affirmative Action creates an opposition between Latinas/os, African-Americans, and Asian-Americans. Latinas/os and African-Americans may find commonality in opposing the end to such programs, but what are we to make of attempts to deploy Asian Americans as 'victims' of Affirmative Action (along with White males)? What could this mean?" (1997: 189). Also see Omi and Takagi (1996) and Gee (2001).
7 Jo (1992) and Umemoto (1994). Also see the *Amerasia* journal's special issue on the relationship between Asian (Korean) Americans and African Americans, vol. 19, no. 2 (1993).
8 For discussion of the local identity, see Kosasa (1994); Chang (1996); Fujikane (1994, 2000); Rosa (2000); Edles (2004); Okamura (1980, 1994, 1998); Yamamoto (1979); Sumida (1991); Ohnuma (2002); Kwon (1999); Carroll (2000); and Kanuha (1999).
9 Some Asian American scholars recognize the importance of shifting Asian American focus away from their victimhood. As Sucheng Chan notes, for example, Cambodian refugees in the United States are "not just victims." Although Chan is referring to survival of mass killing in Cambodia in the 1970s, and not white racism in the United States, her new focus on agency of Asian Americans is refreshing. See Chan (ed.) (2003).

REFERENCES

Almaguer, T. (1984) Racial domination and class conflict in capitalist agriculture: the 1903 Oxnard sugar beet workers' strike. *Labor History* 25: 325–50.

Aoki, K. (1997) Direct democracy, racial group agency, local government law, and residential racial segregation: some reflections on radical and plural democracy. *California Western Law Review* 33: 189.

Azuma, E. (1994) Interethnic conflict under racial subordination: Japanese immigrants and their Asian neighbors in Walnut Grove, California, 1908–1941. *Amerasia* 20(2): 27–56.

Azuma, E. (1998) Racial struggle, immigrant nationalism, and ethnic identity: Japanese and Filipinos in the California Delta, 1930–1941. *Pacific Historical Review* 67(2): 163–99.

Carroll, D. (2000) Hawai'i's "Local" Theater. *TDR* 44(2): 123–52.

Chang, J. (1906) Local knowledge(s): notes on race relations, panethnicity and history Hawai'i. *Amerasia* 22(2): 1–29.

Chan, S. (ed.) (2003) *Not Just Victims: Conversations with Cambodian Community in the United States*. University of Illinois Press, Urbana, IL.

Edles, L. D. (2004) Rethinking "race," "ethnicity," and "culture": is Hawai'i the "model minority" State? *Ethnic and Racial Studies* 27(1): 37–68.

Espiritu, Y. L. (1992) *Asian American Panethnicity: Bridging Institutions and Identities*. Temple University Press, Philadelphia.

Foley, N. (1997) *The White Scourge: Mexicans, Blacks, and Poor Whites in Texas Cotton Culture*. University of California Press, Berkeley.

Forbes, J. D. (1993) *Africans and Native Americans: the Language of Race and the Evolution of Red-Black Peoples*. University of Illinois Press, Urbana.

Friday, C. (1994) *Organizing Asian American Labor: The Pacific Coast Canned-Salmon Industry, 1870–1942*. Temple University Press, Philadelphia.

Friday, C. (1999) Competing communities at work: Asian Americans, European Americans, and Native Alaskans in the salmon canneries of the Pacific Northwest. In: Matsumoto, V. and Almendinger, B. (eds.) *Over the Edge: Remapping the History of the American West*. University of California Press, Berkeley, pp. 307–28.

Fujikane, C. L. (1994) Between nationalisms: Hawaii's local nation and its troubled racial paradise. *Critical Mass: A Journal of Asian American Cultural Criticism* 1(2): 23–57.

Fujikane, C. L. (2000) Asian settler colonialism in Hawai'i. *Amerasia* 26(2): xv.

Grinde, D. A., Jr. and Taylor, Q. (1984) Red vs. black: conflict and accommodation in the post Civil War Indian territory, 1865–1907. *American Indian Quarterly* 8: 211–25.

Gee, H. (2001) Why did Asian Americans vote against the 1996 California Civil Rights Initiative? *Loyola Journal of Public Interest Law* 2: 1–52.

Ichioka, Y. (1997) The meaning of loyalty: the case of Kazumaro Buddy Uno. *Amerasia* 23(3): 45–71.

Jo, M. H. (1992) Korean merchants in the Black community: prejudice among victims of prejudice. *Ethnic and Racial Studies* 15(3): 395–411.

Jung, M.-K. (2002) Different racisms and the differences they make: race and "Asian Workers" of prewar Hawai'i. *Critical Sociology* 28(1): 77–100.

Kanuha, V. K. (1999) Local and gay: addressing the health needs of Asian and Pacific Islander American (A/PIA) Lesbians and Gay Men in Hawai'i. *Hawai'i Medical Journal* 58(9): 239–93.

Kosasa, E. (1994) Localizing discourse. In: Ng, F. et al. (eds.) *New Visions in Asian American Studies: Diversity, Community, Power.* Washington State University Press, Pullman, pp. 211–21.

Kwon, B. (1999) *Beyond Keʻeaumoku: Koreans, Nationalism, and Local Culture in Hawaiʻi.* Garland, New York.

Lee, R. G. (1994) Imagined communities: Asian America in the 1990s. *Journal of American–East Asian Relations* 3(2): 181–91.

Leiker, J. N. (2002) *Racial Borders: Black Soldiers Among the Rio Grande.* Texas A&M University Press, College Station, TX.

Liestman, D. (1999) Horizontal interethnic relations: Chinese and American Indians in the nineteenth century American West. *Western Historical Quarterly* 30 (Autumn): 327–49.

Littlefield, D. (1978) *The Cherokee Freedman: From Emancipation to American Citizenship.* Greenwood, Westport, CT.

May, K. (1996) *African Americans and Native Hawaiians in the Creek and Cherokee Nations, 1830s to 1920s: Collision and Collusion.* Garland Publishing, New York.

Nomura, G. (1994) Within the law: the establishment of Filipino leasing rights on the Yakima Indian Reservation. In: McClain, C. (ed.) *Asian Indians, Filipinos, Other Asian Communities and the Law.* Garland Publishing, New York, pp. 49–67.

Ohnuma, K. (2002) Local haole. A contradiction in terms? The dilemma of being white, born and raised Hawaiʻi. *Cultural Values* 6(3): 273–85.

Okamura, J. Y. (1980) Aloha Kanaka Me Ke Aloha ʻĀina: local culture and society in Hawaiʻi. *Amerasia* 7(2): 119–37.

Okamura, J. Y. (1994) Why there are no Asian Americans in Hawaiʻi: the continuing significance of local identity. *Social Process in Hawaiʻi* 35: 161–78.

Okamura, J. Y. (1998) The illusion of paradise: privileging multiculturalism in Hawaiʻi. In: Gladney, D. G. (ed.) *Making Majorities: Constituting the Nation in Japan, Korea, China, Malaysia, Fiji, Turkey, and the United States.* Stanford University Press, Stanford, pp. 264–84.

Omi, M. (1997) Racial identity and the state: the dilemmas of classification. *Law and Inequality* 15: 7–23.

Omi, M. and Takagi, D. Y. (1996) Situating Asian Americans in the political discourse on affirmative action. *Representations* 55: 155–62.

Rodriguez, R. (1999) The study of whiteness. *Black Issues in Higher Education* 16(6): 20–5.

Rosa, J. P. (2000) Local story: the Massie case narrative and the cultural production of local identity in Hawaiʻi. *Amerasia* 26(2): 93–116.

Stephan, J. J. (1997) Hijacked by utopia: American nikkei in Manchuria. *Amerasia* 23(3): 1–42.

Sturm, C. (2002) Blood politics, racial classification, and Cherokee national identity. In: Brooks, J. F. (ed.) *Confounding the Color Line: the Indian–Black Experience in North America.* University of Nebraska Press, Lincoln.

Sumida, S. H. (1991) *And the View From the Shore: Literary Traditions of Hawaiʻi.* University of Washington Press, Seattle.

Takaki, R. (1983) *Pau Hana: Plantation Life and Labor in Hawaii.* University of Hawaiʻi Press, Honolulu.

Takaki, R. (1989) *Strangers from a Different Shore: A History of Asian Americans.* Little, Brown, and Co., Boston.

Umemoto, K. (1994) Blacks and Koreans in Los Angeles: the case of LaTasha Harlins and Soon Ja Du. In: Jennings, J. (ed.) *Blacks, Latinos, and Asians in Urban America: Status and Prospects for Politics and Activism.* Praeger, Westport, CT, pp. 95–118.

Umezawa Duus, M. (1999) *The Japanese Conspiracy: the Oahu Sugar Strike of 1920,* translated by Beth Cary. University of California Press, Berkeley.

Warren, J. W. and Twine, F. W. (1997) White Americans, the new minority? Non-blacks and the ever-expanding boundaries of whiteness. *Journal of Black Studies* 28(2): 200–18.

Wu, F. (2003) The arrival of Asian Americans: an agenda for legal scholarship. *Asian Law Journal* 10: 1–12.

Yamamoto, E. K. (1979) The significance of local. *Social Process in Hawai'i* 27: 101–15.

Index